CONNECTIVITY, NETWORKS AND FLOWS

Conceptualizing Contemporary Communications

THE HAMPTON PRESS COMMUNICATION SERIES
Communication, Globalization and Cultural Identity
Jan Servaes, series editor

The Dao of the Press: A Humanocentric Theory
Shelton A. Gunaratne

Connectivity, Networks, and Flows: Conceptualizing Contemporary
Communications
*Andreas Hepp, Friedrich Krotz, Shaun Moores
& Carsten Winter* (eds.)

Viewing the South: How Globalization and Western Television
Distort Representations of the Developing World
Emma Miller

forthcoming

New Voices Over the Air: The Transformation of South African
Broadcasting in a Changing South Africa
Eric Louw

Cultural Citizenship and the Challenges of Globalization
Wenche Ommundsen, Michael Leach & Andrew Vandenberg (eds.)

Serbian Spaces of Identity: Narratives of Belonging by the Last
"Yugo" Generation
Zola Volcic

Media and Power on the Margins of Europe: The Public Negotiation
of the Breton Language and Cultural Identity
David P. Winterstein

CONNECTIVITY, NETWORKS AND FLOWS

Conceptualizing Contemporary Communications

edited by

Andreas Hepp
University of Bremen

Friedrich Krotz
University of Erfurt

Shaun Moores
University of Sunderland

Carsten Winter
*Hanover University
of Music and Drama*

**HAMPTON PRESS, INC.
CRESSKILL, NEW JERSEY**

Library of Congress Cataloging-in-Publication Data

Connectivity, networks and flows : conceptualizing contemporary communications / edited by Andreas Hepp ... [et al.].
     p. cm. -- (The Hampton Press communication series.
     Communication, globalization and cultural identity)
    Includes bibliographic references and index.
    ISBN 978-1-57273-856-0 (hbk.) -- ISBN 157273-857-5 (pbk.)
1. Mass media--Social aspects. 2. Communication. I. Hepp, Andreas.
    HM1206.C665 2008
    302.23--dc22
                        2008017246

Hampton Press, Inc.
23 Broadway
Cresskill, NJ 07626

CONTENTS

1   Connectivity, Networks and Flows   1
    Andreas Hepp, Friedrich Krotz, Shaun Moores
    & Carsten Winter

2   Media Connectivity: Concepts, Conditions   13
    and Consequences
    Friedrich Krotz

3   Translocal Media Cultures: 33
    Networks of the Media and Globalization
    Andreas Hepp

4   "Your Life—To Go": The Cultural Impact   59
    of New Media Technologies
    John Tomlinson

5   The TIMES Convergence of Mediality of Communication   69
    as Change in Cultural Solidarity: Convergent Mobile
    Telephones and Laptops and New Flows, Networks
    and Connectivity
    Carsten Winter

6   Actor Network Theory and Media: 93
    Do They Connect and on What Terms?
    Nick Couldry

7   Network Theory and Human Action: 111
    Theoretical Concepts and Empirical Applications
    Thorsten Quandt

8   Undercurrents: Postcolonial Cyberfeminism,   135
    a Mailing List and the Network Society
    Maren Hartmann

9   Towards a Network Sociality   157
      Andreas Wittel

10 Conceptualizing Place in a World of Flows   183
      Shaun Moores

About the Authors   201

Index   205

CONNECTIVITY, NETWORKS AND FLOWS

Andreas Hepp
Friedrich Krotz
Shaun Moores
Carsten Winter

Contributors to this co-edited book are concerned, in one way or another, with conceptualizing contemporary communications in the context of a changing world, and they each employ at least one (sometimes all three) of the terms that appear in the title—connectivity, networks and flows. There is no single, shared theoretical line running through the various chapters. However, what the authors have in common is a critical engagement with these key concepts, in order to try to understand various social transformations today—technological, institutional, experiential, temporal and spatial. The book is located at the intersections of social theory with media, communications and cultural studies.[1]

---

[1]Most of the chapters published in this volume are extensively revised versions of papers prepared for presentation at a workshop held in Erfurt, Germany in 2003, which was organized by the Media Sociology section of the German Communication Association. The editors wish to thank Caroline Düvel and Julia Vetter for their assistance in arranging the workshop, the German Communication Association for supporting the translation of a number of the chapters from English into German (for publication in the German-language edition of this book), Matthew Merefield and Juliane Wagner for their advice to some of the German authors on English-language issues, and Jan Servaes as editor of the Hampton Press book series, 'Communication, Globalization and Cultural Identity.'

Chapters in the pages ahead range from those that are broad in scope, reviewing theoretical debates and perspectives, to those offering more focused case studies, in which key ideas are applied to particular instances of communication and social organization. Throughout the book as a whole, though, there are numerous discussions of contemporary media and cultural practices—featuring examples such as the uses of mobile phones and the Internet, situations of online working and socializing, and constructions of liveness in electronically mediated encounters. There is a good deal of talk here about globalizing and deterritorializing processes, and of the increasing significance of mobilities in (late) modern existence—yet this is also a book about the continuing importance of locality, senses of place and face-to-face, physically copresent interaction in circumstances of daily living. Indeed, several of the authors suggest that it is precisely the interface between locality and mobility, or else between physical copresence and technologically mediated communications, which now requires careful analysis.

Before introducing the chapters to follow, it is first necessary to outline briefly some existing uses of the three terms in the book's title, beginning with the concept of connectivity—a concept that is found not only in academic writings but increasingly in industry and popular discourses, too. In his work on globalization and culture, John Tomlinson (1999, pp. 1-2), who is one of the contributors to this volume, employs the idea of 'complex connectivity': 'By this I mean that globalization refers to the rapidly developing and ever-densening network of interconnections and interdependencies that characterize modern social life' (note that his basic definition of globalization already incorporates the notion of a network, which extends 'across national borders'). At the same time, he is keen to stress that, on its own, a statement of the 'empirical condition' of complex connectivity is not enough. The concept and the condition therefore need to be elaborated further.

According to Tomlinson (1999), connectivity is related to—although not simply coterminous with—the theme of 'global-spatial proximity', to take an example. Academic discourses of globalization are 'replete with metaphors' of such proximity, he observes. There has been much talk, then, of how an intensified transnational 'interconnectedness'—an extension or 'stretching' out of social relationships across potentially vast distances (Giddens, 1990, 1991)—leads to a (phenomenologically) 'shrinking world', to feelings of 'time-space compression' (Harvey, 1989) and circumstances of 'time-space convergence' in which physical places 'move closer together . . . in travel or communication time' (Janelle 1991, p. 49). Of course, as Tomlinson (1999, p. 131) recognizes, it is crucial to qualify this kind of talk about connectivity and global-spatial proximity by acknowledging that globalization is highly 'uneven' in its social consequences, 'not just in that it involves "winners and losers" or that it reproduces many familiar configurations of domination and subordination, but also in the sense that the cultural experience it distributes is highly complex and varied.'

Doreen Massey (1994) has insisted that experiences of time-space compression need 'differentiating socially.' There is what she calls 'the power geometry of it all', with some groups of people ('the jet-setters, the ones . . . holding the international conference calls, the ones . . . organizing the investments and the international currency transactions') being 'in a sense in charge' of current transformations, whereas others are more 'on the receiving end' of social change (Massey, 1994, p. 149). A similar argument about inequality and unevenness has been made by Andrew Leyshon (1995, p. 35), who suggests that rather than converging 'some places have moved further apart in relative space', as the people who live there are excluded from the 'ever-densening network of interconnections' described by Tomlinson. For those who are subject to exclusion from global-spatial proximity, in economic terms or in terms of their relative lack of access to technologies of physical transportation and electronic communication, there is 'an undeniable, stubbornly enduring physical distance . . . which the technological and social transformations of globalization have not conjured away' (Tomlinson, 1999, p. 4). Indeed, even for affluent 'First Worlders' who can purchase tickets for long-haul flights or interact with each other virtually instantaneously at a distance via the telephone or Internet, this physical distance is still a material fact of life. Friedrich Krotz (2001), too, in his work in the German academic context on 'mediatization', has argued that old power relations are being reproduced and new ones articulated on a global scale.

In recent social theory, the next key term in the title of the book (networks) is associated especially with Manuel Castells' thesis on the 'rise of the network society' (Castells, 1996).[2] Castells (1996: 470-471) offers a definition of his concept of network in the following passage:

> A network is a set of interconnected nodes. . . . What a node is, concretely speaking, depends on the kind of concrete networks of which we speak. They are stock exchange markets, and their ancillary advanced services centers, in the network of global financial flows. . . . They are television systems, entertainment studios, computer graphics milieux, news teams, and mobile devices generating, transmitting and receiving signals, in the global network of the new media . . . in the information age. . . . Networks are appropriate instruments for a capitalist economy based on innovation, globalization and decentralized concentration . . . and for a social organization aiming at the supersession of space.

---

[2] Of course, there are other approaches where the concept of network is important, too—such as actor network theory and social network analysis, which are of considerable interest to some of the contributors below.

Many of the strands running through that definition are already quite familiar from previous academic work in this area. Like Giddens (1990, 1991), Castells sees money and media of communication as two of the significant 'disembedding mechanisms' in (multidimensional) globalizing processes, and, like Harvey (1989), he is particularly interested in capitalist economic transformations and in the overcoming of spatial barriers that is made possible by—among other things—the movement of information at the speed of light. The distinctive feature of his analysis is the framing of these shifts within a model of what he names the network society: 'Networks constitute the new social morphology . . . processes in the information age are increasingly organized around networks' (Castells 1996, p. 469). There are writers, such as Michael Schenk (1995), Tom Standage (1998) and Armand Mattelart (2000), who contend that the principle of 'networking' has a very long history—yet Castells (1996, p. 469) believes contemporary social circumstances provide, for the first time, a unique basis 'for its pervasive expansion throughout the whole social structure.'

From Castells' perspective, capitalism is now going through a period of 'profound restructuring.' For example, there is the emergence of what he names the 'network enterprise', involving a new organizational 'logic' for businesses in the global economy. In turn, this general logic is converging and interacting with a new 'technological paradigm' (Castells, 1996, p. 152), which is associated with the 'information technology revolution.' The Internet, then, is perhaps the most obvious symbol of Castells' network society (see Castells, 2001). Its technological design is, in the words of his definition of a network, a 'set of interconnected nodes', where the 'distance' between the nodes in operational—as opposed to physical—terms is effectively 'zero.' There is the potential for a virtual 'temporal immediacy' of technologically mediated communications. Furthermore, Castells (2001, pp. 130-132) contends that the development of 'cell-telephony' and Internet interaction 'provides an appropriate material support for the diffusion of networked individualism'—thereby enhancing 'the chances for networked individualism to become the dominant form of sociability.' Here, in pointing to emergent 'cellular' and personalized 'structures of sociability', he draws on the earlier social network analysis of Barry Wellman (for instance, see Wellman, 1997).

When Castells advances his arguments about the rise of the network society, he also employs the last key term in the title (flows). His account associates a network society with the expansion of 'the space of flows': 'flows of capital, flows of information, . . . flows of organizational interaction, flows of images, sounds and symbols' (Castells, 1996, p. 412). Taking a similar line, John Urry (2000) proposes a new field of investigation in which the emphasis would be on the analysis of 'global fluids'—of various kinds of flow across 'porous borders.' This would involve making the 'social as mobility' a central focus of study, getting beyond what Ulrich Beck calls the 'methodological nationalism' of the social sciences (see Beck, 2001, Beck & Willms, 2004).

As well as the flows listed by Castells, Urry (2000, p. 50) understands physical mobility or 'corporeal' travelling as a highly significant fluid in the contemporary period:

> The scale of such travelling is awesome. There are over 600 million international passenger arrivals each year. . . . International travel now accounts for over one-twelfth of world trade. It constitutes by far the largest movement of people across boundaries . . . in the history of the world.

In considering these 'awesome' figures, though, it is necessary to remember that the borders of nation-states are far more 'porous' for some social groups than they are for others. Although there is usually what Zygmunt Bauman (1998, pp. 92-3) terms a 'green light for the tourists', there is typically a 'red light' for those groups he labels 'the vagabonds' (for whom staying put 'does not seem a feasible option'). Indeed, members of the latter groups—such as the Mexicans who are making, on foot, 'a perhaps fatal dash for it across the border into the US' (Massey, 1994, p. 149)—may often not find their way into the official travel statistics quoted by Urry.

When transnational migrations of people do occur, one of the interesting features of this physical mobility is to be found in its relation to the 'flows of information, . . . images, sounds and symbols' identified by Castells (1996, p. 412). Arjun Appadurai (1996, p. 4) suggests that attention should therefore be given to the links between media and migration:

> As Turkish guest workers in Germany watch Turkish films in their German flats . . . and as Pakistani cabdrivers in Chicago listen to cassettes of sermons recorded in mosques in Pakistan or Iran, we see moving images meet deterritorialized viewers. . . . Neither images nor viewers fit into circuits . . . that are easily bound within local, national or regional spaces.

These transnational (and translocal) flows of people and images (of sounds, too) give rise to 'diasporic communications' (Dayan, 1999), in which media technologies help to sustain particular cultural connections despite the wide geographical dispersion of populations. In his examples above, Appadurai refers specifically to migrant viewers (or listeners) as being 'deterritorialized.' However, Tomlinson (1999) insists that a 'mundane experience of deterritorialization' is also widely available outside of diasporic cultures—including to many members of physically less mobile populations. So even where there is evidence of 'geographical sedentarism' (Morley, 2000), there is still likely to be a 'penetration of local worlds by distant forces' and an 'ever-broadening horizon of relevance in people's routine experience' (Tomlinson, 1999, p. 115)—at least partly as a result of their technologically 'mediated proximity' with others and elsewhere.

Friedrich Krotz, in the first of the single-authored chapters in this collection, takes a critical line on recent social theorizing that has highlighted the concepts of connectivity and networks. Although he is sympathetic to certain aspects of the work of theorists such as Tomlinson and Castells, his concern is with what he regards as the limitations of current thinking on complex connectivity and the network society. For example, Krotz proposes that although these ideas are helpful in accounting for 'specific functional features' of an 'emergent society', they tend to marginalize older (now less fashionable) lines of thought on 'cultural hegemony' or 'cultural imperialism' that in his view deserve continued consideration. Moreover, he contends that the concepts of connectivity and networks alone take insufficient account of 'meaning-making' and the 'lifeworld elements of everyday life.'[3] He insists, then, that what Castells calls the 'global network of the new media' has to be understood as 'intertwined and intermingled' with the networks of physically co-present, face-to-face encounters in routine circumstances of daily living. Krotz also advocates a return to some of the interests of well-known thinkers such as Peter Berger and Thomas Luckmann, Norbert Elias and Jürgen Habermas, whose concerns with the 'social construction of reality', the 'civilizing process' and the 'public sphere' should not, he believes, be allowed to slip from the theoretical agenda just yet.

Andreas Hepp draws on Krotz's characterization of globalization as one of the significant 'metaprocesses' in contemporary social life, but his approach has a greater degree of sympathy with recent theoretical discussions of connectivity and networks (of flows too). He begins on a cautious note, however, recognizing the potential pitfalls of searching for a 'universal' theory of global social change and suggesting, rather modestly, that the metaphorical concepts in the title of this book could be helpful in developing more context-sensitive ways of thinking about communications. Hepp's chapter goes on to offer definitions of (and outline distinctions among) connectivity, networks and flows as key concepts, proposing that the idea of network is best seen as relating to the 'structuring aspects' of complex connectivity, whereas the notion of flow

---

[3]In Tomlinson's work on globalization and culture (Tomlinson, 1999), there is an attempt to extend the discussion of connectivity in precisely this direction—towards an exploration of the phenomenological dimension of 'global modernity' (see also Tomlinson, 1994).

can help in coming to terms with its 'processing aspects.' The main argument of his chapter, though, involves linking these concepts to a provisional theorization of 'translocal media cultures', because 'translocality' has, to his mind, a 'central place' in thinking about the consequences of 'communicative deterritorialization.' Hepp asserts that 'the local' still matters today, yet he focuses on how media are contributing to a transformation of localities, because they serve to intensify the communicative connections between different locales. Finally, he turns to questions of social inequality and power, considering issues of production, representation and appropriation in the constitution of translocal media cultures.

John Tomlinson, whose important work on globalization and culture was reviewed earlier, provides an interesting new twist on debates about complex connectivity in his contribution to this book. In his chapter he looks at how there is, at least for those people who have access to new media technologies, the possibility (perhaps even the expectation) of immediate social contact with others at a distance, even in situations of physical mobility. Yet he reads the cultural impact of such technologies as ambiguous. So if, on the one hand, they could be regarded as ways of 'extending cultural horizons' or else as 'exit portals' from the limits of locality, then on the other hand they may be interpreted as offering a (networked) 'security of cultural location'—a sense of 'fixity' in the context of a 'culture of flow.' Tomlinson understands mobile phones, for example, not simply as 'globalizing' media but as 'technologies of the hearth', because the talk they facilitate tends to produce a certain sort of 'dwelling' or 'belonging' while on the move (and see Morley, 2003). Indeed, much mobile phone use appears to have to do with the coordination of quite routine and mundane activities within fairly localized areas, such as the calls made by urban commuters to their loved ones in order to report that the train home is running late.

Carsten Winter sets the development of mobile phones and laptop computers, which he calls 'convergent media', in a broad historical context. In his contribution to the volume, he also refers to these as 'quaternary media', distinguishing them from 'primary' ('human media' such as priests or religious preachers), 'secondary' (books and newspapers) and 'tertiary' (radio and television) media that came before. Comparing the quaternary with the tertiary, for instance, he notes that mobile convergent media can be distinguished from broadcasting by their 'protocol and transfer technology', which 'turns transmitters into receivers' and vice versa. As Winter explains, though, it is not only a matter of making distinctions between new and 'old' media, but of analyzing the new 'in the light of the old.' One feature of this analysis is an argument about the shifting historical attachments of love; so whereas in the past communicative connectivity has been associated, for example, with 'love of God' or 'love of country', advertisers now encourage love of 'the medium itself', as in the 'Apple iBook' slogan: 'Is it possible to fall in love with a computer? Oh yes.' Interestingly, in the course of his chapter, Winter also presents a critique of an aspect of Urry's work, where the social theorist discusses the notion of 'inhabited machines' (see Urry, 2003).

Nick Couldry provides a positive critique of an approach known as actor network theory, which is associated with the writings of academics such as Bruno Latour and John Law, asking in his chapter about the potential contribution that this perspective could make to media studies. Actor network theory, he explains, is concerned with the establishment of particular 'networks of connections' involving both human and non-human 'actants' (a technology, for instance, would be thought of as an 'actant' within that framework)—and so, one might imagine, actor network theory is 'perfectly placed' to conceptualize the 'connectivities that media enable.' He observes, however, that this perspective is 'ironically . . . not "networked" with media theory.' In his careful critical assessment of actor network theory, Couldry notes that it has several key strengths—not least of which are its skepticism towards any 'essentialized notions' of the social and the technical, and its attention to the spatial organization of 'stretched-out networks.' Yet this approach also has significant limitations, he argues, especially when it comes to applying actor network theory in thinking about technologically mediated communications. There is insufficient attention paid there, in his opinion, to issues of 'time, power and interpretation'—to the 'long-term consequences of networks' for distributions of power, and to the ongoing construction and reconstruction of meanings in networks of connections (involving, in the case of media, those interpretations that are made by audiences or users).

Thorsten Quandt contributes a chapter to the book that is distinctive for two main reasons. Firstly, having reviewed some of the varied ways in which the concept of network has been employed in social analysis, he proposes that it is possible in the social sciences to make use of certain techniques that are derived from 'mathematical graph theory.' Secondly, using tools including 'data mining software', he analyzes material arising from his detailed empirical study of a new type of labor in the media industry—online journalism—focusing on what he terms a 'network of action elements' in the day-to-day routines and practices of a number of journalists working in different institutional settings. This research entailed lengthy periods of observation, during which the actions (and sequences of action) of the online journalists were coded and recorded. In presenting the findings of his research, Quandt looks to demonstrate 'some striking similarities' in the journalists' everyday 'rules of action' and 'uses of resources.' His study identifies 'recurring patterns' of action, then, that may, in turn, be forming 'orientation horizons for further action.'

Maren Hartmann also engages with network theory by means of a specific case study (like Quandt), although her chapter returns to Castells' ideas on the network society and her study is of an Internet forum named 'Undercurrents.' She contends that the principal 'nodes' in this international 'mailing list' network are the 'people who participate in online communication.' The topics of discussion in the online forum she investigates are framed by the fact that this list was explicitly set up for participants to share views on issues relating to 'cyberfeminism' and the 'racial politics of "net.culture".' Hartmann is especially interested in the moments of 'rupture' or 'disturbance' that emerge within the network, where there is conflict and where some participants feel 'silenced' by others. Her central point is that such conflict illustrates the limitations of Castells' argument concerning the space and power of flows, which, according to her interpretation of his work, has a tendency to assume harmonious relations within networks. In addition, she makes a further point that the offline social locations of the participants in the mailing list help to shape their online expressions and responses to others' views; as she puts it, the 'situatedness of the nodes is important.'

Andreas Wittel maps the rise of a 'network sociality', which, he hypothesizes, is set to become the 'paradigmatic social form of late capitalism.'[4] His reference to the 'rise' of this social form clearly echoes Castells' wider concerns with the emergence of a network society (and seems to relate closely to Castells' own notion of 'networked individualism'). Wittel's hypothesis is once again based on case study material, as it is grounded in qualitative research on the 'new media industry' in London. Drawing on that study, as well as on a range of developments in contemporary social theory, he identifies the characteristic features of network sociality. It can be defined, in his view, in contrast to the concept of 'community'—including recent ideas about 'virtual community'—and it is marked, for example, by 'ephemeral but intense encounters' and by a blurring of the boundaries between work and play. Wittel describes his overall aim as one of elaborating a 'micro-sociology of the information age', in which the main object of analysis is 'the making of networks' and 'networking as a practice.'

Shaun Moores, in the last of the contributions to the collection, asks how we are best to conceptualize place in an increasingly globalized 'world of flows', exploring a theme that was of particular interest to Hepp (the transformation of 'experiences of locality'). In searching for answers, he begins by engaging directly with the thoughts of Castells and Urry that were initially discussed in the opening part of this introductory chapter. His commentary then proceeds to examine the reflec-

---

[4]An earlier version this chapter has appeared as an article in *Theory, Culture and Society*. The author is grateful to the journal for permission to revisit the concerns of that piece here.

tions of Massey (whose name was also mentioned above), Joshua Meyrowitz and Paddy Scannell on place as 'permeable, marginalized or pluralized.' Moores insists that he is not advocating a 'media-centered approach' to understanding social change, but towards the end of his chapter he does come to focus on the ways in which electronic media are involved in the creation of 'new sorts of social situation for interaction.' Here, though, his argument is that it is always necessary to see how a media setting 'overlays' the physical place which a media user inhabits, with a consequent 'doubling' of being and interaction. He believes it is crucial, then, to locate what goes on in the 'virtual' places of Internet or telephonic encounters in relation to offline social life.

REFERENCES

Appadurai, A. (1996). *Modernity at large: Cultural dimensions of globalization.* Minneapolis: University of Minnesota Press.

Bauman, Z. (1998). *Globalization: The human consequences.* Cambridge: Polity Press.

Beck, U. (2001). *What is globalization?* Cambridge: Polity Press.

Beck, U., & Willms, J. (2004). *Conversations with Ulrich Beck.* Cambridge: Polity Press.

Castells, M. (1996). *The information age: Economy, society and culture. Vol. 1: The rise of the network society.* Malden, MA: Blackwell.

Castells, M. (2001) *The internet galaxy: Reflections on the internet, business and society.* Oxford: Oxford University Press.

Dayan, D. (1999). Media and diasporas. In J. Gripsrud (Ed.), *Television and common knowledge.* London: Routledge.

Giddens, A. (1990). *The consequences of modernity.* Cambridge: Polity Press.

Giddens, A. (1991). *Modernity and self-identity: Self and society in the late modern age.* Cambridge: Polity Press.

Harvey, D. (1989). *The condition of postmodernity: An enquiry into the origins of cultural change.* Oxford: Blackwell.

Janelle, D. (1991). Global interdependence and its consequences. In S. Brunn & T. Leinbach (Eds.), *Collapsing space and time: Geographic aspects of communication and information.* London: Harper Collins.

Krotz, F. (2001). *Die Mediatisierung des Kommunikativen Handelns: Der Wandel von Alltag und sozialen Beziehungen, Kultur und Gesellschaft durch die Medien.* Opladen: Westdeutscher Verlag.

Leyshon, A. (1995). Annihilating space? The speed-up of communications. In J. Allen & C. Hamnett (Eds.), *A shrinking world? Global unevenness and inequality.* Oxford: Oxford University Press/Open University.

Massey, D. (1994). *Space, place and gender.* Cambridge: Polity Press.

Mattelart, A. (2000). *Networking the world, 1794-2000.* Minneapolis: University of Minnesota Press.

Morley, D. (2000). *Home territories: Media, mobility and identity.* London: Routledge.

Morley, D. (2003). What's 'home' got to do with it? Contradictory dynamics in the domestication of technology and the dislocation of domesticity. *European Journal of Cultural Studies, 6*, 435-58.

Schenk, M. (1995). *Soziale Netzwerke und Massenmedien: Untersuchungen zum Einfluss der persönlichen kommunikation.* Tübingen: Mohr.

Standage, T. (1998). *The Victorian internet: The remarkable story of the telegraph and the nineteenth century's online pioneers.* London: Weidenfeld and Nicolson.

Tomlinson, J. (1994). A phenomenology of globalization? Giddens on global modernity. *European Journal of Communication, 9,* 149-72.

Tomlinson, J. (1999). *Globalization and culture.* Cambridge: Polity Press.

Urry, J. (2000). *Sociology beyond societies: Mobilities for the twenty-first century.* London: Routledge.

Urry, J. (2003). *Global complexity.* Cambridge: Polity Press.

Wellman, B. (1997). An electronic group is virtually a social network. In S. Kiesler (Ed.), *The culture of the internet.* Hillsdale, NJ: Erlbaum.

MEDIA CONNECTIVITY

Concepts, Conditions, and Consequences

Friedrich Krotz

FROM GLOBALIZATION DISCOURSE TO NETWORK AND CONNECTIVITY CONCEPTS

If one looks from outside at the discourse on globalization, it is a striking fact that globalization today is mainly discussed as a new form of social life. Connectivity concepts and an understanding of society as a network frame the discussion, whereas topics like the economic dimension or the problems of cultural hegemony have largely disappeared. Thus, two questions arise: Is this enough to constitute a theory of globalization? And if not, what can be done to make the theoretical approaches more convincing?

The following essay is concerned with these questions and develops some ideas about them. First, the character of the theoretical concepts *network* and *connectivity* is discussed. We do so together with a discussion of the question of what it is that constitutes the *new* of the social life under the conditions of globalization. The particular problem here is that *network society* is a formal concept that only refers to the mechanisms of some specific fields of social life. Because of this the concept fails to grasp the full reality of the manner in which people are socially positioned and live their lives. Further, some additional theoretical approaches are suggested, by which the view of social life under the conditions of globalization can be complemented. Second, the concepts of complex connectivity and of network society refer to expected states of the social and cultural life in the future. Thus they predict what will be instead of starting to analyze the existing developments of today in their full complexity. In its main part, the chapter will develop some ideas to understand the upcoming forms of life as the products of different metaprocesses, especially as products of globalization, mediatization, individualization and commercialization. What results from this is still an open question. But we should take into consideration that it might be a development that may be influenced by politics and, in particular, by civil society. This will be explained in the following parts of this essay.

THE FORMAL CHARACTER OF NETWORK AND CONNECTIVITY

In a rather rough overview, one can say that the discourse on globalization started with an economic view on what is changing in the world. In particular, financial flows have been at the center of discussions of globalization (Giddens, 1990, 2001; Mattelart & Mattelart, 1998). The so-called antiglobalization movement ATTAC (Association for the Taxation of financial Transactions for the Aid of Citizens) provided an answer to the financial problem of globalization in the form of the proposal of a tax on this international flow, which is commonly called the Tobin Tax. Another complex theme of the last decades that was close to the issue of globalization was the concern about *cultural hegemony* and the disappearance of weaker cultures, as given in the idea of the "McDonaldization of cultures."

Today, these topics have been rather marginalized. Instead, concepts such as the network society (Castells, 1996) and *complex connectivity* (Tomlinson, 1999) seem to attract much more interest. In addition, the highly differentiated descriptions of what happens worldwide by Arjun Appadurai (1998), Martin Albrow (1998) and others (cf. Duerrschmidt, 2002) have provoked a lot of discussion. Subsequently, the question about the forces that cause globalization is evidently no longer a central topic of concern; it seems enough if academic research knows how the social life in a globalized world may function. Even the word "globalization" has widely disappeared from academic discussion.

Partly, this is a justified development, as all empirical indicators show (see also the chapter by Andreas Hepp in this volume). What happens under the label of globalization is a multidimensional process and does not depend on the economy alone. In addition, if we look at the work of Manuel Castells and the connectivity concept of John Tomlinson, it seems plausible that the theoretical conceptualization of social, cultural, and economic developments must be described in new ways. Following John Tomlinson we understand complex connectivity as the rapidly developing and increasingly dense network of interconnections and interdependencies that characterize modern social life (Tomlinson, 1999). Insofar as connectivity is concerned with all processes that are not confined to a national, regional, or cultural area, the emergence of this concept in the context of the discussion about globalization is evident.

At present, two assumptions are part of this shift from globalization to network society and complex connectivity. The first is that that the manners in which social life and the economy are functioning today have changed fundamentally compared with former times. Social life and the economy cannot henceforth be described by traditional concepts. Moreover, the interdependencies and interconnections between people, social institutions, and economic enterprises, and also the existing channels and flows of energy, goods, debts, and money; of activities of service industries and knowledge of police departments or governments; and of emotions and personal relations have all changed and now take place as a set of networks, in opposition to what was true in former states of society.

The second assumption is that complex connectivity and network society describe the core of what is really new compared with former times and characterize the economy and social life of the future. Only such an assumption would justify the use of the term "network society" for the present and future forms of social life. But why should this be the case? At this point in this rather roughly sketched theoretical development, it is important to remember what type of concepts network and connectivity are: they are formal concepts that describe social and cultural life in terms of nodes and channels, accumulations and flows. They symbolize interconnections and interdependencies and how these work. In addition, social life in a globalized world thus appears as a net of networks.

In the rest of this essay we will present some empirical and theoretical arguments for why this is only partly helpful if one intends to construct a broader theory. Those concepts and the assumed social changes need to be understood in more detail. The general problem is that the character of what a network is made of is no longer of importance insofar as we speak of network society and connectivity. Sociology has always dealt with social aggregates such as family, group, community, class, institution or enterprise. Each of these social aggregates may be seen as a network, as each consists of nodes and connections, channels and actual flows. But in traditional sociology family, group, community, and other aggregates are not only networks. Instead each such aggregate has a detailed inner structure that cannot be reduced to its functional or working principles as can the network concept. Thus, any theory of contemporary social life must explain why the inner structures—for example, any adhesion that is not only functionally defined—should no longer be considered important.

It does not seem plausible that whatever is behind a contemporary or future social aggregate does not matter any longer. This is because social reality does not have only a functional character, but also consists in lifeworld-based action. The functional character of social life thus provides a helpful view on what takes place, but it does not represent the whole and therefore is not enough to give a theoretical concept of what takes place today.

To understand this better let us look at the work of Norbert Elias, who analyzed the process of civilization in Europe. Elias characterized this process as a twofold development, and thus even when considering the past, in a much more complex way than, for example, Castells. First, he described the historical development of nations that centralized and demonstrated in this context the growing dependence of people, institutions, and economy on increasingly complex interconnections and interdependencies. To make this clearer, Elias distinguished between social, economic, affective, and spatial interdependencies (Arnason, 1987; Baumgart & Eichner, 1991, p. 110; Elias, 1972, 1993, 1994; cf. also Featherstone, 1987 and Krotz, 2003). Here, it is evident that these interdependencies can already be described by a network concept, at least in part. But a network concept alone would not grasp the full conditions of social life, which are the focus of Elias' approach.

Elias also showed in his examination of history that a specific type of person becomes necessary (and then normal) to be able to live in such a type of society—a sort of industrial-age personality. Such persons cannot, for example, solve their problems by violence or on the basis of affects, because this would disturb the functioning of society and the economy. Thus other forms of living, new forms of inner control, etiquettes and so on become necessary. In the view of Elias we thus have a strong duality between the social and cultural behavior of the individual and his or her definition of self and everyday life and the functionally described organization of economy and society. Social life and its development, when framed in this manner, cannot become reduced to the network concept, even if parts of Elias's theoretical concepts, such as *figuration,* are close to that concept. The description of all social aggregates as networks thus ignores the fact that people also act on the basis of sensibilities, meaning making and lifeworlds; the formally described interconnections are only adequate for specific areas of economy and, only in part, for social life. I cannot see any plausible argument to suggest that this may have changed today.

A further theoretical reference that may serve as a base to analyze this problem in more detail is provided by Juergen Habermas. As is well known, he developed the concept of the public sphere, which in prior phases of capitalism and the nation-state constituted the basis of democracy, freedom, and justice (Habermas, 1990). In some sense, the *public sphere* may be described as a net of communication flows, as it consists of interpersonal communication on the one hand, and of informational media flows on the other (cf. Jarren & Krotz, 1998). But the public sphere is not only a functional net, as it may be assumed to be when referring to the concept of, for example, network society. This becomes clear if one takes into account Habermas' later work on communicative action (Habermas, 1987). Here he differentiates between the traditionally grown lifeworld of the people and the systemic structures of life in modern societies, which may be understood as complex connectivity. Simply explained, lifeworld is the area in which communication aims at understanding, whereas the systemic structures of economy and society are areas of instrumental communication guided by other aims. Both forms of orientation and organization—the lifeworld and interpreted self on the one hand and the systems of economy and politics on the other—are engaged in a constant struggle, and this struggle is characteristic for society in the second half of the 20th century. In the theory of a contemporary globalized world, lifeworld elements and their crucial role for the constructing of the everyday are widely ignored and seem to have become a sort of more-or-less irrelevant appendage of the connectivities and flows. If we argue that the former theory of society must be replaced by a network theory of social life in a global world, we run into the problem of explaining why all those historically and culturally engendered relationships have become trivial—which is not very plausible.

Let's finally argue in a third way, referring to *media connectivity*, which we discuss here in the context of communication research. One way to define media connectivity is in an analogous way, as the nets and connections, the flows and nodes of communication in all existing forms—an emerging net of communication and the media. If we do so, it is evident that we must analyze this in more detail, because the complex ways of communication by media, with media and also without media together characterize human communication in developing media environments. Not only the functional modes and uses of communication are relevant—communication also exists in a lifeworld-oriented interpersonal mode.

We will discuss this in more detail later, but we will begin to emphasize the importance of this argument here. This is because humans are beings who exist in and depend on interaction, communication, and social relations (Cassirer, 1994; Habermas, 1987; Krotz, 2001; Mead, 1967). Insofar as media connectivity changes the forms of communication, interaction and, in consequence, the forms of social relations in which people live, the core of what human beings are is affected. Because of this, we must consider the conditions and consequences of communication organized as a functional network or a complex connectivity; but we must also consider communication as the base of the everyday lifeworld in the sense of Berger and Luckmann (1980/1969), following Alfred Schutz and George Herbert Mead.

We conclude, so far, that the globalized forms of social, cultural, and economic life described by the concepts of the network and complex connectivity refer to a fundamentally different type of economic and social organization and thus to a fundamentally different meaning of media and communication. But this, too, is only partly the case: the lifeworld of the people is, on the one hand, the basis of culture, sense making, and meaning production. On the other hand, it also exists as a basis for and at the same time in a fundamental opposition to the functional, systemic, and network character of the economy and the organizational and institutional levels of social life. But it is not an automatic consequence that industrial culture and the mass media, that meaning mediated by advertising and by labels and other systemic influences, are successful in overcoming the lifeworld and thus make it disappear or become trivial.

This means that we accept the first of the assumptions mentioned above, but not the second. The reduction of social and cultural life to a network society or a complex connectivity concept is too narrow. It must therefore be discussed in more detail. In addition, all the abovementioned theories are in some sense speculative, as they start with assumptions about the future states of social life: network society, for example, is nothing more than a prediction. Instead, we should analyze contemporary developments in order to collect indicators that might help us to understand what takes place and with what it is connected. The purpose of the rest of this essay is demonstrate that it is more helpful to understand the developments of today as the intertwining of rather fundamental and global developments like globalization, individualization, commercialization, and mediatization.

SOCIETY AS DEVELOPMENT: METAPROCESSES

Traditionally, sociological and cultural thinking starts with the assumption that we live in a given culture and society. On the basis of the discussion of globalization and of the work, for example, of Albrow (1998), one may doubt whether it today makes sense to speak of culture and society as an entity. But to the same degree, one may also doubt that the usually made assumption of the stability of cultural and social environ-ments is still valid. Stable states exist only for moments in a constant flow of history and development. The conclusion thus is that only in starting from an understanding of society and culture as a product of long-term processes can we begin to understand what takes place in the culture and society of today.

But, even if we want to do so, we lack adequate concepts. Tradition-ally, the concept *process* is used to describe developments (e.g., Elias, 2000). But process is usually defined as a temporal sequence of more-or-less different states that are thought to belong together. Such processes have a clear starting point and a defined direction and may be empirically analyzed by quantitative methods. A good example for what may be understood as a process is that of the diffusion of innova-tions, as it is described by Everett Rogers (1995) in the frame of commu-nication research. Here, we have a clearly defined invention that is assumed to have a clear advantage for people. The frame for the diffu-sion is given by a fixed region, most often a country, a fixed culture and society, and the people living in that culture. If this is the case, we can describe the diffusion process as a sequence of different states over time in the region. Culture here is to be understood as slowing down or accel-erating the respective diffusion process; in the countries of the so-called "Third World," for example, culture is mostly seen from outside as not very functional in relation to its ability to successfully acquire the goods and institutions of the Western economy (cf. Lerner, 1962)—for exam-ple, the distribution of new medicines, or of new media such as the PC or the internet.

It is evident that such a concept of process is not a good way to understand developments such as the enlightenment, industrialization, globalization, or individualization. Developments such as those may last for decades or even centuries and are not necessarily confined to a sin-gle area or a given culture. It is also not clear at which point in time they begin or end. It is not even clear whether they have a defined goal and direction and what they do or do not consist in. Thus, such develop-ments are not processes in the sense defined above. But nevertheless they exist in the following sense: they are constructs that describe and grasp theoretically specific economic, social, and cultural dimensions and levels of actual development. If one uses one of these concepts, it is generally possible to analyze it in more detail and to find out whether or not it makes sense to use it in an academic discourse.

Thus, it is helpful to use the term *globalization* to sum up a lot of dif-ferent, but probably connected developments, as is done by Albrow (1998), Duerrschmidt (2002), Giddens (2001), and others. Of course, one may ask whether this is a fruitful and theoretically adequate concept, but only if we operate with the concept can we analyze it empirically and study its implicit and explicit conditions and consequences. And the use of such a concept makes clear that the developments of today are different from the developments of the last 50 years, as in those times other concepts for other phenomena with other implications have been used successfully. It may be that we decide not to use the globalization concept any longer, but then we should find a better concept. Probably, in the case of globalization, we must describe the respective development in more detail and use different concepts such as connectivity and network society, but also additional ones, as we have argued above.

Thus there exist long-term developments that are not processes in the above sense, because they are not confined to an area, culture, or society and do not have a starting point or a direction. For such developments we here will use the term *metaprocess*. Globalization, individualization, commercialization, and *mediatization* (see below) thus are at least four metaprocesses of today that influence social life, culture, politics, economic, and other conditions of life, at least in the long run. Thus, these metaprocesses are of interest for any answer to the question about future forms of social life. It is evident that these metaprocesses are important for people on the micro level, for institutions and organizations on the meso level, and for culture and society on the macro level. It is also evident that there are complex relations among these four metaprocesses. In the next sections of this essay, we will consider some of these metaprocesses.

But before we move on to them, let us briefly indicate why we should use the concept of metaprocess: the reason is that the dynamics of contemporary change have increasingly come to have greater impact and importance. We do not live in a stable culture and society, but in a rapidly and fundamentally changing world. The concept of metaprocesses gives us the advantage of being able to concentrate on the change instead of looking for final states: metaprocesses already exist today and we can analyze them today. If, instead, we aim to describe the final states of what may emerge, such as an expected body of knowledge, information, or a postindustrial society, we run the risk of overemphasizing specific points and aspects we hope for or fear.

GLOBALIZATION, INDIVIDUALIZATION, AND CONNECTIVITY

So now let us briefly discuss globalization and *individualization* as metaprocesses and comment on their relations to complex connectivity and network society. The thesis at which we will arrive in this and the following section is as follows: The tendency that social, cultural, and economic interconnections and interdependencies, the communicative and also the personal and social relations of people can increasingly be characterized in functional terms by network and connectivity concepts as a consequence not only of globalization, but also of individualization, mediatization and commercialization. It is a general and overall tendency of social life. But as we have argued above, it is a development that is not valid in every area of social and cultural life and does not include the disappearance of the lifeworld as the basis of reality construction.

Globalization is a concept that originally started as a description of the development of financial markets (Albrow, 1998; Appadurai, 1996; Duerrschmidt, 2002; Giddens, 2001; Hepp, 2004; and others). It more generally refers to market actors (Mattelart & Mattelart, 1998) and thus could be understood as a theory of financial, economic, and later political and cultural developments. A lot of definitions and a lot of outlines for globalized forms of social life in the future exist—for example McLuhan and Powers (1995) with their idea of a global village or Cohen and Kennedy (2000) with their emphasis on a global world sociology.

Furthermore, it is well known that we can describe different aspects of globalization; for example, globalization can be conceived of (a) as a changing understanding of time and space and in consequence of changes in people's meaning making and actions; (b) as an increase of interactions among cultures; (c) as an increase of problems that concern all people of the world; (d) as an increasing network of transnational actors and organizations that become more and more influential both on the global economy and on political decisions.

A broadly discussed question is whether the metaprocess of globalization makes different cultures more homogeneous or even causes some to disappear. There are many indicators which show that this is not directly the case, as cultural contact is not primarily a threat but rather a new possibility to think and to live (cf. Krotz, 1994; Martin-Barbero, 1993; Tomlinson, 1991). In general, contact among cultures alone does not affect them negatively. Instead, it makes culture broader and more complex, which must be seen as an advantage. In particular, academics in the tradition of Cultural Studies have made this clear. The problem here is that today cultural contacts in the age of globalization as in the age of imperialism are always also economic contacts—we come back to this point in the last section of this essay. (We have already discussed the role of concepts such as network society and complex connectivity for the globalization metaprocess, in the first sections of this essay).

A second important metaprocess that we will discuss here is *individualization*. This development has already been described and analyzed by Emile Durkheim and his successors. Following Ulrich Beck, a new form came into life after the Second World War (Beck, 1983, 1986, 1994; cf. also Beck & Beck-Gernsheim, 1994; Krotz, 1999). In Beck's view, individualization takes place on three levels: (a) We are increasingly free from integration in social aggregates such as neighborhood, village life, relationships and so on. So, we are therefore increasingly free from traditional concepts of how to live, to act, to think, and to feel. Thus we are responsible for finding our own way, which also means that there is a loss of institutionally guaranteed forms of living; (b) there is a loss of traditional orientations such as beliefs, values, and norms; and (c) there are also new forms of reintegration as people become increasingly dependent on market conditions and societal institutions.

This metaprocess refers to the expansion of the range of goods that must and can be bought and paid for and services that must or can be ordered and paid for; more and more people are becoming actors in the market rather than members of society. And it refers to the expansion of the influence of institutions to define reality for people. For example, health insurance, schools, and education are organized more and more by government, as are as institutions for pension schemes and so on. They increasingly define the life, biography, and career of each single person. For example, they decide that 6-year-olds should become students and that people of 65 are no longer necessary to the economy.

The metaprocess of individualization thus does not only consist in people becoming free from traditionally given relations in both a positive and in a negative sense, as we are free to choose a lifestyle, but also have no income if there are no jobs. There are also mechanisms for reintegration into society. For example, it's increasingly the case that we can/must buy things and services that in former times were produced in another way or were guaranteed by existing nonformal social aggregates, such as the provision of shelter, everyday-life help, or psychotherapy.

Evidently, this metaprocess of individualization is also a construct, which helps to analyze, to describe and to understand the developments of social life and to discuss and study them. And it is evident that individualization tends to replace traditionally given relations between persons and persons and between persons and organizations, institutions or enterprises by way of abstract interdependencies and interconnections that can be described in a satisfactory way by network and connectivity terms.

Thus, we can sum up that both the metaprocesses of globalization and individualization claim to be important for our understanding of the contemporary and future social and cultural life. This is because they change the relations, the memberships and orientations, the habits, and the values of the people. They do so by making them into something that you can choose or not, as both processes offer more alternatives and weaken the traditionally given binding forces. Other kinds of relations and relations to other people become possible and more important. For example, the traditionally important neighbors with whom you live in close proximity lose their importance, and the same is true for the community you live in, for your working conditions, and for your relations to societal institutions and enterprises. A description of social life in terms of (functional) networks and connectivities thus seems more adequate—for both metaprocesses. People are increasingly integrated into social and cultural life by the market, by being part of a social life that is functionally divided into specialized jobs and their necessary organization, by being points in financial nets and social institutions run by governmental operations, and so on.

Thus, the formally oriented views on the function of networks and connectivity are a consequence of both metaprocesses. In this sense, as we have already stated, the descriptions of Tomlinson and Castells are not wrong. But the question remains of whether the lifeworld elements of everyday life (Berger & Luckmann, 1980/1969) disappear in general and automatically, as we argued above. This is a theoretical question of whether a society conceived of only as a network and a functional connectivity may function without being dependent at least partly on the autonomous lifeworld of each individual, as described by Habermas and Schutz, Mead, and Berger and Luckmann. There are many good reasons to doubt this.

MEDIATIZATION AS A FURTHER METAPROCESS

Here, we define a further metaprocess, that is of special interest with regard to communication and the media. By mediatization we mean the historical developments that took and take place as a result of change in (communication) media and the consequences of those changes (cf. Krotz, 2001, 2003). If we consider the history of communication through music, or the art of writing, we can describe the history of human beings as a history of newly emerging media and at the same time changing forms of communication. The new media do not, in general, substitute for one another, as has been recognized in communication research since the work of the Austrian researcher Riepel (cf. Krotz & Hasebrink, 2001).

Theoretically, we can refer to the so-called *medium theory* (e.g., Barck, 1997; Carey, 1975; Giessen, 2001; Goody, Watt, & Gough 1986; Krotz, 2001b; McLuhan, 1967; Meyrowitz, 1985). Medium theory is "the historical and intercultural analysis of different cultural environments produced by the communication media," as Meyrowitz (1994) defined it. It is concerned with the role of media technologies and consequently with changing human communication. Of course, this is not a technologically determined process, but a man-made one. We can argue that mediatization changes human communication by offering new possibilities of communication to individuals, economies, societies, and cultures. If, in the frame of their respective culture and societies, they accept these for their own purposes, they in consequence change the way they communicatively construct their world. Today, we can say that mediatization means at least the following: (a) changing media environments (as they become more complex); (b) an increase of different media (as is the case of the digital media); (c) the changing functions of old media (e.g., using TV is vastly different today from watching TV in previous decades); (d) new and increasing functions of digital media for the people and a growth of the importance of media in general; (e) changing communication forms and relations between the people on the micro level, a changing organization of social life and changing nets of sense and meaning making on the macro level.

The specific relevance of mediatization lies in the fact that it is a metaprocess that changes communication and so the core of human action. Through communication, we construct our everyday life (Berger & Luckmann, 1980), ourselves (Mead, 1967) and our society (Habermas, 1987) or social life, our culture, meaning, and sense of action. Media then, can be seen as changing communication. This means that mediatization, like other metaprocesses, includes the idea of changing structures of the individual, of changing interpretations and reconstructions of the world and so on through changing forms of communication as a form of social action. In the history of humankind, four general forms of communication come up:

1. *Face-to-face communication* is the basic form of communication, as it is learned by every individual as a baby (and by the human race at the beginning of its history). This does not mean that other beings do not communicate, but the complexity of human communication and interaction is specifically human and a characteristic of the species. Later in the history of humans new forms of communication arose through the invention of media.
2. The first we will mention is *communication by media*, as is the case in the writing or reading of letters and e-mails, or in the case of speaking by phone to other persons.
3. The second we mention is *communication with media*, as takes place in the case of TV, of a book, a picture, an internet website or any other standardized media product that is not addressed to a single person or a small, personally known group of persons. Here, we usually speak of media reception.
4. Thirdly, the emerging new form of media is so-called *interactive communication*, which takes place inside of computer games, with robots, tamagotchis and those football-playing robot dogs called AIBOs, or with GPS and speaking navigation systems that appear with increasing frequency in cars and other devices.

Thus, the communicational environment of the people changes through the emerging digital media, and this has consequences for the communication and through that for everything else that depends on communication. Today, digital media also change the other, already existing media. And they do not only affect leisure time, political information, and entertainment, but all areas of everyday life, of culture, and society. Thus, we can speak of an emergent mediated complex net of communication via the digital media (Krotz, 2003).

Of course, this includes the fact that we can observe that people using the digital media become part of new communicational networks that may be described by network and connectivity concepts. But at the same time we must keep in mind the fact that the face-to-face-communication in the given lifeworld we are born into and live in has not been superseded by the new developments. Digital media, like every new media, are integrated into the everyday life of the people. But to use them you need the competence to communicate, and you learn this in the interpersonal face-to-face-world with which you are familiar. Communication may acquire a new shape and function through the digital media, but has its basis in lifeworld-oriented face-to-face communication, which aims towards understanding.

Let's thus sum up with the conclusion that *media connectivity* may be understood as an ever-thickening net of communication possibilities and communication flows of the people who, to an ever-increasing extent, live in a complex media environment.

Thus a net of digital media overlays the familiar and traditional net of everyday life communication such that both are intertwined and intermingled. Increasingly, this digital media net gains importance, and the media connectivity given by that includes the interpersonal, predigital communication as a part, but only as a part.

THE INTERTWINING OF THE METAPROCESS COMMERCIALIZATION WITH THE OTHER METAPROCESSES

Here, we will rather briefly deal with the interrelations of the three sketched metaprocesses and then discuss their common basis, the metaprocess of commercialization. Evidently, each of the introduced metaprocesses is more or less independent from each of the others. But they all belong together with regard to our question here, as all may be described as tendencies that lead into the emerging world of the future. In particular, all three are developments that lead towards a social and cultural life that may be described by connectivity and network concepts. But the mediatization metaprocess makes it especially clear that interpersonal communication and social relations and activities, the sense making, the construction of everyday life and of the communicatively based self and identity cannot be totally replaced. Thus, the lifeworld of the people will go on existing as a dialectic contrary of functional networks and complex connectivity—as a base and an opposite.

If we ask for the specific relations among the metaprocesses, a differentiated picture emerges. Individualization and globalization produce more mediated communication, as people increasingly need mediated information and communication to be informed, to be integrated, and to be in connection with related people. Thus, both metaprocesses promote mediatization. This even means that mediatization is, therefore, a condition for individualization and globalization, as media, for example, make it possible to live in one culture and to act in another one, to conserve long-distance interpersonal face-to-face-relations, to give them new forms and shapes, or to become part of a market. On the other hand, globalization and individualization define conditions such that mediatization comes into life as media become increasingly necessary. Thus these metaprocesses are intertwined and intermingled, but may have very different effects:

1. Globalization, individualization and mediatization have *unidirectional effects*, in that traditionally given embeddings in social units and cultural orientations are of less importance in the nets produced by those metaprocesses.
2. Media may promote globalization and individualization as, for example, they make globalization more acceptable. This is because you may stay in contact with others far away. Thus these metaprocesses evidently may have *complementary effects*. Also, globalization and individualization promote mediatization, as we have shown above.
3. However, the three metaprocesses may lead in different directions and have *conflicting consequences;* media are problematic for globalization, as people need more credible information in a globalized world, but they will not get it, because the information function of the media becomes less credible and more problematic.

The background of this is that each metaprocess has its own logic of how it develops, and that in capitalism, all such metaprocesses depend on economic development. Thus we must analyze the relation of the three metaprocesses to the metaprocess commercialization. The thesis here is that commercialization is the *basic* process, which is close to each of the other three. Basic here means that economy gives the people a continuous reason to act whereas, for example, media are just a possibility and not a general motive. We can explain this here only by way of some remarks, referring to mediatization as an example.

An important property of mediated communication is the following: if two people communicate in a common face-to-face situation, they are generally free to communicate as they like. Communication takes place as an interaction process, which of course is influenced by situational qualities, but these are also influenced by participants' definition of the situation. On the other hand, media are generally organized by enterprises and controlled by institutions. This means that in each media communication something like a third person participates, and so further interests are involved. If you talk by phone, your provider wants you to go on speaking. When you watch television, the screen communicates with the goal that you stay until the next block of advertisements appear. When you read a magazine, the editor tries to influence you to buy the next edition as well. In each of these cases, we can say, following Habermas (1987), that communication does not aim only towards a basic understanding, but also works in terms of the further instrumental influences set out by institutions, markets and enterprises.

Media thus are part of the economy and politics, and not only of the cultural network of tradition and meaning. And this gives any mediated communication a different character, as it is also an element of the costs of production and energy use, connecting people to societal and political institutions. This difference is most often overlooked, but remains important. More generally, we thus can say that in a prominent way the metaprocess of mediatization also means that it involves people in markets (cf. e.g., Giessen, 1998; Krotz, 2001; Krotz & Eastman, 1999; McAllister, 1996). Communication by media is organized communication and is controlled by economic and governmental institutions: advertising agencies, Telecom enterprises, software and media producers, and regulatory institutions are participating with you when you phone a friend or watch the news. Communication by media is therefore basically different from communication without media, as it introduces instrumental interests into each communication. Because of that, we can refer to the work of Herbert Schiller (1989, 1994) who wrote about the corporate take-over of public expression (cf. Krotz, 2001a). The other theoretical line here is the work of the so-called *critical theory* of Theodor W. Adorno and Max Horkheimer and their concept of cultural industry, which remains important today.

Thus we can say that in general the metaprocess of commercialization is a core process behind all those metaprocesses, as we have argued here in the case of mediatization. The same is probably true for globalization as the beginning of new connections in capitalist societies has the strong motive of the pursuit of profit. And it is also true for individualization, as the required mobility, as well as the time problems of successful persons, and other developments, may show (Sennett, 1999). This of course does not mean that the above-named metaprocesses depend mainly and fully on economy. They are still multidimensional developments, which take place on different levels. But it means that we still live in a capitalistic society, and here the motive of every formalized activity is to follow one's interests, which in the last instance refer to money. Thus culture and social life are conditions for economic activities. If they change, this may be used to accumulate profit, and if this is possible, it will happen.

This has two important consequences. The first one is important for the question of cultural hegemony and globalization. It should be clear that economic rather than cultural hegemony is the problem in the case of the contact of cultures. All the developments discussed today have a strong basis in the economy, and more and more of our social and cultural life today is understood as being a part of the economy. Because of this we can say that cultural autonomy in general is expensive when seen from the view of economy, and that this is dangerous because the economy tries to reduce costs.

The second consequence is that commercialization may have the power to make the lifeworlds of the people irrelevant. This metaprocess thus may lead into a society that may with far greater certainty be described as a functional systemic network. But this is not certain and therefore must be observed and analyzed.

CONCLUDING REMARKS

Let's sum up. We have shown that network and complex connectivity are concepts that are adequate to describe specific functional features of the emergent society. But they are—at least today—not valid for everything. This becomes clear if instead of using the final states of an expected development as the basis of analysis, we analyze the already existing metaprocesses that lead to the social and cultural life of the future.

Here, we have analyzed globalization, individualization, and mediatization. Together with commercialization, which in the capitalistic society must be understood as a basic metaprocess, as it describes the core motives of individual action in a network society, all these developments can be said to have an impact on social life such that they may be described and theoretically understood by using connectivity and network terms and concepts. But the mediatization metaprocess in particular makes it clear that lifeworld-specific communication remains the basis of communication and meaning in general. In this context, the digital media can be described as a digital net of possibilities and flows, which increasingly becomes intertwined and intermingled with previously existing forms of communication. The construction of everyday life and social relations, of meaning, sense, identity, and self then takes place inside the full communication environment. Thus the form of the individual, but collectively produced lifeworld retains its character as a basis and counterposition to the systemically organized, structured network, or connectivity areas of modern life.

Of course, the developments offer us new possibilities, but what we might do with them depends on society and culture. Rather than concluding that we should fear further developments, we should do more empirical research and participate—with reference to Habermas—in the discussion process of civil society. The civil society must decide what takes place, not the political elite, not the industry, and not the economy or the media, as social and cultural life belong to humanity's core agendas.

REFERENCES

Albrow, M. (1998). *Abschied vom Nationalstaat*. Frankfurt a. M.: Suhrkamp.

Appadurai, A. (1996). *Modernity at large: Cultural dimensions of globalization*. Minneapolis: University of Minnesota Press.

Arnason, J. (1987). Figurational sociology as a counter-paradigm. *Theory, Culture & Society, 4*, 429-456.

Barck, K. (Ed.). (1997). *Harold A. Innis—Kreuzwege der Kommunikation. Ausgewählte Texte*. Wien, New York: Springer.

Baumgart, R., & Eichener, V. (1991). *Norbert Elias zur Einführung*. Hamburg: Junius.

Beck, U. (1983). Jenseits von Stand und Klasse? In R. Kreckel (Ed.), *Soziale Ungleichheiten. Soziale Welt, Sonderband 2* (pp. 35-74). Göttingen: Schwartz.

Beck, U. (1986). *Risikogesellschaft*. Frankfurt a.M.: Suhrkamp.

Beck, U. (1994). The debate on the individualization theory in today's sociology in Germany. *Soziologie, 3*, 191-200.

Beck, U., & Beck-Gernsheim, E. (Eds.). (1994). *Riskante Freiheiten. Individualisierung in modernen Gesellschaften*. Frankfurt a.M.: Suhrkamp.

Berger, P. L., & Luckmann, T. (1980). *Die gesellschaftliche Konstruktion der Wirklichkeit*. Frankfurt a.M.: Fischer. (Original work published 1969)

Carey, J. W. (1975). Canadian communication theory: Extensions and interpretations of Harold Innis. In G. J. Robinson & D. Theale (Eds.), *Studies in Canadian communications* (pp. 29-59). Montreal: Programmes in Communications, McGill University.

Cassirer, E.(1994). *Wesen und Wirkung des Symbolbegriffs*. Darmstadt: Wissenschaftliche Buchgesellschaft.

Castells, M. (1996). *The rise of the network society*. Oxford: Blackwell.

Cohen, R., & Kennedy, P. (2000). *Global sociology*. Houndsmills: Palgrave.

Duerrschmidt, J. (2002). *Globalisierung*. Bielefeld: Transcript.

Elias, N. (1972). *Über den Prozeß der Zivilisation* (Vols. 1 and 2, 2nd ed.). Frankfurt a.M.: Suhrkamp.

Elias, N. (1993). *Was ist Soziologie?* (7th ed.). Weinheim, München: Juventus.

Elias, N. (1994). *Die Gesellschaft der Individuen* (2nd ed.). Frankfurt a.M.: Suhrkamp.

Elias, N. (2000). Prozesse, soziale. In B. Schäfers (Ed.), *Grundbegriffe der Soziologie* (6th ed., pp. 271-277). Opladen: Leske und Budrich.

Featherstone, M. (1987). Norbert Elias and figurational sociology: Some prefatory remarks. *Theory, Culture & Society, 4,* 197-212.

Giddens, A. (1990*). The consequences of modernity.* Cambridge: Polity Press.

Giddens, A. (2001). *Entfesselte Welt. Wie die Globalisierung unser Leben verändert.* Frankfurt a.M.: Suhrkamp

Giessen, H. W. (Ed.). (1998). *Long term consequences on social structures through mass media impact.* Saarbrücken: Vistas (Reihe der LAR).

Giessen, H. W. (2001). Harold W. Innis: Kommunikation als Schlüsselbegriff zum Verständnis der Menschheitsgeschichte? *Medien & Kommunikationswissenschaft, 50*(2), 261-273.

Goody, J., Watt, I., & Gough, K. (1986). *Entstehung und Folgen der Schriftkultur.* Frankfurt a.M.: Suhrkamp.

Habermas, J. (1987*). Theorie kommunikativen Handelns* (Vols. 1 and 2, 4th ed.). Frankfurt a.M.: Suhrkamp.

Habermas, J. (1990). *Strukturwandel der Öffentlichkeit* (2nd ed.). Frankfurt a.M.: Suhrkamp.

Hepp, A. (2004). *Netzwerke der Medien. Medienkulturen und Globalisierung.* Wiesbaden: VS.

Jarren, O., & Krotz, F. (Eds.). (1998). *Öffentliche Kommunikation unter Vielkanalbedingungen.* Baden-Baden: Nomos

Krotz, F. (1994). Eine Schule am Marktplatz des globalen Dorfes? Globalisierung und Europäisches Bildungsfernsehen. *Publizistik, 4,* 409-427.

Krotz, F. (1999). Individualisierung und das Internet. In M. Latzer, G. Siegert & T. Steinmaurer (Eds.), *Die Zukunft der Kommunikation. Phänomene und Trends in der Informationsgesellschaft* (pp. 347-365). Innsbruck, Wien: Studienverlag.

Krotz, F. (2001). *Die Mediatisierung kommunikativen Handelns. Wie sich Alltag und soziale Beziehungen, Kultur und Gesellschaft durch die Medien wandeln.* Wiesbaden: Westdeutscher Verlag.

Krotz, F. (2001a). Die Übernahme öffentlicher und individueller Kommunikation durch die Privatwirtschaft. Über den Zusammenhang zwischen Mediatisierung und Ökonomisierung. In M. Karmasin, M. Knoche, & C. Winter (Eds.), *Medienwirtschaft und Gesellschaft 1* (pp. 197-217). Münster: LIT.

Krotz, F. (2001b). Marshall McLuhan Revisited. Der Theoretiker des Fernsehens und die Mediengesellschaft. *Medien- und Kommunikationswissenschaft, 49*(1), 62-81.

Krotz, F. (2003). Zivilisationsprozess und Mediatisierung: Zum Zusammenhang von Medien- und Gesellschaftswandel. In M. Behmer, F. Krotz, R. Stöber, & C. Winter (Eds.), *Medienentwicklung und gesellschaftlicher Wandel* (pp. 15-38). Wiesbaden: Westdeutscher Verlag.

Krotz, F., & S. Eastman (1999).Orientations toward television outside the home in Hamburg and Indianapolis. *Journal of Communication, 49*(1), 5-27.

Krotz, F., & Hasebrink, U. (2001). Who are the new media users? In S. Livingstone & M. Bovill (Eds.), *Children and their changing media environment. A European comparative study* (pp. 245-262). Mahwah, NJ: Erlbaum.

Lerner, D. (1962). *The passing of traditional society.* Glencoe: The Free Press.

Martín-Barbero, J. (1993). *Communication, culture and hegemony.* Newbury Park, CA: Sage.

Mattelart, A., & M. Mattelart (1998). *Theories of communication: A short introduction.* London: Sage.

McAllister, M. P. (1996). *The commercialization of American culture. New advertising, control and democracy.* Thousand Oaks, CA: Sage.

McLuhan, M. (1967). *Understanding media: The extensions of man.* London: Sphere Books.

McLuhan, M., & Powers, B. R. (1995). *The Global Village. Der Weg der Mediengesellschaft in das 21. Jahrhundert.* Paderborn: Jungfermann.

Mead, G. H. (1967). *Mind, self and society.* Chicago: University of Chicago Press.

Meyrowitz, J. (1985). *No sense of place.* Oxford: Oxford University Press.

Meyrowitz, J. (1994). Medium theory. In D. J. Crowley & D. Mitchell (Eds.), *Communication theory today* (pp. 50-77). Cambridge: Polity Press.

Rogers, E. M. (1995). *Diffusion of innovations* (4th ed.). New York: The Free Press.

Schiller, H. I. (1994). *Mass communications and American empire* (2nd ed.). New York: Kelley.

Schiller, H. I. (1989). *Culture, Inc.: The corporate takeover of public expression.* New York: Oxford University Press.

Sennett, R. (1999). *The corrosion of character.* New York: Norton.

Tomlinson, J. (1991). *Cultural imperialism.* London: Pinter.

Tomlinson, J. (1999). *Globalization and culture.* Cambridge: Polity Press.

TRANSLOCAL MEDIA CULTURES

Networks of the Media
and Globalization

Andreas Hepp

Focusing on media theory and globalization steers us to a tricky situation: on the one hand theory is the thing in academia that travels best
globally, or what is thought of as globally—the English speaking, international community. The reason for this may be that theory seems to be
more universal than context sensitive studies are. Because of this
assumed *universality* we often have the impression that we can do
something with a theory across different (cultural) contexts. But when
discussing media theory in the time of globalization we have to realize
that theory is not something universal. From a linguistic perspective
George Lakoff and Mark Johnson (1980) argued more than two decades
ago that our thinking is, to a strong extent, based on (culturally specific) metaphors. In a comparable perspective focused on the way of doing
cultural studies Stuart Hall has argued that all theories have to be contextualized and that we should develop a practice of ongoing theorizing
rather than seek a universal theory (Hall, 1988; for the same arguments
on audience studies see Ang, 1996). In media theory in particular, such
a focus on *universal theory* may tend to Western-centrism, as there is
a kind of "self-absorption and parochialism of much Western media
theory" (Curran & Park, 2000, p. 3): many of the key concepts of Western

media theory are based on historically specific metaphors of Western cultures, which are constructed as universal and used as a guideline to evaluate processes of media communication around the globe.

In this situation one should be careful when arguing that *connectivity, network*, and *flow* are appropriate concepts for media and cultural studies in the time of globalization *in general*. As John Urry has pointed out, one has to accept that these concepts also refer to a metaphorical thinking, which, we have to add, is culturally situated (Urry, 2003, p. 50f.). If we accept the general critique of poststructuralism and deconstructionism, it is impossible to develop that "universal theory" of media and cultural globalization. Nevertheless, I would like to pick up the argument that connectivity, network, and flow are theoretical concepts that help us to develop *a* way of theoretical thinking, which is especially appropriate for media and cultural studies focusing on questions of globalization. With these concepts it becomes possible to theorize media cultures in the time of globalization not because they are universal, but because they allow a self-reflexive way of thinking that is highly productive in questioning a Western-centric point of view. To clarify this approach, I want to propose a three-step argument: First, I want to give some comments on the concepts of (global) connectivity, networks, and flows. Secondly, taking these reflections as a starting point I want to develop a theorization of translocal media cultures. This provides the base for the third step of my argument, which presents a discussion of contemporary global media inequality. Although my argumentation is in many parts rather abstract, I hope that this abstract thinking provides a basis for a more concrete critique of specific aspects of media globalization, without losing the opportunities offered by this process at the same time.[1]

GLOBAL CONNECTIVITY, NETWORKS, AND FLOWS

Recent work on globalization in sociology and cultural studies tends to culminate in the argument that globalization is best understood as the metaprocess of an increasing, multidimensional worldwide connectivity. This formulation seeks to conjoin at least three different arguments: In the first place, if we understand globalization as a "meta-process" (Krotz, 2005), this indicates that the concept *globalization* does not designate something we could observe in the sense that it is an empirical object which can be situated in a specific context. Rather, globalization

---

[1]The arguments I am developing in the following pages summarize the basic ideas of my book *Netzwerke der Medien. Medienkulturen und Globalisierung* [Networks of the Media. Media Cultures and Globalization], which was published in 2004.

is a theoretical concept like *individualisation* or *commercialisation*, which helps us to understand contradictory and paradoxical subprocesses as a whole.

In the second place, this process is multidimensional (Giddens, 1990, p. 70; Tomlinson, 1999, p. 13). This indicates that globalization operates on different *process levels* or *scapes*. Whatever concept of globalization we support the different arguments agree that globalization can't be reduced to one main dimension (for example, the economic one) that determines the others. The different subprocesses of globalization seem to have their own logic or forces, which have to be conceptualized before relations between them can be understood. Nevertheless there seem to be many relations among the different process levels, whose "disjuncture" (Appadurai, 1996, p. 27) is relative.

This refers to the third point, which is associated with the term connectivity. In the arguments of John Tomlinson (Tomlinson, 1999, pp. 3-10), the term connectivity indicates a wariness of what we can conclude from the metaprocess we call globalization: Whereas early work on that topic had the tendency to argue that globalization might imply an increasing global standardization, homogenization, a kind of "McDonaldization" (Ritzer, 1998), or—in short—a "global culture" (Featherstone, 1990), we now know that cultural proximity *can* be one result of globalization in specific contexts. But processes of increasing conflicts, misunderstandings and cultural fractions are also part of globalization: "globalization divides as much as it unites; it divides as it unites" (Bauman, 1998, p. 3). This is especially a central argument in the field of media communication: an increasing communicative connectivity does not bring people inevitably together, as Marshall McLuhan's utopian idea of the global village has outlined (see McLuhan & Fiore, 1968), and has not resulted in a *worldwide Americanization* as an unquestioned consequence. Rather the increasing worldwide media connectivity indicates, on the quantitative level, a high number of ongoing communicative processes. These processes have a very different character when seen from a qualitative point of view. We must analyze in detail what the consequences of media globalization are by focusing on specific processes within specific contexts.

Up to this point my arguments bind together present academic thinking on globalization. One can say that the globalization of media communication is one dimension of the metaprocess of globalization, and this dimension is best understood as an increasing communicative connectivity. For sure, this process is not homogenizing but is marked by different inequalities and conflicts. Also it can't be reduced to the economic activity of global media industries because media products are not only commercial but also cultural commodities. As cultural commodities they can't separated from processes of meaningful articulation, which have to be contextualized within everyday life.

However, keeping this academic debate on globalization in mind, there is one further argument that is important in the context of present media theory: This is the argument that the global connectivity of globalization makes it necessary to re-evaluate the theoretical concepts we are used to. It was Anthony Giddens (Giddens, 1990, pp. 10-17) who pointed out the extent to which sociology as a modern discipline is connected with the concept of "society" as a reference point for describing social processes as productive of "integration" within the frame of a territorial, bounded nation-state. But with ongoing globalization, we ought to question this frame if we want to capture modernity—or better—the present modernities. As Giddens noted, "if we are adequately to grasp the nature of modernity, [...] we have to break away from existing sociocultural perspectives" (Giddens, 1990, p. 16). The same arguments can be found in the writing of other thinkers. Ien Ang, for example, criticized the sociological focus of *national integration*, which seems to be inappropriate when focusing on contemporary cultures (see Ang, 1996, pp. 162-180). Arjun Appadurai argues for a "transnational anthropology" (Appadurai, 1996, p. 48f.) that should analyze the cultural dynamics of what is now called *deterritorialization*.[2] Ulrich Beck has pointed out that globalization makes a new "sociology of globalization" (Beck, 1997, p. 48) necessary, which operates beyond the territorial frame of a container theory of society. Comparable arguments can be found in the work of John Urry, who advocates a "sociology beyond societies" (Urry, 2000, 2003), or in Manuel Castells' attempt to describe a society "structured around a bipolar opposition between the net and the self" (Castells, 1996, p. 3). All these arguments were made for media and cultural studies in a globalized world, too (see Hepp, 2004, pp. 17-21).

If we accept these claims for new concepts in the time of globalization as correct, we are confronted with one problem: how can we theorize them as part of the global connectivity? It seems that there are at least two perspectives from which such an undertaking can be done. First of all, this is the perspective of the *structuring* aspect of globalization, which can be related to the already mentioned term "network"; secondly it is the *processing* aspect of globalization, which can be related to the term "flow" (see Figure 3.1).[3] It seems to me that it is important to keep both aspects in mind when we discuss questions of globalization.

---

[2]Again, this is a critique of the social science tradition, if we understand anthropology as part of this: "The terms of the negotiation between imagined lives and deterritorialized worlds are complex, and they surely cannot be captured by the localizing strategies of traditional ethnography alone" (Appadurai, 1996, p. 52).
[3]It seems to be inconsistent to name an aspect of a metaprocess itself processing. But this is not as contradictory as it seems at first blush: In the first case the focus is on a metaprocess as an interpretative frame on the whole; in the second, the focus is on a rather contextualized and situated process. However we have to keep in mind that we are not dealing with the epistemological level, but rather the level of viewing perspectives.

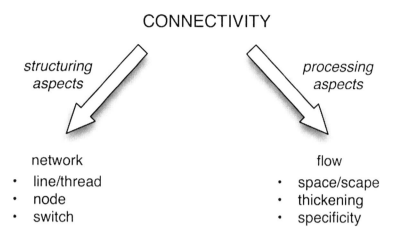

CONNECTIVITY

structuring aspects

processing aspects

network
- line/thread
- node
- switch

flow
- space/scape
- thickening
- specificity

Figure 3.1. Theorizing Global Connectivity

Networks: Structuring Aspects

The term network offers a clear view of the structuring forces of globalization.[4] To make this comprehensible, I want to quote Manuel Castells' definition of network, which meets with many others. For Castells networks are:

> open structures, able to expand without limits, integrating new nodes as long as they are able to communicate within the network, namely as long as they share the same communication codes (for example, values or performance goals). (Castells, 1996, p. 501)

This quote clarifies some of the important aspects of *theorizing networks*. In a specific sense, it is tautological to argue that networks consist of connections (links, threads, curves and so on) that are connected at nodes. This is just a description of a network as an everyday metaphor. But in recent theory, these terms have been loaded with specific meanings. It is increasingly obvious that the connectivity of a network is constituted within a specific *code*. Structures of (social) networks are not just there, but reproduced in an ongoing contextualized process. This, for example, makes it possible that one and the same person may be part of different networks: he or she can be part of the net-

---

[4]In contrast to John Urry (Urry, 2003, p. 59), I wouldn't argue that the "structural view of concepts" is obsolete with an increasing global connectivity. Globalization seems also to be a structuring power, which makes it necessary to develop theories to describe these aspects. On the other hand, this does not, of course, minimize the relevance of a point of view that focuses on flows and fluidity.

work of friends (where a specific kind of social relation might be the *dominant code*), and he or she can be part of the network of a social movement (where specific cultural values and political aims are the dominant code).[5] This seems to be the reason why network structures are so open and the borders of networks are so blurred, while nevertheless working as structuring forces: A network of friends places demands on us, just as our political engagement in a social movement closes other opportunities for political action.

These remarks help to theorize what we can understand by the term *nodes*. At a neutral level one can say that a node is the point where the connection (ties, links, threads, curves and so on) of a network traverses itself.[6] From an initial perspective, formulations like this seem to be irritating; nevertheless they help us to understand the important point, that nodes within network structures can be completely different things. We can understand communication as a process of establishing a specific kind of connectivity, in which the speaking persons are the main nodes. But nodes can also have other social forms. For example, we can describe local groups as nodes in the network of a wider social movement, or we can understand organizations such as local companies as nodes in a wider corporation network. *Network structures* can be seen on completely different levels, and that is the reason the concept offers the chance to describe and compare structuring powers across these different levels.

A third term that seems to be important when we discuss the structural aspect of global connectivity is the term *switch*. Again, it was Manuel Castells who introduced this term into the academic discussion. For Castells, a switch is a specific kind of node, which links different networks. The term "switch" refers to the idea that this node must be able to switch the code of one network into the code of another. To make this clearer, it will help to have a look at the nodes Castells describes as switches. The examples he focuses on in this context are the networks of capital, information and decision making (see Castells, 2000, p. 502). Their different structures are linked via specific switches—in these cases located in so-called global cities. Switches are in this sense the location where central aspects of power are concentrated in network structures, and this idea opens an additional aspect of analyzing power

---

[5]To base this argument on person-centered networks: although all of these different networks are working along the code friendship, the focus of "friendship" ("friendship," with whom) shifts over the network. This is exactly the reason we can't argue unambiguously and in detail where the "border" of a personal network is. Along this line, we can also say that the small-world theorem works (even if two persons do not have a friend in common, they are separated only by a short chain of intermediaries; see Watts, 2004).

[6]Of course, it is important to differentiate between strong and weak ties in different networks. See, for example, the classical arguments by Granovetter (1983).

relations within (global) networks: Whereas power relations are rooted in the totality of social networks, as Michel Foucault has pointed out (Foucault, 1996, p. 43), the concept of the switch helps us to understand where power relations are concentrated in networks—at the position where different networks interact.

The *network thinking* that I have outlined offers a way of describing structural aspects of connectivity, which explains the paradox of the *openness* and *closedness* of connectivity. On the one hand, the structures of networks are open in the sense that networks can (more or less) easily integrate new nodes and grow without losing their *stability*. From this point of view networks are open. On the other hand, networks are also closed, as these processes of extension operate across specific codes, which define the specificity of a network and its power. But again there seems to be a certain openness of networks at this point, as switches offer the opportunity to communicate across the coding borders of networks. This is the point where the network metaphor seems to be more productive than, for example, the *system* metaphor in current functional theory. Systems are, as in the writing of Niklas Luhmann (1997), thought of as closed structures which reproduce themselves in an "autopoetic way." Because of their autopoetical structure, there is no possibility for systems to interact in a direct way; they are linked, instead, by structural coupling. Although these concepts of functional system theory may offer a coherent theoretical framework, their weakness lies in their focus on unambiguous system borders and system integration. Network as a concept seems to offer a much more open way of thinking, which is appropriate for the paradoxical structures of globalization (see Karmasin, 2004, for the concept of paradox in media studies).

Flows: Processing Aspects

As I have argued, focusing on networks is only one way of discussing global connectivity. As important as this structural aspect is the processing point of view. The main term used to describe these processes is flow or fluid; I prefer to use the concept of flow.[7] These flows operate across specific network structures; for example, the *flow of news* has to be conceptualized on the base of different media networks (see Boyd-Barrett & Thussu, 1992; Boyd-Barrett & Rantanen, 1998), while the flow of migrants operates across person(al) networks (see Pries, 2001).

---

[7]The reason for this is that fluid does not only refer to liquid but also gas. Certainly, this opens a productive field of metaphors, as Zygmunt Bauman (2000) has shown in his book *Liquid Modernity*. Nevertheless there remains the risk of missing the structural aspects of globalization by focusing only on the dissolution of the traditional institutions of modernity, instead of on their transformation into new structures.

John Urry, in particular, has argued that the concept of the flow or fluid[8] seems to be highly important for describing social and cultural processes in the time of globalization, because these concepts offer the possibility for a new kind of sociology that can conceptualize the increasingly mobile cultural forms. Urry argues that the "development of a mobile sociology demands metaphors that view social and material life as being like the waves of a river" (Urry, 2003, p. 59). Based on this idea, Urry favors a concept of *global fluids*, emphasizing that fluids undoubtedly involve networks, but nevertheless the specificity of these global fluids is that they transgress networks and are "in part self-organizing, creating and maintaining boundaries" (Urry, 2003, p. 60). These arguments are very interesting from my point of view as they are helpful and problematic at the same time. They are helpful because of the accentuation of the transgressing character of flows: Flows like the flow of specific information "transgress" different networks, and this is the reason why the concepts of network and flow can't be interwoven. On the other hand, this argument seems to be problematic, as Urry is deducing from this—partly despite his critique of the functionalist tradition—a self-organizing aspect of global flows. However, if we break down such an abstract theoretical perspective to the level of everyday experience, we notice, at least, that global communication flows are not autonomic phenomena, but are structured through communication networks along which they have to "travel"—and these structuring processes have something to do with power. What I want to argue is that Urry is certainly right in emphasizing the complexity of (global) flows. What remains problematic is his tendency to give up asking about structuring aspects in global complexity and how these are interwoven with power relations. In spite of their tentative character, theoretical concepts such as the aforementioned concept of the switch as a power-marked transgression point of different networks are a more appropriate way of thinking about power in global complexity than talking about self-organizing aspects of flows. It is exactly these switches that are very manifest in everyday life: If we discuss media flows, we have to have a look at the power position of globally acting media companies while acknowledging that they are at the same time part of an increasing global capitalism that produces uncertainty and ambiguity rather than a collective understanding (see Ang, 1996, pp. 171-180).

Based on this we can conclude that flows are not an instantaneous occurrence, but constitute long-term conglomerations of processes. There are different terms that have been established to describe these conglomerations, such as *space* in Castells' (2000, pp. 407-459) concept of *space of flows* or *scape* in Arjun Appadurai's (1996, p. 33) well-known differentiation of ethnoscapes, mediascapes, technoscapes, finance-

---

[8]Urry uses both terms interchangeably. I prefer the term "flow," as I have already explained.

scapes, and ideoscapes. Theoretical frameworks such as these try to capture the idea that different (global) flows constitute complex landscapes that have to be described in their appropriate logic. The flows of globalization do not exist as an isolated singularity but constitute one part of a more complex whole.

Although we can see how powerful spatial concepts are to describe long-term conglomerations of flows (see for this the chapters in Couldry & McCarthy, 2004; and in general, Morley, 1996, pp. 327-331), one specific theoretical concept seems to me very helpful in discussing the processes involved in a conglomeration of flows. That is the concept of *thickening* (see, for example, Löfgren, 2001). If we understand our present world as being marked by an increasing global connectivity of networks and flows that merge into each other and have uncertain borders, we have to answer the question of how we should think of the nevertheless still existing cultural, economic, and other conglomerations. If we understand them as "meaningful thickenings" of flows along and across networks, we emphasize on the one hand the specificity of such a conglomeration, and emphasize at the same time their blurred borders. It is striking that "thickening" accentuates the open character of networks and flows but at the same time the specificity of the space or scape of long-term conglomerations: thickenings are a focused and meaningful specificity with disappearing borders. The specificity of thickenings is based on the character of its constituting flows, their direction and extent.

Up to now, I have tried to outline the basis of a connectivity-based theorization of globalization, especially the globalization of media communication. But there is still at least one question to answer: Does there not remain, implicit in such a theoretical model the problematic trajectory of a universal theory of globalization? Ien Ang and Jon Stratton, in particular, have emphasized how problematic such a trajectory would be. In discussing the impossibility of global cultural studies, they point out one already mentioned problematic of sociology as a "predecessor" (Stratton & Ang, 1996, p. 364) of present cultural studies. Sociology was focused on the development of generally applicable concepts, which had a tendency to "construct a world of separate, clearly demarcated 'societies' whose differences can be contained as mere variations of the same" (Stratton & Ang, 1996, p. 364). Although this trajectory is criticized nowadays in the sociology of globalization itself, Ang and Stratton conclude from this discursive pattern of (functional) sociology[9] a central aspect of cultural studies in the time of globalization: These can't be global cultural studies in the sense of developing a generally applicable

---

[9]One has to restrict the arguments of Ang and Stratton in this way, as there always has been other tendencies in sociology, especially within cultural sociology, which has a lot in common with cultural studies. See for this Long (1997, p. 15).

and universal metalanguage, which generalizes cultural specificity. But it also does not make sense to develop different national cultural studies projects, as this just would reproduce the segmenting patterns and logic of functional sociology. Rather, cultural studies should focus on the process of articulating particularities themselves, based on a context-specific and continuous mode of theorizing. In Ien Ang's and Jon Stratton's own words, "what cultural studies needs to do if it wants to avoid universalization is not just valorize any asserted particularity, but reflect on the concrete processes of particularization itself, and to interrogate its politics" (Stratton & Ang, 1996, p. 367).

In my perspective, this is the point where theorizing with the concepts of connectivity, network, and flow makes sense: This offers one conceptual base for reflecting the processes of particularization or, as I want to call them, thickening. Of course there are and have to be other possibilities of theorizing. But from my point of view, the model outlined above seems quite helpful. In this sense the named concepts don't refer to a universal theory but to one way of theorizing, particularity in the time of globalization, and of focusing cultural and media studies on this theory. To make my arguments clearer, I now want to discuss contemporary media cultures in the frame of this theoretical framework.

TRANSLOCAL MEDIA CULTURES
AND GLOBAL CONNECTIVITY

On an abstract level, one can discuss any medium as an instrument of establishing connectivity. Language, for instance, is a tool people use to connect communicatively. So one can understand, as Werner Faulstich and Carsten Winter do (Faulstich, 1996; Winter, 1996), itinerant preachers as *human media*, because these travellers make communicative connections among people in different regions. Furthermore, electronic media such as film, television, radio and the internet can also be understood as tools for establishing connectivity. Their representations construct symbolic links among different people and cultures.

These examples can be used to illustrate the following two aspects. Primarily, connectivity is a general avenue of communication. It is not new or specific to electronic media or the internet.[10] Rather it helps us to conceptualize the idea that communication refers to establishing a specific kind of link or relation, which can result in understanding, but could also result in misunderstanding. Secondly, something has changed in the process of establishing connectivity in the course of media histo-

---

[10]This is important because many present theories—for example, the already mentioned network theory of Manuel Castells (2000, pp. 31-38)—tend to neglect this.

ry. The first forms of communicative connectivity were strongly based on physical aspects, as is the case, for example, in the obviously physical nature of a person's travels. By contrast, the forms of connectivity becoming important in the course of the past two centuries are forms with reduced physical aspects. Of course internet connections still have a physical basis in electronic cable networks, but the forms of connectivity are more and more *delinked* from this base.

If we focus on the cultural change of globalization, it is exactly that ongoing delinkage of cultural forms that has been identified. Néstor García Canclini (1995, p. 229), for example, argues that the cultural change caused by globalization is deterritorialization; hence, we can see a growing loss of the apparently natural relationship among culture and geographical and social territories that is mediated by the process of globalization.

But having my general arguments on conceptualizing connectivity in mind, I would argue that the concept of deterritorialization needs further classification in order to be a basis for analytical and empirical work on current media cultures and the changes they are undergoing. The main problem with García Canclini's work is that the different aspects of deterritorialization are mixed. First of all, you see something one can call *physical deterritorialization* on which García Canclini's and the arguments of others focus (see, for example, Appadural, 1996, pp. 27-65). In the time of globalization many people are moving, travelling, and migrating, and the world as a whole is much more mobile than in previous centuries. García Canclini focuses on this when he speaks about the cultural changes in Latin America or the United States, specifically using the example of migrants. But we can also see an increase of these forms of mobility within Europe.[11]

Besides this, there is a second type of deterritorialization, one that can be named *communicative deterritorialization*. The cultural change of globalization does not only refer to an increasing mobility of people and goods, but to the ongoing process of media globalization—an increasing global communicative connectivity—and the cultural changes involved that are very important in everyday life. An increasing number of products that are available in different territories are media products (see, for example, Hall, 1997).

Physical and communicative deterritorialization cannot be set against each other, but are interwoven on different levels, especially if we discuss migration and other forms of mobility. Taking diasporas as an example for physical deterritorialization, it is obvious that they can only be stable "exemplary communities of the transnational moment" (Tölölyan, 1991, p. 3), because their members share common cultural representations. These common cultural representations are mediat-

---

[11]For statistical data on this see European Commission (2003).

ed—based on a communicative connectivity.[12] Nevertheless, it is important to draw a distinction between physical and communicative deterritorialization for the following three reasons:

1. *Speed*: Communicative deterritorialization seems to take place much faster than its physical counterpart. Media flows can be shifted much more quickly and cheaply than flows of goods or people. This is particularly the case for the internet.
2. *Volatility*: Communicative deterritorialization often seems to be much more volatile than physical deterritorialization. If we take migration as a prominent example of physical deterritorialization, this process is very manifest in a local neighborhood. A person who is there as a stranger irritates through his or her everyday practices on a deep level, and this may be exactly why classical sociology is deeply interested in the social type of the stranger. In contrast to this, many aspects of communicative deterritorialization are difficult to enact; for instance, nationalized formats of soap operas or quiz shows on television, which are normally regarded as national television although the format itself is actually deterritorialized (see Moran, 1998; Müller, 2002). Comparably, the national(ized) internet portal of a transnational provider might be seen as something of one's "own." In this sense the existing forces of communicative deterritorialization are more volatile—in the sense of ephemeral and charged—than physical ones.
3. *Degree*: In contrast to this, the degree to which communicative deterritorialization is involved in everyday life is paradoxically much higher than the degree to which physical deterritorialization is. Although in Europe, as in many regions of the world, mobility in the sense of "moving house" is lower than one would expect, the access to media products from many different regions of the world via the local communicative connectivity is evident (see Morley, 2000, pp. 86-104). Because of its speed and volatility, communicative deterritorialization pervades everyday life on many levels.

To bring these three aspects together, one can argue in the first place that the concept of communicative deterritorialization as a consequence of increasing global communicative connectivity makes it possi-

[12]Marie Gillespie has shown this in detail for the Punjabi diaspora (see Gillespie, 1995, 2000, 2002 and my arguments later in the section on appropriation). Comparable arguments are developed by Aksoy and Robins (2000); Ang (2001, 2003); Bromley (2000); Clifford (1994); Dayan (1999); Mercer (1988); Papastergiadis (1998); Zips (2003).

ble to understand the change of media cultures in the time of globalization, a change that has already taken place. More and more media products are mediated across various territories; for instance international news (see, for example, Boyd-Barrett & Rantanen, 1998; Paterson, 1997; Volkmer, 1999; Zelizer & Allan, 2002), as well as Hollywood[13] and Bollywood[14] blockbusters. And in a specific sense one can understand the internet as the most deterritorialized medium, as its WWW contents at least on an ideal level can be accessed from everywhere. But how can we analyze this communicative deterritorialization in detail? And how can an understanding of communicative connectivity be focused upon in this context?

On the basis of the theoretical framework developed above, I would give the following answer: by focusing on *translocality* (Hepp, 2004, pp. 163-194). First of all, the word "translocal" or "translocality" is an analytical concept used to study the communicative connectivity of the media. There are two reasons for this concept that are appropriate and that one can link with the word "locality" and its prefix, "trans." Locality emphasizes that in the time of media globalization the local world does not cease to exist. Irrespective of how far the communicative connectivity of a locality goes, this does not prompt questions of whether a person is living his or her life primarily locally. As a physical human being he or she must reside somewhere. Surely this place changes its meaning with growing communicative connectivity, especially if this connectivity tends to be global. But the centrality of locality is not minimized in the time of globalization. "Trans," as a prefix, guides the focus from questions of locality (on which, for example, media anthropology focuses in particular) to questions of connectivity. If research is centered on translocality, this emphasizes, on the one hand, that local issues still matter, but that on the other hand today's locales are connected physically and communicatively to a very high degree. And that is the reason why that which is local does not cease to exist, but rather, changes.

But besides this, translocality also refers to a specific understanding of culture. Some time ago, Jan Nederveen Pieterse (1995) divided principal understandings of culture into two: territorial and translocal. To put his arguments in a nutshell, one can say that territorial concepts of culture are inward-looking, endogenous, focused on organicity, authenticity and identity. Translocal concepts of culture are outward-looking, exogenous, focused on hybridity, translation and identification. On the basis of my arguments on connectivity it seems helpful to me to under-

---

[13]Concerning Hollywood, see During (1997); Hickethier (2001); Miller et al. (2001); Olson (1999).

[14]For the Indian film industry see, for example, Chakravarty (1993); Dhaliwal (1994); Kazmi (1999); Pendakur (1990); Pendakur and Subramanyam (1996), and increasingly a lot of popular writing.

stand cultures in general in a translocal frame: all cultures are more or less hybrid, and had to translate, change their identities, and so on. In contrast to this, what is problematic for a general territorial conceptionalization of culture is that it refers to the already criticized "container-thinking" of nation states. Within this concept, cultures are from the beginning interpreted as national cultures of territorial states. More helpful than such territorial bordering is to consider how cultures—as the sum of the classificatory systems and discursive formations on which the production of meaning draws (see Hall, 1997, p. 222)—transgress the local without being necessarily focused on territoriality as a reference point of their meaning articulation. In this sense, cultures are a kind of thickening of translocal processes of the articulation of meaning. Such a theorization opens the possibility of understanding territorialization and its analogue, deterritorialization, as contested practices through which specific cultures are articulated in their particularity by the media and beyond.

This way of thinking allows the theorizing of media cultures in a new way. When speaking about media cultures I include all cultures whose primary resources of meaning are accessible through technology-based media. From this point of view, all media cultures have to be theorized as translocal, inasmuch as media make translocal communicative connections possible. With respect to the context of a connectivity theory, media cultures in general have to be theorized as translocal phenomena. But in some cases, they are rather territorialized (national media cultures), and in some cases rather deterritorialized (media cultures of diaspora).

By focusing on this framework, it will be possible to describe the change of European media cultures during the last hundred years in a different way. One can take, for instance, the works of Benedict Anderson (1983), Orvar Löfgren, (2001) or David Morley (2000) as examples of this. The rise of national cultures is related to the diffusion of the so-called mass media. When different locales are very intensively connected by media, different people can be involved in a communicative process and the construction of a common "imagined community" (Anderson, 1983), "home territory" (Morley, 2000), or "cultural thickening" (Löfgren, 2001). Such reflections refer to the level on which questions of territory pertain to translocality. One can take television history as an example. First, television was marketed in the 1950s as global, when it was called a "window to the world." Secondly, television had to be appropriated locally, that is, it had to find its place in local life. And thirdly, the horizon of its first representations had the tendency to be nationally territorial, because the first important television events were national celebrations, national football games, or national serial productions; but also, the borders of TV network broadcasting were the borders of nations. Like the print media and the radio before it, television helped to construct the territorialized "imagined community" of a nation.

David Morley's metaphor of the "home territory" is, at this point, important in a dual sense. On the one hand, it shows the specificity of these national media cultures. It is possible to describe national media cultures whose translocal communicative thickening has been territorialized in such a way that national frontiers are the main borders of many communicative networks and flows. The process of thickening of the national imagined community was territorially bound. On the other hand, Morley's metaphor of the home territory shows us quite clearly that this territoriality of the media-influenced home no longer exists in a pure form. In the time of globalization, communicative connectivity is becoming more and more deterritorialized. With the distribution of media products across different national borders and the emergence of the internet global communicative connectivity grows, which makes the thickenings of national media cultures relative. One must contextualize them as part of different networks of the media.

This means that the borders of the cultural thickenings we belong to do not necessarily correspond with the territorial borders, while at the same time territories still have a high relevance as a reference point of constructing national community. However, deterritorial thickenings nevertheless gain relevance with increasing global media connectivity. If we take the case of the media cultures of today, we can say that we have both moments at the same time: on the one hand, we still have rather territorially focused thickenings of communicative connections, which is why it does make sense to talk about mediated regional or national translocal communities as a reference point of identities.[15] But at the same time, we have on the other side communicative thickenings across such territorial borders, thickenings, which offer the space for deterritorial translocal communities with corresponding identities. Analytically, here, we can make a three-level distinction based on ethnic, commercial, and political aspects. On the level of ethnicity we have an increasing number of communicative thickenings of minority groups and diasporas. On a commercial level we have an increasing number of deterritorialized popular cultural communities such as youth cultures or scenes. On a political level we have an increasing number of deterritorialized social movements such as the critical globalization movement. One can argue that all of these examples are based on translocal media connectivity and specific cultural thickenings, which offer an important resource point for current identities.

---

[15]One example would be the identity of different German federal states like Bavaria or Bremen, another example the different national identities within Europe. In addition, the construction of Europe itself is a space of communicative connectivity and the originating European identity is historically a territorially bound process (see Kleinsteuber & Rossmann, 1994; Morley & Robins, 1995).

THEORIZING GLOBAL INEQUALITY

At this point the different arguments presented can be tied to the perspective that in current times translocal media cultures should best be viewed as specific cultural thickenings, which are occasionally territorialized, but increasingly not. But is such a theory not hypocritical inasmuch as it tends to overlook those power conflicts and inequalities that, for example, the theory of cultural imperialism highlights? Doesn't such a perspective tend to harmonize or gloss over these problems?

Such arguments are important, as a number of theories of connectivity appear to have overly harmonizing tendencies. But the concept of translocal cultures offers a new way of theorizing inequality within the globalization of media, because inequality in global communicative connectivity is best understood as an "inequality in translocal connectivity." This can be seen on the levels of production, representation and appropriation. At all of these three levels the arguments I have developed become—(I hope)—more concrete.

Nodes of Production

If one were to ask which media organizations produce the media products constituting communicative connections *across* different territories, one realizes that the number of these organizations is limited, and that a rather small number of media companies are acting globally; that is, they produce products that have access to a wide range of cultural contexts (see, for example, Hachmeister & Rager, 2002; Herman & McChesney, 1997).

Taking a closer look at the specifics of media corporations such as Sony, Time Warner, or Bertelsmann, one realizes that these corporations are not integrated organizations but rather complex networks of subsidiaries and joint ventures. One has to conceptualize their structure translocally and not territorially. The main subsidiaries and joint ventures of these deterritorial media corporations can be found in various cities worldwide, no matter which of them one analyses. These cities can be categorized as "global media cities" (Figure 3.2) (Krätke, 2001; 2002) on three levels.[16] First, these cities are the central nodes in the networks of deterritorial media organizations. The global media cities are not only those localities where many deterritorial media products

---

[16]Having the view of global media cities above raises the question of whether there isn't a Euro-centrism behind the criteria of such a categorization, as a high number of the global media cities are located within Europe. I would nevertheless argue that in spite of such a problematic it offers helpful insights into why we should discuss questions of media production in times of globalization in a translocal rather than a territorial frame.

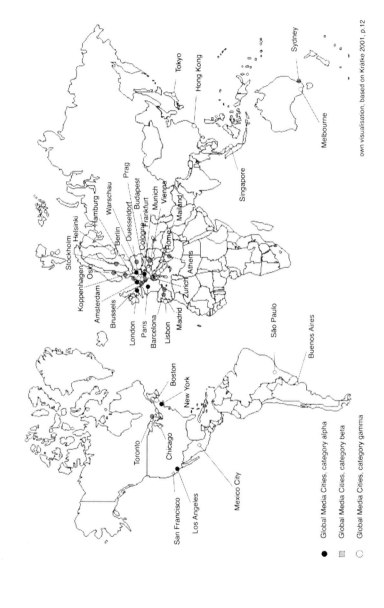

own visualisation, based on Krätke 2001, p.12

Figure 3.2. **Global Media Cites**

49

are developed, but also where the decision making within these deterritorial media organizations is centered. Secondly, global media cities are the central nodes in the networks of infrastructure and distribution of global connectivity. And third they are the nodes of global finance networks and flows (see Sassen, 2000) on which the actions of deterritorial media companies are based. In this perspective, global media cities can be understood as the location of the switches within deterritorial media corporations.

At this point it is important to note that only a translocal approach can account for such inequalities within global media production. This cannot be culturally territorialized in the manner of the cultural imperialism paradigm. Is Sony Pictures Japanese or American? What is Bertelsmann's Random House? German? Rather, these companies are networks across specific territorial and deterritorial translocal cultures, thickened at the nodes of specific global media cities. They do not act just in the frame of an increasingly global capitalism, but focus on commercial success across different cultures.

The example of global media cities and media organizations shows why the inequalities of globally orientated media production should be described as translocal phenomena. On one hand, globally orientated media production takes place in deterritorialized networks. On the other, the power relations within these networks are concentrated in specific global media cities, which are not equally spread out across the world. A translocal approach makes it possible to discuss such inequalities, but in a way that does not territorialize from the beginning.

Layers of Representative Thickening

At the beginning of the last section it was argued that national media cultures can also be viewed as translocal, but with one specification: the media connectivity of these cultures is territorialized; it has territorial boundaries. This argument can be formulated more precisely if one says that the media representations within these national media cultures are primarily communicated within specific borders and develop their discourses in an unmarked national frame. But this articulation of media representations as territorially specific, and therefore unequal, is only one aspect of the representation of translocal media cultures. In a translocal frame one can see other inequalities.

By viewing media cultures translocally, it is possible to separate different layers of agglomeration within the connectivity of media representations. Primarily, there are still regional and national thickenings of media representations. If one takes television as an example, present studies show that the prime-time serial productions in different regions of the world are national representations with respect to their availability and represented topics (see Hallenberger, 2002; Sinclair, Jacka, &

Cunningham, 1996). But besides this, further television representations gain relevance as globalization continues. Examples of this are transnational regional representations such as Indian television fictions, which are also available in neighboring countries (see Pendakur & Subramanyam, 1996). At the same time, Indian television productions are also examples of the increasing relevance of what one can call *deterritorial representations*. Deterritorial representations are accessible in different territories, but focused on specific cultural communities such as diasporas or lifestyle communities. Many Indian television productions are accessible through channels such as *Zee-TV* or *B4Y* and are viewed outside of India, in particular by the Indian diaspora, and therefore one can see them as deterritorial representations.

At this point the argument is again that it is not possible to reason in a time of globalization exclusively within a territorial frame. Although one can say that territorial aspects still have relevance in the form of national representations, there are other kinds of media representations, which construct connectivity transculturally across territorial borders that are equally relevant. Because of this, it is necessary to understand that representations form a complex landscape. This landscape has different thickenings, which can be territorially bound as, for example, regional or national coagulations. But besides these, there are also increasing numbers of combinations, which are deterritorial. Inequality gets increasingly complex in this translocal frame of discussion as the crossing of different thickenings comes into focus. We have to discuss the question of whether because of this, such a thickening tends to exclude and has to be criticized contextually, without losing the focus on the global landscape of communicative thickenings.

Infrastructure and Practices of Appropriation

A further aspect of the inequality of connectivity can be seen at the level of the infrastructure and practices of appropriation. This is the level on which questions of inequality are usually treated in the so-called "digital divide" discussion (Norris, 2001). It is a discussion that is focused, for example, on the question of how many computers with internet access are diffused in a specific country; how many television sets, dishes, or VCRs can be found, and so on (see, for example, the visualizations in Balnaves et al., 2001, or Le Monde Diplomatique, 2003). The focal point here is that these statistics are often not particularly helpful, because the infrastructure and processes of cultural appropriation are territorialized too early and too easily within such statistics. It is obvious that there are differences between countries, but as soon as one focuses exclusively on territorial concepts, one cannot find substantial numbers of further inequalities. One can prove this argument by theorizing, for example, net communication translocally, which means avoiding the territorialization of differences in connectivity too soon but focusing on locality, its mediated connectivity, and thickenings.

At this point one sees a paradox within the infrastructure. First, differences of the infrastructure of connectivity are local rather than territorial phenomena. Localities with a high infrastructure of connectivity are generally cities in Africa, Latin America, or Asia, but also include areas in Europe (see Afemann, 2002a, 2002b). Although it is technically possible to get access to the internet everywhere, there is proof that the infrastructure of net communication is more densely concentrated in big cities than in the countryside. This is not surprising in the so-called Third World because cities are the area where one finds telephone lines, a working power supply, and sufficient numbers of people who can afford a computer. But one can find, for example, rural-urban differences in Germany, too (see Vogelgesang, 2002). Focusing on translocality makes these inequalities more accessible than focusing on territoriality.

Secondly, it does not seem to be reasonable for an approach that is focused not on translocality in general but on translocal media cultures to discuss the infrastructure of connectivity only on such a technical level. As with any aspect of technology, the infrastructure of connectivity is culturally embedded. On this level one must have something one can call the appropriation of inequality, which does not eliminate differences in the infrastructure of connectivity, but which makes it possible to understand that a lower infrastructure of connectivity does not necessarily exclude the globalization of media. Ethnographical reports show that the connectivity of net communication in Africa is appropriated in a specific way (see for example Cornu, 2002). On the one hand, the internet is used much more frequently in urban netcafés or public points of access than, for example, in Europe (see for this in general, Jensen, 1999, 2001, 2002). The localities of net communication are public spaces. On the other hand, these possibilities of access are localized by a specific set of cultural practices that link the connectivity of net communication to the connectivity of everyday face-to-face-interaction. In countries in Central Africa one can pay taxi drivers to take messages and send them via the internet to a given address. If one lives in a village and does not have access to the internet but wants to send a message to a family member abroad, this system is both feasible and useful. The drivers take the message with them, send it, and later give you the reply, if there is one. Similar examples can be found for television in rural India, where the rate of ownership of television sets is rather low, but the rate of access is high (see Johnson, 2000). In both cases these circumstances can be interpreted as forms of cultural *appropriation* of the infrastructure of connectivity.

But cultural appropriation goes much further. In the core of the expression, appropriation refers to processes of localizing meaning construction. One central point of this localizing meaning construction is that this itself is mediated by discourses, referring here to discourses of everyday talk. To make this argument clearer, one can refer to a number of studies on transcultural communication performed in recent years. Whereas early explorations showed the difference of meaning construction of deterritorial distributed media production in general (for the example of *Dallas* see the well-known studies by Liebes & Katz, 1993, 2002), recent ethnographic work shows how this process works in detail. Marie Gillespie (1995, 2000, 2002), for example, could show that the cultural change within the youth of Punjabi diasporic communities in London-Southall is to a considerable degree procured by Indian and British media, which provide a central resource for the everyday talk of the London Punjab youth. Gillespie uses the term "TV-talk" to characterize the conversation of these young people, in which they negotiate their own British-Asian identity based on mediated resources of Indian and British (satellite) television and their everyday experience. On the one hand this identity is stamped by the (ethnic) conflicts and cultural contradictions the youth is confronted with; on the other hand the translocal media resources are offering (utopian) spaces for meaning construction. Through everyday talk media appropriation itself is a mediating process of translocal and local discourses. In another empirical study Chris Barker has shown the same central role of everyday talk for media appropriation (see Barker & Andre, 1996; Barker, 1997, 1999). He uses the term "television talk" to characterize the conversation through which young Asian and black British people negotiate the translocal mediated television contents with their everyday discourses. By all means, this process can be problematic, when, for example, liberal views of homosexuality in the media are rejected on the basis of everyday discourses on sexuality. In my own research on talk while watching TV (see Hepp, 1998), I showed that these processes of communicative appropriation already started in the viewing situation itself.

In this sense one can argue that appropriation also refers to a process of local meaning construction, a process in which the discourses of the local are set in relation to the translocal discourses of the media—especially through locally situated everyday conversation. This demonstrates that patterns of inequality are much more complex than a territorially constructed perspective suggests. Certainly there are substantial differences of infrastructure that probably reflect inequalities that are, in most cases, economic. However, taking public and collective use and further communicative appropriation as specific cultural practice into account, it is not possible to conclude that the increasingly global connectivity of the media on an everyday level is only a Western phenomenon.

In concluding my chapter with these examples, my arguments have offered a rather abrupt insight into what I call a translocal theorization of media cultures. I've tried to show that such an approach is appropriate in linking questions of globalization with a historical view on the change of media cultures. For this, a change of perspective towards a transcultural frame is necessary, a frame in which the concept of translocality has a central meaning. Focusing on questions of translocality makes it possible not only to state that we live in a globalized world of complex media connectivity, but also allows one to analyze this connectivity, its networks and flows in detail and, as a consequence, the cultural change of communicative deterritorialization of media cultures on various levels. In addition, such a frame makes it possible to discuss communicative deterritorialization as the cultural change of media globalization without losing national media cultures as a point of reference. Because of this, the concept of translocality is an appropriate tool to analyze critically the different networks of the media. But we have to keep in mind that such an understanding shouldn't focus on a universal theory of (media) globalization. It is rather a tool for context-sensitive media and cultural studies in an increasingly globalized and contested world.

REFERENCES

Afemann, U. (2002a). E-velopment-Entwicklung durch Internet. *epd-Entwicklungspolitik, 11*, 32-36.

Afemann, U. (2002b). Stellenwert neuer Medien und neuer Technologien in Lateinamerika. Paper presented to conference on *Europa-Lateinamerika: Zwischen Geschichte und Gegenwart*.

Aksoy, A., & Robins, K. (2000). Thinking across spaces. Transnational television from turkey. *European Journal of Cultural Studies, 3*, 343-365.

Anderson, B. (1983). *Imagined communities: Reflections on the origins and spread of nationalism*. New York: Verso.

Ang, I. (1996). *Living room wars. Rethinking media audiences for a postmodern world*. London, New York: Routledge.

Ang, I. (2001). *On not speaking Chinese. Living between Asia and the West*. London: Routledge.

Ang, I. (2003). Im Reich der Ungewissheit. Das globale Dorf und die kapitalistische Postmoderne. In A. Hepp & C. Winter (Eds.), *Die Cultural Studies Kontroverse* (pp. 84-110). Lüneburg: Zu Klampen.

Appadurai, A. (1996). *Modernity at large*. Minneapolis: University of Minnesota Press.

Balnaves, M. et al. (2001). *The Penguin atlas of media and information: Key issues and global trends*. Harmondsworth: Penguin.

Barker, C. (1997). Television and the reflexive project of the self: Soaps, teenage talk and hybrid identities. *British Journal of Sociology, 48*, 611-628.

Barker, C. (1999). *Television, globalization and cultural identities*. Milton Keynes: Open University Press.

Barker, C., & Andre, J. (1996). Did you see? Soaps, teenage talk and gendered identity. *Young: Nordic Journal of Youth Research, 4*, 21-38.

Bauman, Z. (1998). *Globalization. The human consequences.* Cambridge, Oxford: Polity.

Bauman, Z. (2000). *Liquid modernity.* Cambridge, Oxford: Polity.

Beck, U. (1997. *Was ist Globalisierung? Irrtümer des Globalismus—Antworten auf Globalisierung.* Frankfurt a. M.: Suhrkamp.

Boyd-Barrett, O., & Rantanen, T. (Eds.). (1998). *The globalization of news.* London, Thousand Oaks, New Delhi: Sage.

Boyd-Barrett, O., & Thussu, D. K. (Eds.). (1992). *Contra-Flow in global news.* London: John Libbey.

Bromley, R. (2000). *Narratives for a new belonging. Diasporic cultural fictions.* Edinburgh: Edinburgh University Press.

Castells, M. (1996). *The rise of the network society. The information age: Economy, society and culture* (Vol. 1). Oxford: Blackwell.

Castells, M. (2000). *The rise of the network society. The information age: Economy, society and culture* (2nd ed., Vol. 1). Oxford: Blackwell.

Chakravarty, S. S. (1993). *National identity in Indian popular cinema 1947–1987.* Austin: University of Texas Press.

Clifford, J. (1994). Diaspora. *Cultural Anthropology, 9,* 302-338.

Cornu, J.-M. (2002). How people use the internet today in Africa. *UNESCO Webworld.* Retrieved May 4, 2002, from http://www.unesco.org/webworld/points_of_views/180302_cornu.shtml

Couldry, N., & McCarthy, A. (Eds.). (2004). *Media space: Place, scale and culture in a media age.* London: Routledge.

Curran, J., & Park, M.-J. (Eds.). (2000). *De-Westernizing media studies.* London, New York: Routledge.

Dayan, D. (1999). Media and diasporas. In J. Gripsrud (Ed.), *Television and common knowledge* (pp. 18-33). London, New York: Routledge.

Dhaliwal, A. K. (1994). Introduction: The travelling nation: India and its diaspora. *Socialist Review, 24,* 1-11.

During, P. (1997). Popular culture on a global scale: A challenge for cultural studies? In H. Mackay & T. O'Sullivan (Eds.), *The media reader, continuity and transformation* (pp. 211-222). London: Sage.

European Commission (2003). *Analysis and forecasting of international migration by major groups* (Part III). Luxembourg: Office for Official Publications of the European Communities.

Faulstich, W. (1996). *Die Geschichte der Medien Band 2: Medien und Öffentlichkeiten im Mittelalter (800–1400).* Göttingen: Vandenhoeck & Ruprecht.

Featherstone, M. (Ed.). (1990). *Global culture: Nationalism, globalization and modernity.* London: Sage.

Foucault, M. (1996). Wie wird Macht ausgeübt? In M. Foucault & W. Seitter (Eds.), *Das Spektrum der Genealogie* (pp. 29-47). Frankfurt a. M.: Philo.

García Canclini, N. (1995). *Hybrid cultures. Strategies for entering and leaving modernity.* Minneapolis: University of Minnesota Press.

Giddens, A. (1990). *The consequences of modernity.* London: Polity.

Gillespie, M. (1995). *Television, ethnicity and cultural change.* London, New York: Routledge.

Gillespie, M. (2000). Transnational communications and diaspora communities. In S. Cottle (Ed.), *Ethnic minorities and the media* (pp. 164-178). Buckingham: Open University Press.

Gillespie, M. (2002). Transnationale Kommunikation und die Kulturpolitik in der südasiatischen Diaspora. In A. Hepp & M. Löffelholz (Eds.), *Grundlagentexte zur Transkulturellen Kommunikation* (pp. 617-643). Konstanz: UVK (UTB).

Granovetter, M. (1983). The strength of weak ties. A network theory revisited. *Sociological Theory, 1*, 203-233.

Hachmeister, L., & Rager, G. (Eds.). (2002). *Wer beherrscht die Medien? Die 50 größten Medienkonzerne der Welt*. München: Beck Verlag.

Hall, S. (1988). The toad in the garden. Thatcherism among the theorists. In C. Nelson & L. Grossberg (Eds.), *Marxism and the interpretation of culture*. London: University of Illinois Press.

Hall, S. (1997). The centrality of culture: Notes on the cultural revolutions of our time. In K. Thompson (Ed.), *Media and cultural regulation* (pp. 207-238). London: Sage.

Hallenberger, G. (2002). Eurofiction. Fiktionale Fernsehsendungen in Europa. In A. Hepp & M. Löffelholz (Eds.), *Grundlagentexte zur transkulturellen Kommunikation* (pp. 421-435). Konstanz: UVK (UTB).

Hepp, A. (1998). *Fernsehaneignung und Alltagsgespräche. Fernsehnutzung aus der Perspektive der Cultural Studies*. Opladen: Westdeutscher Verlag.

Hepp, A. (2004). *Netzwerke der Medien. Medienkulturen und Globalisierung* (Bd. 1, Reihe Medien-Kultur-Kommunikation). Wiesbaden: VS.

Herman, E. S., & McChesney, R. W. (1997). *The global media. The new missionaries of corporate capitalism*. London: Cassell.

Hickethier, K. (2001). Hollywood, der europäische Film und die kulturelle Globalisierung. In B. Wagner (Ed.), *Kulturelle Globalisierung. Zwischen Weltkultur und kultureller Fragmentierung* (pp. 113-131). Essen: Klartext.

Jensen, M. (1999). Chapter 13: Sub-Saharan Africa. In UNESCO (Ed.), *World communication and information report 1999–2000* (pp. 180-208). Paris: UNESCO.

Jensen, M. (2001). *The African internet—A status report*. Retrieved February 7, 2002, from http://demiurge.wn.apc.org/africa/afstat.htm.

Jensen, M. (2002). *The African internet—A status report*. Retrieved May 3, 2002, from http://demiurge.wn.apc.org/africa/afstat.htm.

Johnson, K. (2000). *Television and social change in rural India*. New Delhi, Thousand Oaks, London: Sage.

Kazmi, F. (1999). *The politics of India's conventional cinema. Imaging a universe, subverting a multiverse*. New Delhi, Thousand Oaks, London: Sage.

Karmasin, M. (2004). *Paradoxien der Medien*. Wien: Wuv.

Kleinsteuber, H. J., & Rossmann, T. (Eds.). (1994). *Europa als Kommunikationsraum. Akteure, Strukturen und Konfliktpotenziale in der europäischen Medienpolitik* (Unter Mitarbeit von Arnold C. Kulbatzki und Barbara Thomaß). Opladen: Leske + Budrich.

Krätke, S. (2001). *Globalisierung, Weltstädte und Globalizing Cities. Ansätze und Ergebnisse der Forschung zum Phänomen der Global City*. Retrieved December 29, 2001, from http://home.t-online.de/home/320024190425/Kraetke/index.html.

Krätke, S. (2002). *Medienstadt. Urbane Cluster und globale Zentren der Kulturproduktion*. Opladen: Leske + Budrich.

Krotz, F. (2005). Von Modernisierungs- über Dependenz- zu Globalisierungstheorien. In A. Hepp, F. Krotz, & C. Winter (Eds.), *Globalisierung der Medien. Eine Einführung* (pp. 21-44). Wiesbaden: Verlag für Sozialwissenschaften.

Lakoff, G., & Johnson, M. (1980). *Metaphors we live by*. Chicago, London: University of Chicago Press.

Le Monde Diplomatique. (Ed.). (2003). *Atlas der Globalisierung*. Berlin: taz.

Liebes, T., & Katz, E. (1993). *The export of meaning* (2nd ed.). Cambridge: Polity.

Liebes, T., & Katz, E. (2002). Über die kritischen Fähigkeiten der Fernsehzuschauer. In A. Hepp & M. Löffelholz (Eds.), *Grundlagentexte zur transkulturellen Kommunikation* (pp. 586-616). Konstanz: UVK (UTB).

Löfgren, O. (2001). The nation as home or motel? Metaphors of media and belonging. *Sosiologisk Årbok*, 1-34.

Long, E. (1997). Introduction: Engaging sociology and cultural studies: Disciplinarity and social change. In E. Long (Ed.), *From sociology to cultural studies. New perspectives* (pp. 1-32). Malden: Blackwell.

Luhmann, N. (1997). *Die Gesellschaft der Gesellschaft* (2 Bde.). Frankfurt a. M.: Suhrkamp Verlag.

McLuhan, M., & Fiore, Q. (1968). *War and peace in the global village*. New York: Gingko Press.

Mercer, K. (1988). Diaspora culture and the dialogic imagination. In M. Cham & C. Andrade-Watkins (Eds.), *Blackframes. Celebration of black cinema* (pp. 50-61) Cambridge: MIT Press.

Miller, T. et al. (2001). *Global Hollywood*. London: BFI.

Moran, A. (1998). *Copycat TV. Globalization, programme formats and cultural identity*. Luton: University of Luton Press.

Morley, D. (1996). EurAm, modernity, reason and alterity. Or, postmodernism, the highest stage of cultural imperialism? In D. Morley & K.–H. Chen (Eds.), *Stuart Hall. Critical dialogues in cultural studies* (pp. 326-360). London, New York: Routledge.

Morley, D. (2000). *Home territories. Media, mobility and identity*. London, New York: Routledge.

Morley, D., & Robins, K. (1995). *Spaces of identity. Global media, electronic landscapes, and cultural boundaries*. London, New York: Routledge.

Müller, E. (2002). Unterhaltungsshows transkulturell: Fernsehformate zwischen Akkomodation und Assimilation. In A. Hepp & M. Löffelholz (Eds.), *Grundlagentexte zur Transkulturellen Kommunikation* (pp. 456-473). Konstanz: UVK (UTB).

Nederveen Pieterse, J. (1995). Globalization as hybridization. In M. Featherstone, S. Lash, & R. Robertson (Eds.), *Global modernities* (pp. 45-68). London, Thousand Oaks, New Delhi: Sage.

Norris, P. (2001). *Digital divide. Civic engagement, information poverty and the internet worldwide*. Cambridge: Cambridge University Press.

Olson, S. R. (1999). *Hollywood planet. Global media and the competitive advantage of narrative transparency*. Mahwah, NJ, London: Erlbaum.

Papastergiadis, N. (1998). *Dialogues in the diasporas*. London: River Oram Press.

Paterson, C. (1997). Global television news services. In A. Sreberny-Mohammadi, D. Winseck, J. McKenna, & O. Boyd-Barrett (Eds.), *Media in global context. A reader* (pp. 145-160). London, New York: Arnold.

Pendakur, M., & Subramanyam, R. (1996). Indian cinema beyond national borders. In J. Sinclair, E. Jacka, & S. Cunningham (Eds.), *News patterns in global television* (pp. 67-82). Oxford: Oxford University Press.

Pendakur, M. (1990). The Indian film industry. In J. A. Lent (Ed.), *The Asian film industry*. London: Christopher Helm.

Pries, L. (2001). *Internationale migration.* Münster: Transcript.

Ritzer, G. (1998). *The McDonaldization thesis.* London, Thousand Oaks, New Delhi: Sage.

Sassen, S. (2000). *Cities in a world economy* (2nd ed.). Thousand Oaks: Pine Forge Press.

Sinclair, J., Jacka, E., & Cunningham, S. (1996). Peripheral vision. In J. Sinclair, E. Jacka, & S. Cunningham (Eds.), *News patterns in global television* (pp. 1-32). Oxford: Oxford University Press.

Stratton, J., & Ang, I. (1996). On the impossibility of global cultural studies: "British" cultural studies in an "international" frame. In D. Morley & K.-H. Chen (Eds.), *Stuart Hall. Critical dialogues in cultural studies* (pp. 361-391) London, New York: Routledge.

Tölölyan, K. (1991). The nation-state and its others: In lieu of a preface. *Diaspora, 1,* 3-7.

Tomlinson, J. (1999). *Globalization and culture.* Cambridge, Oxford: Polity Press.

Urry, J. (2000). *Sociology beyond societies: Mobilities for the 21st-century* (International Library of Sociology). London: Routledge.

Urry, J. (2003). *Global complexity.* Cambridge: Polity Press.

Vogelgesang, W. (2002). "Wir müssen surfen lernen." Ein Beitrag zur ungleichen Internetnutzung von Stadt- und Landjugendlichen. *Medien Praktisch, 1,* 38-43.

Volkmer, I. (1999*). News in the global sphere. A study of CNN and its impact on global communication.* London: University of Luton Press.

Watts, D. J. (2004). *Small worlds: The dynamics of networks between order and randomness* (Princeton Studies in Complexity). Princeton: Princeton University Press.

Winter, C. (1996). *Predigen unter freiem Himmel. Die medienkulturellen Funktionen der Bettelmönche und ihr geschichtlicher Hintergrund.* Bardowick: Wissenschaftler Verlag.

Zelizer, B., & Allan, S. (2002). Introduction: When trauma shapes the news. In B. Zelizer & S. Allan (Eds.), *Journalism after September 11* (pp. 1-24). London, New York: Routledge.

Zips, W. (Ed.). (2003*). African diaspora: Out of Africa into new worlds.* Münster: LIT.

"YOUR LIFE – TO GO"

The Cultural Impact of
New Media Technologies

John Tomlinson

The question that I want to broach in this discussion is that of the cultural impact of what I will loosely—and in fact only provisionally—call *globalizing media technologies*; for example, networked computers, mobile phones, and the convergence of these in, for example, so-called third-generation mobile technology. There is no mistaking the preferred messages of the manufacturers and marketers of these technologies. For example, Apple Macintosh's I-Book is sold with the slogan *Your Life: To Go*—thus, rather elegantly, tying the product, on the one hand, to the urban, modern, mobile lifestyle of its target market and, on the other, to the very condition of human existence itself. Communications technologies, we are led to believe, are indispensable to—indeed constitutive of—a successful modern lifestyle in which the keywords are liberty, mobility, ubiquity, immediacy, and (though, as I will conclude, to a significantly lesser extent) globality. These keywords—understood as cultural values—are never, of course, problematized. Like the physiological pathologies associated with new technologies—from repetitive strain injury to brain tumors—cultural anxieties over such founding values are understandably invisible in marketing discourse.

Not that I think we should dwell on potential cultural pathology—this is so often merely the critical reflex response to what the Frankfurt School described as the "repressive positivity" of the culture industry. The point, rather, is to try to get beyond the rather compelling common-sense discourse of undisturbed convenience and utility that we are being sold, to see what deeper impact these technologies will be having. We can take it as read, then, that buying mobile phones for our children means that we can allow them a little more independence and ourselves a little less anxiety over their safety; that there are conveniences and *maybe* even environmental advantages to doing our shopping on-line; that e-mail has made everyday communication vastly easier for us; and that these technologies have often been exploited in the cause of progressive political activity—as, for instance, in the famous example of the Sandinista guerrillas in Chiapas. And, equally, of course, there are proportionate downsides to all these advantages, which the reader may already have begun to list. But this game of pluses and minuses is clearly a rather shallow approach to cultural analysis. And so, though I will return to the issue of *cultural anxieties* generated by new technologies, I want to approach things in a rather oblique, but perhaps more interesting way.

CHANGING TERMINALS

The way I want to approach things is by thinking about how new technologies may be changing our lived and imagined relationship to *place*. This approach ties the discussion in a general way to the concept of *deterritorialization*, by which I mean the reach of the complex connectivity of globalization into the localities in which everyday life is conducted and experienced. This is at once a perplexing and disruptive and an exhilarating and empowering phenomenon, involving the simultaneous penetration of local worlds by distant forces and the dislodging of everyday meanings from their "anchors" in the local environment—in particular geographical places. Deterritorialization, as I have argued elsewhere (cf. Tomlinson, 1999), is a feature of all societies in the 21st century and, without doubt, a phenomenon of the greatest consequence both for cultural practices and experience. However, here I will not develop this general conceptualization of the cultural impact of globalization, but rather, explore some of the vocabulary by which we may understand the changing significance of places themselves.

So I will begin with the changing image of the *terminal*. The idea of the terminal is, of course, of both a place of departure and of arrival, of beginning and ending—but in either sense it implies a limit, a boundary, a set of fixed spatial co-ordinates for travel or for communication. Once upon a time, in that broad epoch that Zygmunt Bauman (2000) calls the era of "heavy" or "solid" modernity, our understanding of a terminal, or a terminus, was as a feature of the built environment—typically, one of the great railway terminals that were so much a feature of the modern metropolis from the middle of the 19th century.

The grandiosity of the architecture of these early-modern terminals was indicative of a broad cultural assurance about the power–geography of the times. These were the gateways to the great expanding modern metropolises, and indeed, the centers of imperial power, in an era in which, as Bauman says, mechanical, heavy technologies implied a certain reliable *permanence* in time-space location. This early heavy modernity was a period in which "size is power and volume is success: the epoch of weighty and ever more cumbersome machines, of ever-longer factory walls enclosing ever-wider floors and ingesting ever more populous factory crews, of ponderous rail engines and gigantic ocean liners. It was, moreover, a period in which power was perceptibly concentrated in physical locations: embodied and fixed, tied in steel and concrete" (Bauman, 2000, p. 114). One way of reading the iconography of the transport architecture of this period, then, is in terms of simple territorial expansion: the increasing possession of space and the control of time. It suggests the apogee of territorial control and conquest: of colonization, of the regulation (the clocking, and hence the uniformity) of time and of the co-ordination of time-space: the era of the survey, the schedule, the timetable, the control plan.

However, the aesthetics of such terminals also, I would suggest, carried another significant message about the triumphs of mechanical modernity: they were a demonstration of the way in which the premodern vicissitudes of travel—its etymological link with "travail"—painful or laborious effort—were being swept away, particularly, by locomotive power. The grandiosity of railway terminals signified the overcoming of the journey itself. As Paul Virilio (1997, p. 56) observes, the transport revolution of the 19th century reduced the significance of a journey to two points —Departure and Arrival.

And there was a certain cultural heroism involved in this: the valorization of the mechanical effort involved in closing this time-space gap.

Railway terminals, then, can be seen as celebrations of a certain form of mobility, which was at the core of the early modern cultural narrative of technological progress—the emancipation of humanity from nature, here seen as the overcoming of the natural resistance of physical space to the fulfilment of human desire. This narrative—which contained certain quintessentially early—heavy—modern themes—goal orientation, organization and regulation, an heroic image of machinery and labour—has, according to Bauman's analysis, now lost ground to another set of cultural preoccupations and values—hardly a narrative—which he calls "light" or "liquid" modernity.

Our emergence into liquid modernity is into a world in which solidity, fixity, and sheer extension of possessed location is no longer automatically an asset; a world in which capital is fluid and entrepreneurs travel light; where production methods are plastic, sourcing is variable, delivery is "just-in-time," employment is temporary, planning is flexible and adaptable; where logics are fuzzy—the world of dot.com entrepreneurship and call center shift work as opposed to the production relations of Ford or Renault. Here the valuing of permanence and location—in everyday lifestyles, in attitudes and values—gives way to the valuing of portability, flexibility, and openness to change. Constructing, planning and regulating give way to coping with uncertainty and "going with the flow"; durability cedes to transience, the long term to the short term. Above all, in liquid modernity, distance is no object. As Bauman has it, "In the software universe of light-speed travel . . . space no more sets limits to action and its effects, and counts [for] little" (Bauman, 2000, p. 117).

Now this idea that "space no more sets limits to action" seems to me to have a direct implication for the transformation of the terminal. Whereas the terminals of early modernity were precisely points of limit—points of departure and arrival—those that we carry with us—or maybe soon within us—represent a quite different set of principles constellating around the transcendence—or rather the imagined transcendence—of space and place. As Virilio (1997, p. 56) says, the coming of new communications technologies means that, "departure now gets wiped out and arrival gets promoted, the generalized arrival of data." Hence, the terminals of liquid modernity, employing technologies of generalized arrival, trade on more or less an opposite aesthetic to the terminals of solid, mechanical modernity. As it is most evident in the design and marketing of mobile phones, it is an aesthetic of miniaturization, personalization, and discretion, rather than of grandiosity and ostentation that now dominates.

This aesthetic is, of course, linked to the emerging cultural value of *communicational portability* centered on the person as opposed to the eclipsed value of simple early-modern mobility—the overcoming of physical distance—in which place (as the condition of embodiment) still situates and constrains the person in the cultural imagination. Communicational portability, moreover, constellates a range of other values, attitudes, and styles—most importantly the ubiquity of presence, but also the redundancy of effort in communication and a certain related apparent insouciance in communicational style.

The impression we get from the use of new communication technologies—when they are working properly that is—is one of a general effortlessness and ubiquity. Things, and particularly people, do seem to be pretty much immediately available. There is little effort in communicating; there seem to be few obstacles to overcome. The discrete "soft" technology, as if by an act of *legerdemain*, seems to have closed the gap that was preserved in the era of heavy mechanical modernity between here and elsewhere, now and later, desire and its fulfillment.

For all its cultural force, however, this remains only an impression. The constraints of place and embodiment and the concrete realities of distance still, of course, obtain, and their stubborn persistence is evident in the continuing—indeed growing—significance of fixed terminals—bus, rail and air terminals, parking lots—and the associated technologies of the physical transport of people in 21st century culture. The vicissitudes of travel today are, of course, different from the ones that early mechanical modernity liberated us from: now they divide, on the one hand, between the attenuated inconveniences of delays and, on the other, the risk of spectacular catastrophic mishaps or deliberate sabotage. But in either form they attest to the limits imposed by the fragility and sheer existential facticity of the embodied human condition. If we want to encapsulate the prime cultural impact of new communications technologies, then, it might be fair to say that they have produced a kind of false dawn of expectations of the liberation of human beings from the constraints of place. And if we want an image—albeit a banal one—that grasps this overreaching expectation of immediacy, we need only to think of the gesture of frustration with which a crowd of—let's say train passengers—simultaneously pull out their mobile phones in the instant that follows the announcement of a delay to their service.

To summarize: I am suggesting that the possibility of immediate, ubiquitous telemediated communication changes our real and imagined relationship to place but in an ambiguous way that perhaps generates as many cultural anxieties as it offers genuine emancipations.

CULTURAL-TECHNOLOGICAL ANXIETIES

Some of these anxieties are the familiar—and it should be said, reasonable—concerns that are expressed over the possible long-term consequences of our exposure to any new technology. For instance the warning given by the psychologist Susan Blackmore, at a meeting of British vice-chancellors and e-learning specialists in October 2001, was that the internet may actually undermine children's learning capacities by shifting the development of cognitive functions from storing to accessing information (Millar, 2001).

However, more interesting for what they may reveal about our wider contemporary cultural preoccupations are those anxieties about the human condition itself, particularly over the nature and limitations of our embodiment, that are prompted by the introduction of new communications technologies. These are anxieties over the ways in which, on the one hand, we may be tempted, disturbingly, to modify our bodies, and on the other, over how we may be beginning, perhaps even more troublingly, to regard our relationship to our bodies differently. They are anxieties about the culturally acceptable limits of communicational prosthesis and about the imagination of escape from embodiment. Much has been written in the often febrile literature on cyberspace and cyborg culture about these issues and I won't try to broach all these arguments, but just pick out two prominent themes.

The anxiety over communicational prosthesis can be traced back at least to McLuhan's famous description of the media as "extensions of man" (McLuhan, 1964) and in its subsequent theoretical-speculative treatment is often given to hyperbolic formulation. One less heated way of approaching it is actually via the progressive miniaturization of the terminal that I mentioned earlier. The movement from desktop to laptop to palm-held computer and the aesthetic valorization of progressively smaller mobile phones may seem to be simply a matter of portability. However it is not implausible to see in them a trajectory in the body-technology interface, which seems to be aimed at a final integration of person and machine. Paul Virilio, for example, argues precisely that communicational prosthesis like the Walkman and the mobile phone anticipate, according to what he calls the "law of proximity" or of "least effort," "the future transplantation revolution and the ingurgitation of micro-machines" (1997, p. 43). Now it may stretch our everyday sense of the immediate cultural agenda set by communications technologies to take such anxieties very seriously. However, it appears that commercial applications of communicational implant technology are taken as serious possibilities within the industry.

As reported by Radford (2000), researchers at Roke Manor Research, a part of the Siemens technology group, have predicted the commercial development, within the current decade, of a technique to embed microsensors in the optic nerves of television journalists, enabling them to transmit what they see live to our television screens. The fundamental technology, it is claimed, already exists to do this.

There is a certain attraction, if a rather perverse one, in the idea of the direct—*immediate*—communication of images via the human "hardware" of the journalist, but without, presumably, the subjective mediation of their cognition. For this conforms to a certain trajectory in the exploitation of communication technologies, which has formed a normative pattern in modern journalism—in values such as objectivity, realism, immediacy. But what seems so troubling about this is not simply that it would constitute a significant body modification carried out for a purely instrumental—even worse, a perhaps mere commercial—purpose. The more general cultural anxiety over prosthesis is, ultimately, an anxiety over the technological undermining of taken-for-granted notions of the human condition. Despite a certain vogue for cosmetic body modification, from piercing to breast implants, there remains a significant liminal point in our culture—the surface of human flesh itself—at which humanistic discourses of integrity, in both the corporeal and the ethical sense, still generally hold sway. Virilio's fears of what he calls the colonization of the last *territory*—"the tragedy of the fusion of the biological and the technological" (1997, p. 57) are in part protests against the incursions of instrumentality, technique, and control. But they also, I think, suggest fears about human culture losing confidence in its grounding ontological state.

And it is a very similar anxiety that is at the core of worries about the disembodied nature of internet culture. Skepticism over the sunny optimism with which techno-enthusiasts such as Howard Rheingold (1994) speak of "leaving our bodies behind" when we "travel" on the internet centre on the shift in attitude to embodiment that this may imply. As Hubert Dreyfus has argued in his insightful essay *On the Internet* (2001), the concern is that this may be the thin end of a cultural wedge that ends in a confused, even a pathological, relationship with our existential state: the regarding of our bodies as biological encumbrances rather than as integral aspects of our being. Dreyfus' elegant deployment of Nietzsche's celebration of embodiment against the neo-Platonism of contemporary enthusiasts for liberation from the body is by no means an abstract philosophical reflection on ontology. It springs precisely from a recognition of the peculiar cultural options and attitudes that everyday quasi-disembodiment in communication seems to engender.

KEEPING IN TOUCH

What all these anxieties tell us is that the semitranscendence of our embodied existential state offered by communications technologies—the false dawn of expectations that I mentioned earlier—has confused our cultural assurance in not-insignificant ways. Our entry into liquid modernity and deterritorialization has produced both unrealistic cultural expectations and cultural demands. So we might, albeit speculatively, add to the anxieties over embodiment a broader anxiety over maintaining constant communicational contact with each other. To continue the theme of embodiment this time as a metaphor, isn't there a widespread, diffuse anxiety about keeping "in touch"? I'm thinking, for instance, of the peculiar sort of low-level communicational guilt that attaches to not owning or using the technology. Hasn't this now become a token of cultural marginality, something that has to be owned up to or defended as a rather defiant, eccentric circumscription of personal space? Isn't the denial of instant access to ourselves a breach of a tacit communicational duty?

Of course there is a straightforward account of this in terms of the encroachment of the sphere of employment into personal time and space, the institutional colonization of the private sphere that is part and parcel of the flexibility of capitalism in liquid modernity: networked computers in the home; bleakly instrumental networking parties for the entrepreneurs of e-business; the implacable warbling summons of the mobile phone now forever interrupting those brief holidays from the job that used to be a train journey "on business." These are, I think, obvious incursions.

But isn't there also something else going on? Isn't there evidence of an anxiety—maybe that puts it too strongly, an unease—about being out of touch with our friends and family even for the briefest of times? Isn't this a plausible explanation for the remarkable rise in routine, phatic communication—of the "Hello, I'm on the train" variety—that mobile phones have engendered? To exemplify this, I briefly want to step back in time to an earlier, but no less revolutionary, period in communicational history.

In the second volume of *A la Récherche du Temps Perdu*, Marcel Proust writes vividly of the anxieties that attended the use of the telephone in the early years of the last century. This is a particularly interesting description, because Proust begins by observing how quickly telephony, introduced during the 1880s, became taken for granted:

> The telephone was not, at that date as commonly used as it is today. And yet habit requires so short a time to divest of their mystery the sacred forces with which we are in contact, that, not having had my call at once, my immediate thought was that it was all very long and inconvenient, and I almost decided to lodge a complaint. I found too slow for my liking, in its abrupt changes, the admirable sorcery whereby a few moments are enough to bring before us, invisible but present, the person to whom we wish to speak. . . . (Proust, 1981, pp. 133-134)

What he goes on to describe, however, is the perplexity caused by being able to hear the disembodied voice of his ailing grandmother while not being fully, physically, present with her. In a beautiful phrase he describes first hearing his grandmother: "A tiny sound, an abstract sound, the sound of distance overcome." She is "there," yet not there, he imagines her alone in her home in Paris, he can't reach out and touch her. Added to this, there are breaks in the connection and interruptions from the telephone operators. The telephone call finishes abruptly as the line is lost completely, leaving Marcel with that feeling of inconclusion, loss, and wretchedness that is familiar to us even today when the technology, at crucial moments, fails us. Being Proust, this leads to introspections about his relationship with his grandmother, her imminent death—the final separation—and, predictably, his own mortality. His theme, of course, is the existential fear of separation, emphasized, rather than overcome by the technology of the day. Before the telephone, distance meant a more complete, unambiguous separation in which the distant other could not suddenly, phantasmagorically, enter our lifeworld for a few disconcerting moments. Separations had to be endured, but at least there was no troubling trespassing of the absent-mediated other into the present to have to deal with.

Well, couldn't it be argued that the ease with which, today, we routinely gain instant access to each other hasn't really solved this existential problem, but simply ameliorated it? We probably don't agonize too much about the odd communicational glitch, but isn't there a possibility that we may be at risk of losing a certain capacity to dwell comfortably at distance? Couldn't the constant, apparent need, at any time and place, simply to register our continued connection—"Hello, its"—be read in this way?

COSMOS OR HEARTH? THE PHATIC FUNCTION OF NEW TECHNOLOGIES

But let me stop there, for I am in danger of doing precisely what I declared against in my introduction—of pathologizing cultural shifts. So, in conclusion I'll change track a little and offer a metaphor from the cultural geographer Yi-Fu Tuan's (1996) reflective essay on cosmopolitanism and the ties of locality, *Cosmos and Hearth*.

Tuan draws a distinction between talk and conversation. Conversation, he argues, is characteristic of complex modern societies. It "occurs when a serious attempt is made to explore self and world with another" and "it presupposes a degree of socio-psychological independence from the group and its pressures and a willingness to listen to another even though he may not come cloaked in formal authority." It is typically something that happens between strangers and in impersonal public spaces that "encourage individuals to be more themselves, freed from the thick atmosphere of kinship and family." Conversation is thus, for Tuan, "an accomplishment of the cosmos rather than the hearth" (Tuan, 1996, pp. 175-176).

Talk, by contrast, belongs to the hearth. "People sit around a meal, a fire or just a patch of ground. Currents of words move back and forth, weaving individual speakers into a whole. What is being communicated? Nothing much. Social talk consists almost entirely of inconsequential gossip, brief accounts of the experiences and events of the day." Indeed, serious conversation is often discouraged during talk, as it represents a rather threatening "infiltration of the hearth by the cosmos."

Talk, as a communication act, Tuan suggests, is nearer to the almost lost practice of communal singing than to conversation. Its essential function is the phatic one of establishing and maintaining belonging, of binding human beings into identity groups.

Now if we apply Tuan's distinction to the predominant social use of new communications technologies, it soon becomes clear that we might be mistaken in regarding them as globalizing technologies, as tools for extending cultural horizons, as exit portals from the narrow ties of locality, as facilitators of a cosmopolitan disposition. Rather the opposite, they might more plausibly be considered as technologies of the hearth: as imperfect instruments by which people try, in conditions of mundane deterritorialization, to maintain something of the security of cultural location—of fixity in a culture of flow.

REFERENCES

Bauman, Z. (2000). *Liquid modernity.* Cambridge: Polity.

Dreyfus, H.L. (2001). *On the internet.* London: Routledge.

McLuhan, M. (1964). *Understanding media: The extensions of man.* London: Routledge and Kegan Paul.

Millar, S. (2001, October 12). Internet could damage children's ability to learn. *The Guardian*, p. 6.

Proust, M. (1981). *Remembrance of things past: Vol. 2. The Guermantes Way.* London: Chatto and Windus.

Radford, T. (2000, May 1). Robotic future rushes towards us. *The Guardian,* p. 5.

Rheingold, H. (1994). *The virtual community.* London: Minerva.

Tomlinson, J. (1999). *Globalization and culture.* Cambridge: Polity.

Tuan, Y.-F. (1996). *Cosmos and hearth: A cosmopolite's viewpoint.* Minneapolis: University of Minnesota Press.

Virilio, P. (1997). *Open sky.* London: Verso.

THE TIMES CONVERGENCE OF MEDIALITY OF COMMUNICATION AS CHANGE IN CULTURAL SOLIDARITY

Convergent Mobile Telephones and Laptops and New Flows, Networks, and Connectivity

Carsten Winter

This chapter discusses the meaning of convergent mobile media in civil society generally and, particularly, cultural solidarity in the future. Convergent mobile media such as mobile telephones and laptops burgeoned concurrently with the convergence of the five TIMES branches:[1] telecommunication, information, media, entertainment, and security. As convergent media, they are no longer just telephones and computers but contain technologies and competencies of all other TIMES branches. These render the laptop and mobile telephone interesting because they constitute a new, different mediality, which changes the conditions and presuppositions of culture and cultural solidarity.

My starting point is the lack of conceptual comprehension of media in discussions about cultural change and the TIMES convergence, a lack

---

[1]The acronym "TIMES convergence," which designates a coalescence of the five branches by their individual first letters to make a single word—branches that once were quite separate—is the usual term employed today in politics and economics for this greatest transformation and globalization of branches and political economies in history (also see the introduction and articles in Karmasin & Winter, 2005).

I shall explicate before I reconstruct the TIMES convergence and define mobile convergent media. It is against this background that the development of media and the logic of *flows, networks,* and *connectivity* will be situated in relation to changes in cultural solidarity, which I shall explicate by examples from print advertisements about mobile telephones and laptops. Lastly, I shall formulate theses about the interrelation of media and values of solidarity such as love, freedom, and equality as they are in flux. From this, media-critical perspectives of the future of civil society and solidarity will be developed.

MEDIA AS REFERENCE FOR THE CONCEPTUALIZATION OF THE TIMES-CONVERGENCE

At least since Giddens' reference to the development of media as one driver of globalization (1990), without wanting to name any initial starting point, media have become a prime subject in the discussion about cultural and social change.[2] An example is given by Tomlinson (1999) in his quite plausible argument for the significance of "globalizing media and communication technologies" for the diffusion of "deterritorialized cultural experience" or by Bauman's illustration of the "introduction of mobile telephones" as the "symbolic k.o. punch against being bound by space" (Bauman, 2000, p. 18), with a further reference to mobile telephones and laptops as insignia of the new fleeting-liquid capital. Mobile telephones and laptops have taken a central place in sociological attention.[3]

After their arrival there, it was not far to get to Urry's thesis of a 21st century *inhabited machine*,[4] by which he means primarily the mobile telephone and the laptop. Urry's technicist (mis)conceiving of convergent media as inhabited machines show media so explicitly as the construction site of cultural and social theory, that it is necessary to deal more extensively with Urry's ideas. Urry develops his understanding of inhabited machines in his discussion of global complexities, which demonstrates how networks and fluids depend on "new machines and

---

[2]The discussion about cultural change and globalization is the first international and interdisciplinary discussion in the social and cultural sciences where the media have played a role from the very beginning (i.e., since the early 1990s). For the emergence of the discussion on cultural change and globalization, all of which concurrently took media into consideration, see Winter (2000).

[3]"The heavy capitalism held fast to the ground capital and the work done by it. Today capital travels with . . . laptop and mobile telephone" (Bauman, 2000, p. 73).

[4]"The twenty-first century will be the century of what I call inhabited machines" (Urry, 2003, p. 127),

technologies" (Urry, 2003, p. 56) and how these networks and fluids enter into complex, contradictory, and irreversible relationships, constituting new formations of order with increasing disorderliness. Urry's subject is complexity, not culture or cultural change. Above all, he demonstrates that linear conceptualizations of global development are inappropriate, because they do not take into account the complex relationality in and between various orders. I will show below how this relationality and its complexity in respect to *mediality* of media can be developed from postmodern perspectives, to offer empirically as well as normatively a better orientation than concepts orientated toward the computer sciences (Cillers, 1998) or biological and chemical knowledge (Capra, 2002). Mediality has the meaning here of the technical and cultural complexity of relationality of medial connectivity within the framework of communication.

For Urry, this relationality between—as he puts it—"moorings" and "mobilities" conditions the complexity of global processes.[5] This is the point of reference in his thesis that the 21st century will be the century of inhabited machines, of mobile nodes of new orders made up of fluids and networks, which he describes as follows:

> Such inhabited machines are miniaturized, privatized, mobilized and depend on digital power. This power is substantially separate from material form and involves exceptional levels of miniaturization and mobility. Many of these machines are portable, carried around by digital nomads. [. . .]

> Such machines are desired for their style, smallness, and lightness and demonstrate a physical form closely interwoven with the corporeal. Early examples include walkmans, new generation mobile phones, the individual TV, the networked computer/Internet, the individualized smart car, virtual reality "travel," smart small personal aircraft and others yet to emerge. These machines involve interesting reconfigurations of storage: the portals to these machines are carried around with the individual, they are stored on or close to the person and yet their digital power derives from their extensive connectivity. These inhabiting machines enable "people" to be more readily mobile through space, or to stay in one place because of the capacity for "self retrieval" of personal information at any time or space. Through such machines people inhabit global networks and fluids of information, image and movement. "Persons" thus occur as various nodes in these multiple machines of inhabitation and mobility. The storage in such machines is digitized and hence not only

---

[5]"Overall it is these moorings that enable movement. And it is the dialectic of mobility/moorings that produces social complexity. If all relationality were mobile or liquid, then there would be no complexity. Complexity, I suggest, stems from this dialectic of mobility and moorings" (Urry, 2003, p. 126).

"just in time" but also "just in space." There is a person-to-person connectivity that represents a further shift in the dematerialization of information and mobility. . . . The global fluids of "travelling people," "Internet" and "information" increasingly overlap and converge generating irreversible changes that further move social life towards what Wellman (2001) terms "personalized networking." This involves the further linking-together of "physical space" and "cyberspace." This convergence across the various global fluids further transcends divisions of structure and agency, the global and the local. (Urry, 2003, p. 127)

Urry's explication of inhabited machines dispenses with any reference to concrete persons and normative categories: His relational logic of grouped orders with increasing degrees of disorderliness and their "dialectical" complexity of moving and fixed parts is not conceived for an analysis of media and communication—something like that does not occur in his work. Regardless, although his argument may not be historical and empirical, it ought to be plausible. However, their main characteristic, their *extensive connectivity*, does not fit for all seven inhabited machines he names: A walkman connects two persons at most. Furthermore, I fail to recognize its dependence on *digital power*. This dependence is more obvious in individualized television, airplanes, and automobiles, which connected human beings to human beings and things as soon as they came into being. The argument, finally, that inhabited machines are small, privatized, and portable and can be incorporated into their bearers fits for only mobile telephones and laptops.

According to Urry, unequivocally convergent mobile telephones and laptops take on the definitive role in the 21st century. Competent users will become independent of space and time and obtain access to networks and flows of information, images, and social movements of which they, in their turn, (could) become nodes. Resulting from this new, emerging person-to-person connectivity—here I am in agreement—is a new quality of information and mobility: The significance of personal networking and personal networks will substantially grow. The increasing virtuality of networking alters the relationship to the real world and other people. The extensifying of person-to-person connectivity transforms existing structures and ways of life throughout the world.

Despite this, any conceptual understanding of laptops and mobile telephones as machines does not encompass everything involved. It would be wrong to conclude that their capabilities are owed solely to their technical qualities. Their extensive connectivity has for a long time not been a question of technology but of numerous political and economic desires, pressures, and decisions. Convergent media still do not develop their extensive connectivity from their mere existence. It does not come about by owning them: their users can develop digital power and extensive connectivity only by paying (intensively) for them and obtaining (extensive) access to flows and networks making connectivity possible. Convergent mobile telephones and laptops must not be reduced (essentialistically) to technology.

The nontechnological, political-cultural, economic-social presuppositions of their connectivity as mediality should not be masked out, or else the TIMES convergence remains misunderstood. If we want to comprehend the TIMES convergence as well as convergent media, we should not solely follow John Urry's work, which assumes these emergent technological developments and new levels of complexity, just as the novelist William Gibson does in his cyberpunk novels such as *Neuromancer*, *Idoru* and *Futurematic*. The TIMES convergence is not a development no longer accessible to human intervention and action nor is it a biological one, where it is a mere matter of reaction and adjustment.[6] The TIMES convergence and its media, medial flows, networks, and connectivities are the result of technological and economic and political decisions; they did not descend on humanity as an act of nature like a tornado.[7]

A commercial, political, and a clear technological beginning for the TIMES convergence first evolved with the convergence of private and public radio services and that of telecommunication and IT-technology in the development of end devices. The commercial starting point was a saturated media market in America. It was impossible for the shares of any listed media corporation to gain value without first making itself attractive by arguments about its future global success. This commercial option was in fact so vital to the United States that it withdrew from UNESCO due to a dispute about the New World Information and Communication Order.[8] Digitalization was the technological basis for the convergence of telecommunication and computer technology.

In the wake of these developments, conditions and assumptions of communication and media culture have changed quite a bit since the middle of the 1980s. Beginning with the liberalization of radio in the 1980s, the sale of important Internet administrative functions of the National Science Foundation to American companies came about in 1993 based on Al Gore's idea of a *National Information Infrastructure*. By 1994 the amount of commercial hosts (.com) numerically overtook their scholarly (.edu) counterparts and took top rung. It was then that— after the global commercialization of radio and television—the commercialization of the Internet began. It was not limited to supply and content offered on the Net but also encompassed the connections to the

---

[6]The theory of a quasi-biological momentum is characteristic of the current convergence bestseller entitled: *It's Alive: The Coming of Information, Biology, and Business* by Christopher Meyer and Stan Davis (2003).

[7]On the complexity of parallel processes and the utilization and the direction of media development, see especially Krotz (2001, 2003).

[8]For greater detail, see Herman and McChesney (1997, pp. 10ff).

media and expanded with the emergence of multimedia, first to TIM convergence and later, with the emergence of computer games, to TIME convergence. The international Agreement on Basic Telecommunications in 1997 finally ended the regulatory power of the individual countries, which made this agreement concerning conditions under which communication inside their borders would be structured and made available.

For the most part, the boundaries of the branches and their laws, authorities, rules, and so forth were rendered obsolete. New complex formations of new orders and (at first) actual increasing disorder emerged in the TIMES branches. In the 1990s convergence was above all a struggle for size. The development costs of convergent services, products, infrastructure (UMTS), and markets went beyond the budgets of even the largest telecommunication companies. Due to this cost factor, all the companies of the TIMES branches struck alliances and cooperative agreements with one another, bought other businesses or merged with them. This was not a linear process but an open relational, transnational process whose course no corporation could foresee, because it depended on too many different influences, for example, regional and global market developments, end-products and services, the development of the company, and so on. As a result, there emerged globally the most varied translocal *networks of media* (see Hepp, 2004).

The most important production wave of mobile convergent laptops and mobile telephones commenced with the advent of the new millennium. It has become possible gradually to recognize whether and how money can be earned by access to content such as news, weather, and stock market quotations, by downloading and viewing films and video clips, entertainment in the form of games and corresponding security technology—for example, by placement of bets—and whether and in what degree these small medial convergent nodes change people's lives. By these few hints it becomes obvious how the mobile convergent media greatly differ from the media known to us. In principle, they can make a connection at any time and place with people and media and they employ the corresponding protocol and transfer technology by which they can reverse the known process of medial communication: content is recalled on the basis of personalized and privatized profiles, not according to a pre-edited and prepackaged allocation. The (technical) possibility to influence production and allocation of medial communication constitutes a new group of media.

In the media and communication sciences, this new group of convergent media is called quaternary media, according to the technological classification of primary, secondary, and tertiary media. Primary media are media not requiring any technology for communication and cultural orientation, such as theater, or when communication is constituted by role-agents such as priests and preachers. Hence, primary media are termed human media. In contrast, secondary media such as books and newspapers depend on technology for the production of communication. Tertiary media such as radio and television are dependent on technology for production and reproduction. Employing this logic, quaternary media differ from tertiary media in that in addition to the technology used for production and reproduction—in the sense of reception and usage of media—they feature protocol and transfer technology, which turns transmitters into receivers, receivers into transmitters.[9]

With this possibility, convergent media greatly increase the complexity of relationality between *moorings* and *mobilities* of global flows and networks as well as a person-to-person connectivity, as Urry correctly emphasizes. This complexity has until now always been increased by each new medium. But that is not the only thing Urry fails to mention. By putting more emphasis on comparisons than historical beginnings and developments, Urry neglects change as a vital point of reference. The case is not made with any clarity that mobile convergent media's growth of complexity does not lag behind other media's growth in history. And, equally, the fact that new media change our communication as practice of the transmission of social values such as love, freedom, and equality, and how they do, is largely ignored. The significance that makes media fundamentally different from machines lies in their communicative and cultural transmission of individual ways of life and experience together with the social conditions influencing them. Hence, media are constituents of symbolic social relations between human beings, points of reference for community and cultural solidarity, and this will be our focus in the following discussion.

Urry with his postempirical accentuation of scientific metaphors and inhabited machines could have joined a grand tradition of machine-metaphors, especially that of Rousseau. Rousseau, in his famed *Discourse on the Origin of Inequality*, compares the *machine humaine* to the *machine ingenieuse* of the animal (1990). This ingenious machine does not possess the freedom of choice, in contrast to the "machine person" who, as Rousseau points out, does not employ his freedom merely to his advantage but "often to his disadvantage" (Rousseau, 1990, p. 99) as well as for the constitution of social inequality and bondage. Urry's subject is complexity, not human inequality. He does not ask whether these inhabited machines and their digital power and connectivity contribute to more or less inequality among human beings.

The first mobile quaternary media such as laptops and mobile telephones are end points as well as starting points of TIMES-convergence. They are end points, for a great deal worldwide had to be achieved for them to become a reality beyond erstwhile national media and telecom laws. They are starting points, because more and more people have

---

[9]On the definition, see in greater detail my discussion in Winter (2002).

begun organizing their communication and cultural orientation through them. It is a new beginning for everyone, a beginning that will grow in meaning for one's own life, for society and culture as laptops and mobile telephones will become more important in the cultural and economic self-organization and the mediation between one's own way of life and the given social conditions than other media.[10]

THE TIMES CONVERGENCE OF THE MEDIALITY OF CULTURAL CONNECTIVITY IN THE LIFE OF PEOPLE

The change in medial mediation between one's own way of life and the given social conditions happens, so to speak, beneath the relationality of Urry's moorings and mobilities. Cultural meaning and conceptions of freedom, equality and love are communicated in daily life, into which new convergent media like mobile telephones and laptops—as well as other "new" media before them—are integrated by their practical use. Relationships between people and things, social realities and forms of cultural solidarity change by this use.

The first one who recognized and conceptually took account of this was nobody less than Max Weber. His media were not quaternary media but those that interested him in the context of the emergence of occidental rationality: Primary media like sorcerers, priests and prophets, who of course were not called *primary media* by him. In his "systematic sociology of religion"[11] Weber developed his reflections on these important and influential social roles as bearers of cultural rationality of societies—a work he never finished and which was published posthumously. He situated his concept of culture between Marx and Durkheim: Whereas Durkheim demonstrated in his *Elementary Forms of Religious Life* (1994/1912) that religion as a culture cannot exist without commonly lived usages, rituals, and cults, as it is by these alone they have social reality, and whereas Marx emphasized the social and material condi-

---

[10]This change in cultural processes of transmission is the subject of a larger scholarly project I am currently researching about TIMES convergence. See Winter (2002) in regard to new medial surplus services, and for the cultural meaning of convergent media for children's identity and living patterns and living space, see also Winter (2003a). A scholarly college and a multidisciplinary series of lectures *TELEmediaCULTURES* is a part of the project.

[11]The contribution of his systematic sociology of religion deriving from economics and study of society, in contrast to religious-historical studies, should be understood for its positive conceptualization of the development of cultural (religious) rationality. It was published after Weber's death, an unfinished work (see Weber, 1980).

tions of culture and their meaning above all as ideology, Weber raised questions about the transmission of both. He asked how social conditions are naturalized by religious usages and rituals and how their values and norms are transmitted on a concrete level.

Weber recognized that this transmission was accomplished by very concrete social institutions such as the sorcerer and priest, whose study he declared to be the challenge of sociology: The *sociological side* of the historical separation of religion from sorcery was the *separation* of the priest from the sorcerer according to Weber.[12] In these rankings the prophet was a bearer of a new quality of solidarity in ethical religion, and later on, the printed media became the new bearers of cultural rationality. For easily discernible groups and for the time prior to printed media, the idea is plausible that the bearers of the most influential communication and cultural orientation were also bearers of cultural rationality of the group. The cultural rationality of communities whose members use several media for their cultural orientation cannot be characterized by one single medium.

The idea of a *transmission rationality*, however, should not be abandoned; it should be developed further because it does not deny the cultural moment of transmission, which often gets lost in technical concepts. Media are to be understood as this double significance: They are not just technical nodes in relational contexts but—as nodes—bearers of a cultural rationality (not of *communicative rationality* in Habermas' sense, whose concept is inadequate to encompass the complexity and relationality of medial communication; cf. Winter, 2003b). The claim of rationality would no longer be applied to the culture of a community but to medial communication as the context of usage of a medium in the framework of historically specific communication. Of interest is only a very small communicative-medial component of a community's cultural rationality, which is indubitably made up of these components, of course.[13]

---

[12]Weber evolved this conceptualization in the passage going from his first to second chapter: "One may differentiate those forms of relationships to the transcendental powers, which express themselves as supplication, sacrifice, worship, as religion and cult to separate them from sorcery, characterized as magical constraint, and, furthermore, those as gods as the creatures religiously worshiped, while those that are coerced and proscripted by magical means, shall be differentiated as demons." At the conclusion of the second chapter entitled *Sorcerer-Priest* he adds: "But the sociological side is that differentiation characterized by the emergence of a priestly caste as separate from sorcerers."

[13]As is well known, Weber conceived of sorcerers, priests, and prophets as ideal types. An ideal type is not an instrument through which change may be understood and explained. It does not contribute to a comprehension of processes and beginnings but, above all, is a comparative measure, hence comparable to categories of primary, secondary, tertiary, and quaternary media.

This understanding of communication stands in the tradition of those media theorists of an anti-essentialist and empirical bent such as Joshua Meyrowitz (1985) and representatives of cultural studies such as Raymond Williams (2003) and Stuart Hall (1980). Their work may be characterized as an attempt to understand medial communication neither from the perspective of the medium alone nor independent of content, participants, and contexts.

Meyrowitz demonstrated empirically how a new medium such as television changes the information environment of its users, for it provides insights otherwise inaccessible or "not visible" or, as Raymond Williams would add, created only for television and new, ever more prevalent private forms of life, which we shall take up below. Without meaning to impute a cause-and-effect relation, media change their environment by their mere presence when something is done with them in it. Employing this insight, Stuart Hall has studied media, differentiated in their relations to moments and contexts of communication: hence, production, allocation, reception, and social usage as moments and contexts in which—within the scope of communication—something is done with media. Changes in the medial communication process may, I assume, be adequately analyzed and historically compared as changes in these moments and contexts.[14]

This understanding of medial communication as context of production, allocation, reception, and usage of media for communication takes into account the media in their dependence on contexts and their logic, as well as those who, within these, do something with the medium. I understand the relation of human beings with media in various contexts as "articulation," as temporary connectedness, which those involved can dissolve. Communication as the context of various articulations created by dealing with a medium becomes, from a perspective focused on media, *medial connectivity*. Hence, medial connectivity always indicates a conjunction of what is different through, as well as by, a medium. This shows how complex medial communication is. Neither the production of medial communication nor allocation, reception, or usage are communication but only the medial relational connectivity of articulations with media in all its moments and contexts of communication, whereby no single usage of a medium in one of these moments or contexts can be deduced on the basis of another of those moments and contexts. In my view, this relationality and complexity cannot be adequately reconstructed or conceptualized by biological-chemical or by computer-oriented models.

This understanding of medial communication, which has media as its point of reference, allows for a conceptual understanding of the

---

[14]This conceptualization of medial communication further develops the models of Hall (1980) and Johnson (1986), whose conceptual starting points were derived from Marx's outline of the production of goods (cf. Winter, 2003b).

TIMES convergence as change in technical as well as cultural conditions of the mediality of communication and culture, for it allows for a differentiated understanding of the concrete usage of media. This understanding of medial communication could be depicted as follows (Figure 5-1):

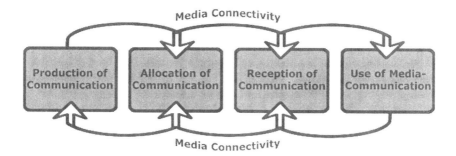

Figure 5.1.   The Media-Connectivity of Communication

The moments and contexts of medial communication are termed *production of communication*, not production of media. This takes into account the fact that usage of a medium as well as medial connectivity is aimed at communication, not at the medium. The usage of media for communication comes about in these contexts and moments, as a rule, on the basis of certain commonly shared cultural assumptions. They change in time along with the media in the context of processes such as the TIMES convergence, within whose framework the conditions and presuppositions of communication are changed by a complex interplay of technical developments and new political and economic imperatives.

Historically this can be understood in the context of the definition of primary, secondary, tertiary, and quaternary media as follows: As a rule, originally the production of cultural orientation was protected in many ways, by cults, temples, rituals and so forth. Not everybody was able or was allowed to communicate. Distribution came about in a framework of rituals; that is, according to specific rules, which often served as control. Maintenance of control was already more difficult with the secondary or printed media. They separated the moments of medial production, allocation, reception, and usage of suprapersonal communication and made allocation, reception, and usage independent of time and place.

During the Enlightenment, print media such as the newspaper were freed from sacral "protection" with which churches up to this day seek to silence "heretic" communication. The production of medial communication became production of the public forum, which, although contested, is guarded by definite rights, especially by freedom of the press. This protection was deemed so important with the new tertiary media radio and television that they received a new status as public goods in most countries of the world and were not allowed to be commercially produced and allocated.

As I discussed in the context of Urry's assertion about the meaning of inhabited machines in the 21st century, my reconstruction of TIMES convergence and definition of convergent media as quaternary media, convergent media laptops and mobile telephones are changing conditions and presuppositions of communication by an emergence of new content flows, media networks and connectivities. A short historical comparison will illustrate how they do this in light of the conditions and presuppositions of civil society and cultural solidarity. The TIMES convergence, with its convergent media, changes the cultural foundations of communication and solidarity because unprecedented direct influence on allocation and production of medial communication has been made possible.

This change, which is certainly no secret, has come about since the evolution of primary media, over secondary and tertiary media, to quaternary and convergent media, and has been discussed as the fragmentizing of public communication and further as privatizing and personalizing of medial communication,[15] whereby with the changes of production and allocation, reception and social usage of communication change too. What I think is important here is not just a critical discussion on what is new but also the loss of meaning of older forms of production, allocation, reception, and social utilization of medial communication. It is not a matter of appraisal, keeping distinct the culturally critical "new" against the "old," but of better dealing with the new in light of the old. In order to do so, we have to know the achievements of those politically and culturally significant primary, secondary and tertiary media. With them, on the basis of specific fundamental cultural assumptions, communicative accomplishments were achieved, which had an influence on community, society and forms of cultural solidarity. These media had their own individual power based on special cultural conditions and presuppositions of the contents, networking and medial connectivity.

The Christian preachers, who made up the most effective medium in the group of primary media, gathered everybody before them as equals (because they were equal before their God) and free to engage in communication with everyone, for the first time in history. But equality and freedom, as incorporated in the medial role of Christian preacher, could only revolutionize conditions and presuppositions of communication when based on Christian charity. This was certainly the most

---

[15]For further reading on fragmentizing, see Winter and Rummel (2005); for privatizing and personalizing, see Winter (2002).

important condition leading more than half of the Roman Empire with its population of 60 million, before recognition of the religion by Constantine, to become Christians, despite the cruelest persecutions. They converted to a community of communication and orientation that had been constituted by newfangled Christian preachers. The intercourse with them had so fundamentally changed the production, allocation, reception, and usage of communication in the Roman Empire that Constantine had no other choice but to take the preachers into government service.

The Christian preacher received his power on the basis of Christian charity, which gave him an opportunity to constitute equality and freedom in the framework of communication. This new "Christian charity," whereby Christians by their love make the love of God for humanity a part of social reality, was a necessary condition for the success of Christian preachers as public and culturally orienting media. Their significance retreated as equality and freedom to communicate, and Christian solidarity in the context of interaction with Christian preachers in a framework of communication, likewise retreated in history. But this is not an object of discussion here.[16]

This basis of communication, whereby Christians gained cultural orientation through the primary medium of the preacher, was for long unopposed. Opposition was only possible when the Church abandoned ever more obviously this foundation of values as a part of social power, commercialized her preachers and brought them into disrepute. But she lost her influence only when printing products were utilized for the constitution of communication and cultural orientation in place of preachers, the human media. A break in the domination by preachers in public communication was when preachers were no longer burned but printed matter was. This change is associated with the Augustinian preacher, Bible professor and bestselling author Martin Luther, of whose printed works in 1520 around 500,000 were sold—more than ever before. It is known that Luther burned printed copies of the papal Bull of Banishment against him after the Catholic Church burned his writings.

The preacher as contemporary, universal, and periodic medium was not replaced until quite later. The medium replacing him in this role was the newspaper. It was the political medium of the Enlightenment and reference point for the demand that what affects everybody must be

---

[16]I have dealt elsewhere with the subject of Christian preachers as mediums. Firstly, in a work about the success of the mendicant orders, unexplained until now, which without money, power and social opportunities in the 13th century swiftly rose to become one of the greatest organizations in contemporary Europe. Then, in an extensive media cultural history of the Christian preacher, where the emergence of the role is reconstructed for the first time, alongside its history up to the present day.

made public. This demand would never have been made at the time
without the medium of the newspaper, nor even (partially) realized
either.[17] The historical realization of this demand changed the character of media, for they made them into more or less public goods. This
status was upheld even when they belonged to individual people as their
private property. The newspaper was a public and concurrently a private good, a cultural as well as an economic good. It could not be
reduced to one or the other.

Like the Christian preacher, the newspaper received its power as
medium not just based on such formal attributes as its contemporaneity,
universality, and periodicity. Its cultural basis was not Christian charity
and thus its contribution to a religious denomination, but rather its contribution to something similar to how the preacher himself constituted
ethical religion: the nation. For its publicity, which distinguished it as a
medium, was national. The new *national publicity* was constituted by
the newspaper as part of the social reality, which became increasingly
national reality (see Anderson, 1991). Its meaning retreated insofar as
its general meaning in the lives of people as citizens retreated. Today,
newspapers still exist as national newspapers beyond a regional basis,
but they have meaning, above all, as a universalistic, contemporary,
periodic, and publicistic medium of the region. Nationally, the significance and credibility of newspapers ranks much below television, which,
as the dominant medium in most societies, has replaced the social media
order specific to printed media, after a brief intermezzo of radio.

Television has molded extensively the medial public space without
adding much more space for the national public forum. The bourgeois
public forum, which Habermas (1993) visualized as the normative bourgeois public space of a nation, became with television a historical, partly public forum. Although television was a cultural medium governed by
public law and in parts still is, it very seldom gathers the nation as a
nation. Television's technologically and culturally newly planned and
mobile flow was the characteristic with which television broke through
as a new medium in the 1970s and 1980s.

Raymond Williams (2003) was the first to describe the attribute
flow. He reflects more systematically than Weber did on the concept of
the medial, demonstrating how television, with its experience of flow,
constitutes a new type of production and allocation connection to the
reception of medial content. Williams does not refer only to the type of
seamless television programming that already was the usual thing by
that time in the United States, in contrast to England, and to the contin-

---

[17]The translation of the German word *Publizität* (publicity) by *Öffentlichkeit*
(public forum) has disguised for a long time its reference to the people. This reference is still contained in the French *publicité* and the English *publicity*, both of
which point to *populus* (Latin for "people").

uous watching of television "without a break," which was the case in the United States. Similar to the view of the preacher and newspaper that I proposed, Williams integrates fundamental cultural aspects that mold television communication, somewhat similar to how Christian communication is strongly affected by equality before God and Christian charity, and how newspaper communication is affected by publicity, which was national publicity and characterized the newspaper as medium of the national and regional public forum.

Williams employs the term *planned flow*[18] for—on the part of television—the planning of connected parts of the program and for the corresponding planning—on the reception side—of these parts of the program as a comprehensive context of experience.[19] As a characteristic of the technological and cultural form of television, its program is still considered *mobile flow* by him. It characterizes the role of television in societies where citizens have become more mobile, must change their residences more often and, above all, are leading private lives. The mobile flow of television renders them independent of the places they live, for it partially replaces the social connection to life at these locations by a life of television stars and television series.

Nowadays flow is no longer understood in Williams' sense as a medium, even though this flow expanded worldwide as the prototype of television experience. Since Appadurai's work (1990), the term "flow" transcends specific media, meaning global *mediascapes* that are no longer the object of an orderly planning of television programming by a manager, that of a recipient who has planned a cozy evening of television viewing. Flows stand for content fluids, driven through locationless flexible TIMES networks, whose smallest nodes are human beings with mobile convergent media, who might well depend on the connectivity with these flows and networks but to which they must no longer be culturally connected, in the sense of *Gemeinschaft*.

Before, cultural connectedness in the form of Christian charity or belonging to a nation considerably raised the probability for communication to succeed, for there was a common foundation, or else a sense of cultural connectedness had been made possible due to a connection with television stars and their various series. Today, in contrast, cultural connectedness can be a problem. Networks whose efficiency lies in

---

[18]"This phenomenon of planned flow is then perhaps the defining characteristic of broadcasting, simultaneously as a technology and as a cultural form." (Williams, 2003, p. 86).

[19]"It is evident that what is now called an evening's viewing is in some ways planned, by providers and by viewers, as a whole; that is in any event planned in discernible sequences which in this sense override particular programme units. Whenever there is a competition between television channels, this becomes a matter of conscious concern: to get viewers in at the beginning of a flow" (Williams, 2003, p. 94).

the speed necessary for their actions and reactions, in contrast to other forms of connection, give more meaning—as Urry would put it—to mobilities than they do to moorings. Hence, the impression can be garnered that with such networks the technical connection of the elements involved, whether they be units of a business, companies, or partners, more strongly determine or alone determine the efficiency of a network. Cultural connectedness, which functions as a common reference point for ways of living, values, practices, and orientations, can slow the speed of a network's action and reaction. Businesses that have become networks have almost no solid structure, having increasingly dissolved into temporary projects without location: their employees no longer have fixed workplaces, just small mobile office units. The organization and business culture of these firms has changed accordingly. The employees take care of their new duties and projects when the old ones end. They must develop a professionalism allowing them and their convergent media to gain immediate connection to the new project and the people involved.

Mobile convergent media such as the mobile telephone and the laptop differ from other media utilized until now in that, although making a connection to human beings and content within a framework of communication, they are no longer dependent on common values. Differing from the preacher, newspaper, and television, mobile convergent media are independent of Christian love, love of country, and love for a television star—to put it in a striking manner. Therefore it is not for nothing that the medium itself, invisible for so long, comes to the forefront more decisively than before. Nowadays, mobile convergent media allow access to connectedness with others, an access possible before by common religion, nation, or at least television star; this love, this cultural mooring, was always a precondition of medial communication, although access to others and other things was not as personal and private as it is nowadays with convergent media.

IT'S POSSIBLE TO FALL IN LOVE WITH A COMPUTER AND THE PEOPLE YOU NEED ARE ONLY A TOUCH AWAY!

The question we are now concerned with is: Where did the love of old go, which people once showed their neighbor, their land as patriots, their idols and favorite series, and what are the interpretations of cultural values such as equality and freedom? This question comes up not merely in the context of the conditions of probability of medial communication, which remain incomprehensible when its "media-cultural" dimensions are masked out, but also because in advertising suggestions are being made in this respect without any inhibition whatever. These aim to pass love on to the medium itself, which nowadays accomplishes that which was possible before only by cultural solidarity, and technologically to re-interpret and transform equality as well as freedom.

I would like to demonstrate through pictures this new situation in which the medium becomes the focus of devotion and interest; much indicates that mobile convergent media are starting to change life and society lastingly. My starting point is an advertisement from a picture-collection series entitled *Fantasy of the Future* (see Plate 1). It shows two women presumably talking on a picture telephone with their children. Although the picture telephone is obviously a fantasy of the future, it is the interaction that stands in the forefront, not the new medium. (This is unequivocally ranked a rung beneath the familial-communal connectedness and practically not touched on.)

The relationship and cultural connectedness in the picture's forefront is between the persons communicating. This cultural connectedness, illustrated so clearly here, can nowadays be found in many ad campaigns for mobile telephones. One example is the Siemens campaign on which everything appears to go wrong for a young girl on her first day in America, who does not need to feel homesick, nevertheless, for her Triband mobile telephone functions in the United States as well. Here the cultural relationship *going home* and *to the parents* is a part of a relationship lived and kept intact in a practical manner by the mobile telephone.

More courageous ad campaigns can do without this connection to people. In these cases, the focus of the campaign, as well as of the life of the people in the illustration, is unequivocally the relationship to the medium. This particular cultural value of the mobile telephone is clearly expressed in a Sony-Ericsson ad campaign (see Plate 2) and additionally by its claim: "The new Sony Z7. You won't be able to let it go any-

Plate 1   Picture from the series Fantasy of the Future

more." That claim relates to an intimate situation in which a woman seduces a man or vice versa—despite it, she does not let go of her Z7.

Siemens plays with another aspect of the cultural dimension of connectedness with a mobile telephone in one ad campaign in which her mobile telephone is a girl's best friend. That makes the significance of the medium even more obvious, even though the claim relativizes the picture: "Sophisticated, sexy and ultimately small. Who can be surprised the CL 50 has a permanent place at your side? In its elegant clamshell design, with its glittering blue display and personal, polyphonic melodies, the CL 50 bewitches everybody, simply like that. And provides more gloss in life" (See Plate 3).

In my opinion, the new cultural significance of mobile convergent media is best expressed in the following Apple advertisement. It asks right up front, without qualms, whether it is possible to fall in love with a computer—and it answers this question: Oh, yes (see Plate 4).

Is it possible for a woman in intimate moments not to let go of her Sony Z7? Is it possible for a Siemens CL 50 to be a girl's best friend? Is it possible to fall in love with an Apple iBook? Advertising would probably not work with these claims if they were totally absurd. My own fieldwork confirms this high cultural significance of mobile convergent media, which when speaking to children and youth ought to be called almost naïve (see Winter, 2003a). That does not concern us, however. What concerns us is: What do TIMES-convergence and mobile convergent media signify for the future of civil society and cultural solidarity? In conjunction with Weber's thoughts to ask questions about the trans-

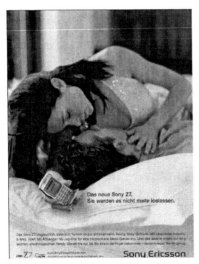

Plate 2   You won't be able to let it go anymore

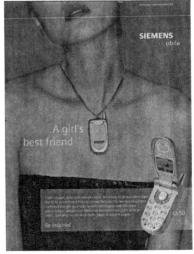

Plate 3   Siemens: A Girl's Best Friend

Is it possible to fall in love with a computer? Oh yes. Introducing iBook.

 Think different.

Plate 4   Apple iBook:
Is it Possible to Fall in Love With a Computer? Oh yes.

mission of cultural practices and conditions of life, we now have to ask: Which practices, in dealings with mobile convergent media reflect which conditions of life in respect to love but also to equality and freedom—and how?

For its many owners, an Apple iBook is a cult; working with it a ritual. That goes for mobile telephones, too, at least for some of them, along with their usage. This quite unequivocally private and personal form of usage of and dealings with laptops and mobile telephones do not quite affect others and the society. Nevertheless, they have significance for our understanding of cultural connectedness, which until now was exclusively a connectedness on the basis of solidarity—into which a person was born or of which, in recent times, a person was able to decide to be a part. A totally new technological connection, termed connectivity, emerges with mobile convergent media, which even has advantages—as we have pointed out—in contrast to this cultural connectedness. Hence, solidarity is no longer an exclusive condition for the connectedness of human beings, as we shall demonstrate below regarding equality and freedom.

Civil society loses significance similarly to the manner in which cultural solidarity loses meaning for greater numbers of human beings as it is "used" less and less. As a cultural community, it is dependent, as Durkheim demonstrated, on common practices, rituals, and cults of civil life and ways of communication. For these, television and its mobile flow offered a practicable replacement that had hollowed out the civil, particularly location-rooted public and communal life. "Civil society" must be lived as a commonly shared and desired form of life. It must be accessible as a communal experience, otherwise it is condemned to failure. In principle, today this would be more possible than ever, for nowadays people whom you need in order to do something are "only a click of a key away" (see Plate 5).

Plate 5   We're Groovy

Once more, the key determinant is not technology itself but the cultural form given to it. It is expressed not just in the claim, "We're groovy," but in the question, "How are you?" It refers to each of us and connects our well-being, whether we are groovy or not, in a subliminal way with whether we belong to those who can send or cannot send a text message to their friends. Thus, the campaign practices cultural exclusion reminiscent of old times believed to be long since forgotten. Here, not everybody is free to communicate, and here, not all people are equal, either. The mobile telephone represents an ideology of freedom and equality that is reminiscent of an era of professed creeds and is nourished by an envy that makes inequality repulsive.[20] The Vodaphone ideology of freedom and equality is not that of a civil and democratic society. It is that of a commercial society in which, above all, cultural equality can be purchased, and it does not function, of course, because purchasing price renders equality more improbable.

After the international Agreement on Basic Telecommunications in 1997 came into effect, TIMES corporations such as Vodaphone have had an ever stronger cultural influence on the conditions under which communication is possible. Vodaphone sets these conditions not just by price but also by public—or, as some still put it—"ad" communication. These TIMES-businesses, controlling the most immense advertising budgets worldwide, are successful in setting forth cultural and identity policies, too, and are starting increasingly to decide who is "in" and "out" and how we communicate or do not. Businesses are aware of this, in my view, as my last example of a new interpretation of freedom as, above all, a technologically determined freedom (see Plate 6) should illustrate.

---

[20]See also Sennett (2003, pp. 89ff), who deals only indirectly with the cultural results of new technology. He is one of the few, however, who develops the categories discussed here; e.g., in 1998 in *The Corrosion of Character*.

Plate 6   We're out

A human being who is really free can only be a networked human being, who uses the network and can free himself from it.

The history of mobile convergent media and their flows, networks, and connectivity has not reached its end, however. And it would be premature to predict an end. Anybody aware of history knows the success of Christian preachers could not have been foreseen. Nobody expected anything other than that religious books would sell well and profane content would never make up more than a few small percentage points of all printed products. Nobody foresaw the newspaper's success and the cultural bond that would be forged by the idea of the nation. Nobody expected media such as radio and television would be organized by public law nearly the whole world over and that the most varied public-law medial attainments would be abandoned so swiftly. Who intuited ten years ago that mobile convergent media would achieve such a global cultural significance this quickly?

TIMES CONVERGENCE, MOBILE CONVERGENT MEDIA, AND THE FUTURE OF CULTURAL SOLIDARITY AND CIVIL SOCIETY

This contribution points out the meaning of TIMES convergence and new mobile convergent media emerging in conjunction with it, a meaning often retreating behind its large economic and political significance. The meaning that the media have for the constitution of community and cultural connectedness among human beings (be it for friendship, family, community, ethnic group, fan group, organization, online community, or just formal and informal network) has hardly been studied until

now. This is also the case for mobile convergent media and the connectivities, flows, and networks constituted by them, which accelerate and
change them further.

My suggestion for researching change in medial communication is
to take seriously media as institutions of transmission in regards to their
cultural and technical aspects, and is aimed toward an understanding of
and research on the values of solidarity such as love, equality, and freedom, not only abstractly but on a practical basis. Media are not merely
machines but are institutions for the transmission of culture and have
significance in this context. People learn solidarity by and with them.
This should be taken into account when we examine new medial flows,
networks, and connectivities by which relationships between people are
freshly constituted. These always have a culturally normative dimension, for they can alter our conceptions of love, equality, and freedom,
as I have hinted in my several illustrations.

Once this media role has achieved due recognition it will be time to
allow it more space in the study of these flows, networks, and connectivities along with their velocities, contents, contexts/locations, and participants. I suggest studying them ethnographically and in respect to
their usage in the four moments and contexts of communication and in
regard to their medial connectivity. By means of this, the complexity
and relationality of media culture will be easier to understand, in my
opinion, than by means of an orientation toward models from computer science or chemistry, which have not yet come to grips with cultural
solidarity and structures such as civil society. Particularities and unexpected developments in regard to content flows, networks, and connectivities can be found to contribute to their better comprehension. It is
often the case that the best critique of change in communication and
media culture is the depiction of these changes and particularities.

The future of civil society and cultural solidarity is the future of specific forms of cultural and medial connectedness. Mobile convergent
media such as laptops and mobile telephones long ago changed these
assumptions and conditions, as they already represent basic conditions
and presuppositions of new forms of connectedness whose specific
rationality and relationality, which depend on how one uses and deals
with them, has for the most part not been researched.

The practices and rituals in dealing with and using new convergent
media must be studied and understood in regard to communication as
the smallest component of civil society and cultural solidarity. This is
necessary if we wish to understand laptops and mobile telephones not
just as technology but as media—as cultural mediators—between ways
of living and their social conditions. This is necessary if we wish to
develop not merely ideas of civil society and cultural solidarity, but want
to work on them so that these will become real in the lives of human
beings.

REFERENCES

Anderson, B. (1991). *Imagined communities. Reflections on the origin and spread of nationalism* (rev. ed.). London, New York: Verso. (Original work published 1983)

Appadurai, A. (1990). Disjuncture and difference in the global cultural economy. In M. Featherstone (Ed.), *Global culture* (pp. 295-310). London: Sage.

Bauman, Z. (2000). *Liquid modernity*. Cambridge: Polity.

Capra, F. (2002). *The hidden connections: A science for sustainable living*. London: HarperCollins.

Cillers, P. (1998). *Complexity and postmodernism. Understanding complex systems*. London: Routledge.

Durkheim, E. (1994). *Die elementaren Formen des religiösen Lebens*. Frankfurt a. M.: Suhrkamp. (Original work published 1912)

Giddens, A. (1990). *The consequences of modernity*. Cambridge: Polity.

Habermas, J. (1993). *Strukturwandel der Öffentlichkeit: Untersuchungen zu einer Kategorie der bürgerlichen Gesellschaft* (mit einem Vorw. zur Neuaufl.). Frankfurt a. M.: Suhrkamp. (Original work published 1962)

Hall, S. (1980). Encoding/decoding. In S. Hall et al. *Culture, media language. Working papers in cultural studies 1972-1979* (pp. 128-138). London: Hutchinson. (Original work published 1973)

Hepp, A. (2004). *Netzwerke der Medien. Medienkulturen und Globalisierung*. Wiesbaden: Verlag für Sozialwissenschaften.

Herman, E. S., & McChesney, R. W. (1997). *The global media: The new missionaries of corporate capitalism*. London: Cassell.

Johnson, R. (1986). What is cultural studies anyway? *Social Text, 16*, 38-80.

Karmasin, M., & Winter, C. (Eds.). (2005). *Konvergenzmanagement und Kommunikationsentwicklung*. München: Fink (UTB).

Krotz, F. (2001). *Die Mediatisierung kommunikativen Handelns. Der Wandel von Alltag, sozialen Beziehungen, Kultur und Gesellschaft durch Medien*. Wiesbaden: Westdeutscher Verlag.

Krotz, F. (2003). Zivilisationsprozess und Mediatisierung: Zum Zusammenhang von Medien- und Gesellschaftswandel. In M. Behmer et al. (Eds.), *Medienentwicklung und gesellschaftlicher Wandel* (pp. 15-35). Wiesbaden: Westdeutscher Verlag.

Meyer, C., & Davis, S. (2003). *It´s alive: The coming convergence of information, biology, and business*. New York: Crown Business.

Meyrowitz, J. (1985). *No sense of place. The impact of electronic media on social behaviour*. New York: Oxford University Press.

Rousseau, J.-J. (1990). *Diskurs über die Ungleichheit. Discours sur l'Inégalité*. (2nd ed., Meier). Paderborn u.a.: Schöningh. (Original work published 1775)

Sennett, R. (1998). *The corrosion of character*. New York: W.W. Norton.

Sennett, R. (2003). *Respect in a world of inequality*. New York: W.W. Norton.

Tomlinson, J. (1999). *Globalization and culture*. Cambridge: Polity Press.

Urry, J. (2003). *Global complexity*. Cambridge: Polity Press.

Weber, M. (1980). *Religionssoziologie*. In M. Weber, *Wirtschaft und Gesellschaft. Grundriss der verstehenden Soziologie* (5th ed. by J. Winckelmann, pp. 245-381). Tübingen: J.C.B. Mohr. (Original work published about 1922)

Williams, R. (2003). *Television. Technology and cultural form.* London, New York: Routledge. (Original work published 1974)

Winter, C. (2000). Kulturwandel und Globalisierung: Eine Einführung in die Diskussion. In C.-Y. Robertson & C. Winter (Eds.), *Kulturwandel und Globalisierung* (pp. 13-73). Baden-Baden: Nomos Verlag.

Winter, C. (2002). Die Zukunft medialer Mehrwertdienste: Eine kommunikationswissenschaftliche fächerübergreifende Einführung. In M. Karmasin & C. Winter (Eds.), *Mediale Mehrwertdienste und die Zukunft der Kommunikation* (pp.9-32). Wiesbaden: Westdeutscher Verlag.

Winter, C. (2003a). Die konvergente Re-Artikulation von Jugendkulturen im Spannungsfeld zwischen spielerischen Taktiken und kommerziellen Strategien. In J. Bug & M. Karmasin, *Telekommunikation und Jugendkultur. Eine Einführung* (pp. 47-75). Wiesbaden: Westdeutscher Verlag.

Winter, C. (2003b). Der Zusammenhang von Medienentwicklung und Wandel als theoretische Herausforderung. Perspektiven für eine artikulationstheoretische Ergänzung systemfunktionaler Analysen. In M. Bremer et al. (Eds.), *Medienentwicklung und gesellschaftlicher Wandel. Beiträge zu einer theoretischen und empirischen Herausforderung* (pp. 65-101). Wiesbaden: Westdeutscher Verlag.

Winter, C., & Rummel, R. (2005). Mediale Kommunikation, Medienöffentlichkeiten und kulturelle Orientierung von Leuten im Wandel—durch TIMES-Konvergenz. In M. Karmasin & C. Winter (Eds.), *Konvergenzmanagement und Kommunikationsentwicklung.* München: Fink (UTB).

ACTOR NETWORK THEORY AND MEDIA

Do They Connect and on What Terms?

Nick Couldry

Actor Network Theory (ANT) is a highly influential account within the sociology of science that seeks to explain social order not through an essentialized notion of "the social" but through the networks of connections among human agents, technologies, and objects. Entities (whether human or nonhuman) within those networks acquire power through the number, extensiveness, and stability of the connections routed through them, and through nothing else. Such connections are contingent and emerge historically (they are not natural) but, if successful, a network acquires the force of "nature": it becomes, in a favorite term of ANT, *black-boxed*. On the face of it, ANT seems perfectly placed to generate a theory of the role(s) of media and communication technologies in contemporary societies: these too have emerged historically, yet over more than a century have acquired the force of nature. Yet this connection has been surprisingly little explored. This chapter asks why, in an attempt to understand the substance as well as the limits of ANT's contribution to how we theorize the connectivities that media enable.

The fact that a stable link between ANT and media theory has not been established—ironically, ANT is not "networked" with media theory—cannot be explained by ignorance. Not only does ANT have

93

a high profile in the social sciences (as indicated by the wide currency of *We Have Never Been Modern*, the main book of one of the ANT founders, Bruno Latour: Latour, 1993), but in the late 1980s studies of how media technologies, especially television, are embedded in domestic and social space were closely aligned with work in the sociology of science and technology influenced by ANT. Particularly important here was the work of the media sociologist Roger Silverstone (Silverstone, 1994; Silverstone & Hirsch, 1992), who took the lead in allying the analysis of television's domestic integration to wider currents in sociology that studied the highly specific ways in which various technologies—from locks to domestic heating— became embedded in social life from the 19th century onwards. However, Silverstone dismisses ANT's term "network" as little more than a metaphor that fails to displace a more fundamental notion of "system"; that is, the systems that structure and are structured by social action. Here is Silverstone's discussion of another founder of ANT, the sociologist John Law:

> Law prefers the term network to system. . . . In relation to the systems metaphor, Law suggests that it tends to underestimate the fragility of the emerging system in the face of the conflictful environments and conditions in which it is embedded. . . . In relation to the construction metaphor, he argues that the privileging of the social which [that metaphor] demands . . . mistakes the complexity of the relationships that need to be understood if the emergence of new technologies is to be explained. . . . However one can grant this and still privilege the social; *indeed one must do so* [italics added], since the natural, the economic and the technical, in their obduracy or their malleability, have no significance except through social action. . . . The socio-technical system is therefore just that: a more or less fragile, more or less secure, concatenation of human, social and material elements and relations, structured in, and structuring of, social action . . . from this point of view the notion of network does not add much to that of system. (Silverstone, 1994, pp. 84-85)

Here ANT and media theory meet and then quickly diverge. Since this passage was written there have been occasional acknowledgements of their potential affinity, especially in relation to computer-mediated communication (Bingham, 1999; Bolter & Grusin, 2000, pp. 50, 62, 67, 77-78; MacGregor Wise, 1997), but these have not been more widely developed. On the face of it, this could be for two quite different reasons: first, that ANT itself is not a substantial or coherent theory and second, that media pose problems, or set limits, to the applicability of ANT, in spite of its general value as a theory. If the first were true, this chapter would be redundant; indeed, whether that is the case would be a matter not for media studies but for a more general sociology of technology. I want, however, to concentrate on the second possibility: taking for granted the substantial nature of ANT as a sociological theory and being open therefore to its contribution to our theorization of media, but also wary of the limits and constraints. There is, I suspect, something important at stake in thinking about ANT in media studies, but what exactly is it?

THE CHALLENGE OF ACTOR NETWORK THEORY

ANT starts from the study of science; for example, Latour and Woolgar's influential study of laboratory life (1979). From the beginning, ANT aimed to deconstruct the implicit idealism of traditional sociology of knowledge: instead of seeing scientific theories and discoveries as ideas that float mysteriously above the surface of social interaction, Latour and Woolgar insisted that the results of science are inextricably embedded in what particular scientists do in particular sites of knowledge production, such as laboratories. Latour and Woolgar's deconstruction is so thorough that it undermines the binary opposition between *ideas* and *matter* itself.

In his later programmatic book *We Have Never Been Modern*, Latour rejects also the distinction between an absolute "Society" and an absolute "Nature", because everything involves hybrids of the two (1993, pp. 51-55). ANT is therefore sociology, but in a paradoxical sense, in that it challenges the existence of sociology's apparent object: society or *the social*. Latour's point is not that there is no social dimension to existence, but rather that the social is always already technical, just as the *technical* is always already social. Latour's aim is:

> . . . to avoid the twin pitfalls of sociologism and technologism. We are never faced with objects or social relations, we are faced with chains which are associations of humans . . . and non-humans. . . . No one has ever seen a social relation by itself . . . nor a technical relation. (Latour, 1991, p. 110)

This fundamental skepticism towards both society (or ideas) and technology (or matter) is, I will argue, a major insight that still resonates for media theory and can help us avoid the implicit functionalism in much media theory.

I will provide more context for this claim later, but first we must address Roger Silverstone's contrasting argument that the notion of network adds little to our understanding of the social, or therefore to our understanding of the social dimensions of technology; for, if correct, that would fundamentally undermine the usefulness of ANT for media theory. Silverstone does not deny that human agents are involved in regular relationships with media technologies that, in turn, form part of the infrastructure of wider social relationships; he is concerned, however, with agency and the necessity (in analyzing the actions and intentions of human agents) of understanding how they are contextualized by more than networks. Networks, by the particular set of links they combine, reinforce certain ways of connecting, while effacing other possibilities, but at most a network sets agents in positions relative to other agents and things (relative, that is, to other *actants,* as ANT calls them, in a term that is deliberately ambiguous between humans and nonhumans: Latour, 1991, p. 123). Those positions limit the possibilities of action in certain ways, but they do not tell us about the dynamics of action. Specifically, the existence of networks does not explain, or even address, agents' interpretations of those networks and their resulting possibilities of action (and it is only human agents that interpret the world, even if, as Woolgar argued, objects and technologies have inscribed within them particular codes and instructions for action: Woolgar, 1991). Networks (and therefore ANT) tell us something important about the embeddedness of social life in media and communications technologies, but they do not offer the basis for a completely new theorization of social order, nor even a new way of analyzing social action, in spite of claiming to do just that. Or, at least, that is Silverstone's argument.

I would not want to disagree with this in one respect. However suggestive are its accounts of how various technologies come to be embedded in social life, ANT does not offer a complete rethinking of society or sociology, in spite of its programmatic ambitions: we will return to some of its limitations in the next section. But to stop at those limitations is to risk missing the continuing importance of ANT's contribution to media theory, which is, in a sense, rhetorical: to warn us at all times against talking as if the everyday workings of media merge seamlessly into the social. ANT's insistence on the necessary hybridity of what we call social relations remains a valuable antidote to the self-effacing, naturalizing potential of media discourse and of much discourse in media studies. In the end, this is a question of power. Let me explain.

I have written elsewhere about the problematic functionalism of much writing in media studies (Couldry, 2005) and will not repeat those arguments here. Put simply, the issue is the tendency in both academic and popular writing about media to speak as if media were the social, as if media were the natural channels of social life and social engagement, rather than highly specific and institutionally focused means for representing social life and channeling social participation. Take this example from Michael Real, who wrote important and pioneering work on the ritual dimensions of media coverage of global sports events such as the Olympics:

> Media serve as the central nervous system of modern society. The
> search to understand these media draws us into a search for the
> centre of all that is life in the 20th century. Our media, ourselves.
> (Real, 1989, p. 13)

My concern here is not whether this captures some of the rhetoric of
and around media—it does, even if the biological metaphor is Real's
own—but the apparent lack of distance from that rhetoric.

By contrast, let us consider the much more skeptical tone of the following passage in which Latour considers the nature of global networks
(he doesn't only have in mind media here, but other passages in the
book make clear he is interested in the properties of media: e.g., 1993,
pp. 1-3):

> The moderns have simply invented longer networks by enlisting a
> certain type of nonhumans . . . by multiplying the hybrids . . . that
> we call machines and facts, collectives have changed their typogra-
> phy . . . we tend to transform the lengthened networks of Westerners
> into systematic and global totalities. To dispel this mystery, it suffices
> to follow the unaccustomed paths that allow this variation of scale,
> and to look at networks of facts and laws rather as one looks at gas
> lines or sewerage pipes. . . . In the case of technological networks,
> we have no difficulty reconciling their local aspect and their global
> dimension. They are composed of particular places, aligned by a
> series of branchings that cross other places and require other
> branchings in order to spread. . . . Technological networks . . . are
> nets thrown over spaces, and retain only a few scattered elements of
> those spaces. They are connected lines, not surfaces. They are by no
> means comprehensive, global, or systematic, even though they
> embrace surfaces without covering them and extend a very long
> way. (Latour, 1993, pp. 117-118)

A little later, he expresses this anti-idealism in terms of a media
metaphor: "Reason today has more in common with a cable television
network than with Platonic ideas" (1993, p. 119). This anti-idealism is
opposed to various apparently comforting abstractions: not just nature
and society but also culture (1993, p. 104) and (as follows, if we read
Real and Latour together) the mythical notion of media as society.
Indeed the tendency to treat mediation as if it were something else (that
is, to make it invisible as such) is, according to Latour, precisely a feature of the philosophical framework of modernity he wants to contest.
Mediation (in the general sense of the process of constructing techno-
logical-social hybrids) is both essential to modernity and rendered
"invisible, unthinkable, unrepresentable" within it (1993, p. 34). So the
mystification of media's social function (which elsewhere I have analyzed as "the myth of the mediated centre": Couldry, 2003a) is not acci-

dental but part of the effacement of technology's embedding within the social that is characteristic of modernity itself.

Media studies, when it speaks of media as if media were society (as it does whenever it thinks in functionalist terms) contributes to this mystifying effacement of the vast linkage of networks that make up the media process. This mystification is not new: it can be traced back to some of the earliest theory about media's social role. To illustrate this, we can go back to Durkheim's less well-known contemporary, Gabriel Tarde, who, like Durkheim, started from the question of social order, or how we develop our sense of ourselves as *social* individuals. Unlike Durkheim, Tarde related this to an analysis of media institutions' role in social cohesion:

> It is . . . essential that each of the individuals [in a society] be more or less aware of the similarity of his judgements with those of others; for if each one thought himself isolated in his evaluation, none of them would feel himself to be (and hence would not be) bound in close association with others like himself. . . . Now, in order for the consciousness of similarity of ideas to exist among the members of a society, must not the cause of this similarity be the manifestation in words, in writing, or in the Press, of an idea that was individual at first, then little by little generalised? (Tarde, 1969, p. 300) [originally published 1898/99]

For Tarde the equation of media with the social fabric is total and seamless:

> The press unifies and invigorates conversations, makes them uniform in space and diversified in time. Every morning the papers give their publics the conversations for the day. . . . But this subject changes every day and every week. . . . This increasing similarity of simultaneous conversations in an ever more vast geographic domain is one of the most important characteristics of our time. (1969, p. 312)

This power of media is unstoppable and, it appears, beyond criticism, because the implicit equation of media and the social is not questioned: "This is an enormous power, one that can only increase, because the need to agree with the public of which one is a part, to think and act in agreement within opinion, becomes all the more strong and irresistible as the public becomes more numerous, the opinion more imposing and the need itself more often satisfied" (1969, p. 318).

What is missing here is any sense of the power asymmetries built into this *mediazation* (cf. Thompson, 1995, p. 46) of the social. It is here that ANT's skepticism provides the necessary critical distance, even if it may be expressed hyperbolically in terms of a questioning of "the social" itself. So Callon and Latour describe the project of ANT as "directing our attention not to the social but towards the processes by which an actor creates lasting asymmetries" (1981, pp. 285-286). This insight is vital in getting a perspective on media. Media institutions, whatever the pervasiveness of their reach and however responsive they are to their audiences, remain the beneficiaries of huge and lasting asymmetries in the distribution of symbolic resources. The idea of media *power* is, of course, a commonplace, but its analysis has been bedeviled by the complex two-way nature of the interactions between media institutions and the rest of the social world (whether in terms of social inputs to media production or in the contribution of media productions to social experience and norms). It is ANT that provides us with the most precise language to formulate how this complex flow nonetheless represents a distinctive form of power. For media institutions, however responsive to audiences and the cultural world around them, remain the "obligatory passing points" (Callon & Latour, 1981, p. 287; cf. Callon, 1986, p. 27) in many, even most, circuits of communication. This is at least a good starting point for an analysis of media power that avoids functionalism and remains fixed on the materiality of flows to, through, and from media institutions (cf. Couldry, 2000, chaps. 1, 2, and 3).

So far I have argued that ANT remains important to media theory as an inspiration to orientate ourselves towards certain approaches to media theory and away from others. As an effective antidote to functionalism, it should stay in our theoretical tool kit. But can ANT be more than this and offer the basis for a more comprehensive theory of media in all its dimensions?

THE LIMITS OF ACTOR NETWORK THEORY APPLIED TO MEDIA

In this section we will see that there are important constraints on ANT's usefulness as a general theory of how media contribute to social experience and social organization. The constraints derive from limitations of ANT itself as an attempt to understand human action, as already suggested in the earlier quotation from Roger Silverstone. These limits are, however, not fatal, and towards that end I want to argue that, provided we step aside from its grandiose claims to be a total and radically rethought account of social action, ANT can be an important part of the panoply of media theory.

So far I have expressed the advantages of ANT in terms of its antifunctionalism and its general skepticism about essentialized notions of the social, the technical, the cultural, and so on. ANT's value for understanding media can also be expressed more directly in terms of its predominant emphasis on space. ANT's appreciation of the spatial dimension of power—the spatial dispersal of power and the instantiation of power not in mysterious substances located at particular points and in particular individuals, but in the workings of stretched-out networks—derives of course from Foucault's reconceptualization of power (Callon & Latour, 1981; Foucault, 1980). ANT's double connection to space and Foucault helps further explain the apparently paradoxical disconnection between ANT and most existing media theory: for it is precisely the spatial dimension of media power that has been long neglected and whose neglect, in turn, explains the relative absence until recently of Foucauldian social theory in accounts of media power (but see now Mattelart, 1996). Yet the neglect of space is clearly unsustainable for an account of media as complex connectivity. As Anna McCarthy and I have argued elsewhere:

> Understanding media systems and institutions as spatial processes undercuts the infinite space of narrative that media appear to promise; it insists that our object of analysis is never just a collection of texts, but a specific and material organisation of space. Media, like all social processes, are inherently stretched out in space in particular ways, and not others. . . . Media, then, emerge as one of the most important of all displacements at work in the relatively centralised "order" of contemporary societies. (Couldry & McCarthy, 2004, pp. 2-4)

Inevitably, however, ANT's spatial virtue is connected with a limitation, which is ANT's relative neglect of time, at least as a dynamic process that continues to transform networks after they have been formed. At one level, it is incorrect to say that ANT neglects time. Considered from the point of view of the set of actants that come to form a particular network, ANT helps us understand the significance of time in two ways: first, in terms of how the coordination of actors around certain chains of action inevitably involves temporal coordination (whether in the submission of experimental results according to laboratory schedules or the production of accounting information to enable the pricing of electricity supply); time is inseparable from the coordination of sequences of actions in networks. Secondly, time features in typical ANT explanations in terms of how networks come to be established as normal, regular, and, gradually, as natural. This is the basis of ANT's profound insight about naturalization that, although not unique to ANT (it is central also to the work of Pierre Bourdieu) is especially relevant to an understanding of media's social dynamics, as we shall see. As Latour and Woolgar put it in *Laboratory Life*, "the result of the *construction* [italics added] of a fact is that it appears unconstructed by anyone"

(1979, p. 240). ANT therefore disrupts the sociology of knowledge by emphasizing both spatial and temporal asymmetries at least to the point where facts get established. Even better, Callon and Latour (1981) leave open, at least in theory, the possibility that facts are reversible and the "black boxes" (that is, the actors such as scientific or media institutions inside which lie collections of hidden networks) may be pried open.

The problem, however, is that ANT remained much more interested in the establishment of networks than in their later dynamics. The closure involved in the establishment of a network is real, but how does it help us understand how a network changes and perhaps becomes destabilized? The answer is that it doesn't—at least not without an addition to the theory. Whereas ANT's bias towards the achievement of actor-networks may be refreshing in its boldness, the overall result of work in this area is, as Barry Barnes has argued, to skew the field of analysis towards a narrative of success (what he calls a "mock-heroic history": 2001, p. 344). Worse, what is celebrated is limited to an account of human agency as extended by technological networks:

> For all that at one level actor-network theory modestly follows the actors and marks no distinction of its own between humans and things, at another level it is a profoundly intrusive monism engaged in the celebration of human agency. (2001, p. 344)

ANT is interested in the celebration of human agency in terms of its entanglement with technology, and not any other dimensions of human agency—all this, in spite of the fact that from other perspectives networks are at most the infrastructure of human action, not its dynamic content.

One problem, then, of building ANT into a fuller account of media is its neglect of time, or rather its concentration on one type of temporal dynamic and historical achievement, at the expense of others. This first limitation is linked to a second: ANT's neglect of the long-term consequences of networks for the distribution of social power. Once again this is not an absolute neglect, but rather a matter of emphasis, which nonetheless is consistent and whose silences are unsatisfactory. As we saw in the last section, ANT offers a precise and nonfunctionalist account of how actors become established as powerful through the stability of the networks that pass through them. The actor (human or nonhuman) that is an obligatory passing-point in a network has power, and the more networks in which that is true, the more power that actor has. As a result, over time, the ability of an actor to act effectively on a larger scale becomes established. Although it requires much further work (cf. Couldry, 2003b), there is the basis here for a useful account of how media institutions have gradually acquired power over large territories through their incremental insertion in an increasingly dense web of communication circuits.

What limits the usefulness of ANT as a research tradition for media analysis and social analysis generally is its relative lack of interest in the long-term power consequences of networks' establishment for social space as a whole and its equality or inequality. For all its intellectual radicalism, ANT comes charged with a heavy load of political conservatism that is, I would argue, directly linked to its professed disinterest in human agency. Power differentials between human actors matter in a way that power differentials (if that is the right term) between nonhumans do not: they have social consequences that are linked to how these differences are interpreted and how they affect the various agents' ability to have their interpretations of the world stick. ANT has much to contribute to understanding the "how" of such asymmetries, but it is strangely silent when it comes to assessing whether, and why, they matter. Its deconstruction of the humanist subject is here disabling—nor is this surprising, because this is precisely the paradox of value at the crux of Foucault's work, as many have argued (Best & Kellner, 1991, pp. 64-65; Taylor, 1986), and, as noted, it is on Foucault's intellectual legacy that ANT is built. MacGregor Wise's criticism of ANT's neglect of both wider power structures and of possibilities of resistance to and contestation of them is therefore well placed (MacGregor Wise, 1997, pp. 31-39). Because media are quite clearly a major dimension of contemporary power structures and also a zone of intense contestation, the limits of ANT as the basis for a general critical theory of media are clear.

These first two limitations share a common pattern: ANT's initial insights into a dimension of social order (spatiality of networks, power asymmetries) are not developed for a network's longer-term consequences for social space and its implications for power. This suggests a third limitation on ANT's usefulness for a general theory of media, which concerns interpretation: its lack of interest in the possibility that networks and their products go on being reinterpreted long after they have been established. This is an especially important problem in relation to networks that produce objects whose main purpose is to generate interpretations (such as media). Once again, ANT was pathbreaking in showing how processes that apparently are purely material (the production of cars or the distribution of electricity) depend crucially on interpretations and contests over interpretation by various actors, and how certain interpretations come to acquire dominance as their picture of the world gets hardwired into the patterning of action. However, this tells us little about the life of objects, such as texts, that are produced to be interpreted, nor about how other objects, as they circulate beyond their original context, remain to various degrees open to reinterpretation by uses, consumers, and audiences. This takes us back to

Silverstone's criticism of ANT, discussed earlier, that it tries to exclude the social process in a way that is impossible, ignoring a large part of how material processes and infrastructures come to have meaning for us. One could equally say that ANT seeks to exclude culture, the realm of symbolic production, except insofar as it contributes to the putting in place of stable networks of actors. If so, ANT cannot tell us enough to generate a broader theory of media.

This becomes even clearer when we look at a rare case which ANT has attempted to discuss not technology but culture (Gomert & Hennion, 1999). Gomert and Hennion's essay, *A Sociology of Attachment: Music Amateurs, Drug Users,* argues that ANT opens up a new approach to cultural production and cultural engagement. This derives from ANT's serious interest in mediation. ANT, Gomert and Hennion argue, moves beyond the analysis of the actions of single human actors to study the action-events that emerge from networks. The competences of actors cannot be understood in an individualistic way but rather "are shaped by the social and material organization of work, the lay-out of . . . institutions, the means of communication" (Gomert & Hennion, 1999, p. 224). All this is developed in ANT without treating "action" by human agents as the main unit of analysis. Instead ANT is able to look more openly at the processes that are really significant: "what happens *only sometimes* [italics added] takes the form of an action that may be distributed to circumscribed sources" (1999, p. 225). This, in fact, is what Gomert and Hennion mean by mediation: "Mediation is a turn towards what emerges, what is shaped and composed, what cannot be reduced to an intersection of causal objects and intentional persons" (1999, p. 226). One example is the emergence of the passion that the music lover feels for music, which, as they point out, cannot be reduced to a simple relation between actor (the music lover) and object (the musical text): "From a long set of mediations (scores, instruments, gestures and bodies, stages and mediums) at certain moments, on top of it all, something might happen" (1999, p. 245). This is an almost mystical evocation of the emergence of musical experience out of a complex chain of mediations and connections. But its lyricism exposes the fact that ANT, as a theory of networks between human and nonhuman actors, has very little to say about processes that come after the establishment of networks: what comes after—the acts of interpretation and attachment—becomes mysterious because, by definition, it cannot be encompassed in an account of how the broad infrastructures of actors and objects (on which, to be sure, it depends) have emerged.

This is not to say that we can learn nothing from ANT about how, for example, music lovers or film lovers understand what they do, but rather that ANT's insights must be extended from a sociology of networks into what Gomert and Hennion seem to want to avoid—a sociology of action and interpretation. We need, in other words, to think about how people's cognitive and emotive frameworks are shaped by the underlying features of the networks in which they are situated. If expressed in these terms, there is a great deal to be learned from ANT in understanding everyday practices around media.

The starting point is that, at the macro level, a medium such as television can be understood as a huge networked space characterized by a fundamental division between producers of meaning (i.e., those acknowledged as such: media institutions and particular actors within them) and consumers of meaning (audiences). It is not that those who work for media institutions are not also consumers of meaning or that audiences do not produce meanings (as audiences research has long emphasized they do), but rather that the space of television is organized so that only under specific and controlled conditions are audience meanings channeled back to media institutions so that they count as meaning production, and even then they remain subordinate to the productions of media institutions. Many of the paradoxes and tensions in how media institutions treat the people who are their audiences can be formulated in the terms that the ANT theorist John Law used to explain the production of knowledge: the "modes of ordering" which position certain types of practices as expert practices and "the relatively consistent pattern of deletion", which disempowers other practices (cf. Couldry, 2000, p. 49; Law, 1994, pp. 110-111). Hall's early (1973) but seminal analysis of how particular people are systematically overaccessed in the production of media narratives, whereas others by the same token are systematically underaccessed, fits well with the language of ANT because it is an attempt to dig beneath the regularities in how media link particular agents and objects into their production process and not others.

This explains why, at the outset, I insisted we should not follow Silverstone in dismissing the insights of ANT as a blind alley in the search for a wider theory of media. On the contrary, ANT offers fundamental insights into the spatiality of networks and into the nature of contemporary power formations, particularly the way important asymmetries of power get hardwired into the organization of action and thought so that they become, precisely, difficult to see and articulate as power. This is a vital starting point for understanding the consequences of media for social and cultural experience. The difficulty is to overcome ANT's self-imposed limitations as a sociology of networks and make the necessary connections to a sociology of action. If we consider media as a distinctive social process that links producers and audiences in a regular set of relationships for the production and consumption of meaning in particular time cycles across large territories, then the organization of those relationships, and particularly their asymmetries, must have consequences for how both media producers and audiences think about their possibilities of action. My own view is that to make progress here we need to look elsewhere in the history of French social thought and draw on Emile Durkheim, particularly as reworked by Pierre Bourdieu. We need Durkheim's notion of social categories, and Bourdieu's notion of *habitus*. This is a line of argument that I have tried to develop through work on people's general orientations to the media process and ritualized aspects of media (Couldry, 2000, 2003a). There is a great deal more work to be done, but ANT remains a useful inspiration. In the next section, I want to illustrate this point through a brief consideration of the familiar concept of liveness from the point of view of networks.

LIVENESS AS CONNECTEDNESS

The term "liveness" has long been recognized in media discourse and in academic writing on media as a central feature of television and certain other media. Television, for example, prides itself on its "live" moments. This quality of television has generally been analyzed in terms of the properties of the televisual text, which characterize liveness. In fact, however, liveness is best understood as a term that stands in for the optimal connectedness of which the usual network between television producers and audiences is capable. As I have argued elsewhere (cf. Bourdon, 2000; cf. Couldry, 2003a, p. 99), liveness is a category that naturalizes the idea that through the media we achieve shared attention to the realities that matter for us as a society. The special status given to live media can therefore be understood in actor-network terms as the time when media's status as mediation is most effectively black-boxed, because of the direct link to events as they happen. Liveness is, in effect, a network value, and it is a value whose applicability across media is increasing (to the Internet, for example).

There is much more that could be said about how liveness works as a category in relation to everyday media, but instead I want to bring out how liveness's categorical weight is now under challenge by other forms of connection that are not linked to a media production center in the same way. We are entering a period in which there is likely to be a dynamic interplay between different modes of liveness and the differently organized networks for which they stand.

Two fundamental shifts in information and communications technologies in the past decade threaten, prima facie, to destabilize liveness in the sense it has been usually understood until now.

The first is what we could call *online liveness*: social copresence on a variety of scales from very small groups in chatrooms to huge international audiences for breaking news on major websites, all made possible by the Internet as an underlying infrastructure. Often, online liveness overlaps with the existing category of liveness; for example, websites linked to reality TV programs such as *Big Brother* that simply offer an alternative outlet for material that could in principle have been broadcast on television, if there had been an audience to justify it. Online liveness here is simply an extension of traditional liveness across media, not a new way of coordinating social experience. Any number of live transmissions can occur online in parallel without interfering with each other, all of them involving the simultaneous copresence of an audience, but in some cases (e.g. website chatrooms) there is often no liveness in the traditional sense, because there is no plausible connection to a centre of transmission. Whether the Internet will, in the longer term, lead to a fragmentation of any sense of a center of transmission remains uncertain, although much, including the Internet's capacity to deliver advertising audiences to fund continued media production, will depend on this.

The second rival form of liveness we might call *group liveness*, but it would not seem, at first sight, to overlap at all with traditional liveness, because it starts from the copresence of a social group, not the copresence of an audience dispersed around an institutional center. I mean here, for example, the liveness of a mobile group of friends who are in continuous contact via their mobile phones through calls and texting. Peer-group presence is, of course, hardly new, but its continuous mediation through shared access to a communications infrastructure, whose entry-points are themselves mobile and therefore can be permanently open, is new. It enables individuals and groups to be continuously copresent to each other even as they move independently across space. This transformation of social space may override individuals' passage between sites of fixed media access, as when school friends continue to text each other when they get home, enter their bedrooms, and switch on their computers. As well as being a significant extension of social group dynamics, group liveness offers to the commercial interests that maintain the mobile telephony network an expanded space for centralized transmission of news, services, and advertising.

What is particularly interesting about the case of mobile telephony is that the same communications space can be the vehicle for two quite different networks, one centralized (for advertising and news transmission purposes) and the other person-to-person, but both in some sense characterized by liveness. Clearly, in the longer term, the meaning of the term liveness may be determined by the different meanings and values given to these rival forms of connection.

CONCLUSION

I have argued that the relationship between ANT and media theory is a significant, if uneasy, one. On the one hand, there are important reasons why ANT cannot offer a total theory of media: these are its insufficient attention to questions of time, power and interpretation. On the other hand, there are important reasons why ANT should be an important part of the media theorist's tool kit. The divergence of ANT and media sociology in the early 1990s, and their relative disconnection from each other, is therefore unfortunate, because ANT remains an important antidote to functionalist versions of media theory and an inspiration towards developing better versions of a materialist approach to understanding what media are and their consequences for the social world and social space.

That this hasn't happened so far is due, perhaps in part, to ANT's political quietism and its excessive hostility to any notion of the social. ANT was right to see that any account of the social that closed its eyes to the social embedding of technology was doomed, but wrong to close down the possibilities of how we might think about the relationship between social and technological to questions of network coordination. In a recent essay, Karin Knorr-Cetina (herself a social theorist with affinity to ANT) has tried to formulate these questions in a more open way in terms of a rethinking of social order that does not rely on notions of social substance (Knorr-Cetina, 2001). The role of technologies such as media in organising forms of attachment and belonging can be analyzed without abandoning our interest in social interaction and its dynamics. Knorr-Cetina's suggestion that we consider computer programs, investment vehicles, and fashion designs (she could easily have added radio phone-ins and lifestyle TV programs) as "unfolding structures of absences" (2001, p. 527) is striking. This captures both the patterned, highly routinized nature of how media contribute to the social world and media's imaginative openness. Crucially, Knorr-Cetina raises the question of interpretation and representation ignored by ANT: we must think, she argues, about "the pervasiveness of the images themselves in a media and information society" and their contribution to what now passes for social order. This is to take on the challenge that media power provides to our understanding of the social, but be ready to admit that this challenge, as yet, remains unsolved:

> The retraction of [traditional] social principles leaves no holes . . . in the fabric of cultural patterns. There has been no loss of texture for society, though what the texture consists of may need rethinking. (2001, p. 527)

In trying to avoid the question of the social through the fix of a reified notion of networks as technical-social hybrids, ANT offered a premature closure of what remain interesting and open issues. But that, as I have argued, is no reason to lose interest in ANT within media theory, for it can still inspire us, even as we push its insights in other directions and over different territory from that which it originally set for itself.

REFERENCES

Barnes, B. (2001). The macro/micro problem and the problem of structure and agency. In G. Ritzer & B. Smart (Eds.), *Handbook of social theory* (pp. 339-352). London: Sage.

Best, S., & Kellner, D. (1991). *Postmodern theory: Critical interrogations.* London: Macmillan.

Bingham, N. (1999). Unthinkable complexity? Cyberspace otherwise. In M. Crang, P. Crang, & J. May (Eds.), *Virtual geographies. Bodies, space and relations* (pp. 244-260). London: Routledge.

Bolter, J., & Grusin, R. (2000). *Remediation: Understanding new media.* Cambridge: MIT Press.

Bourdon, J. (2000). Live television is still alive. *Media, Culture & Society, 22*(5), 531-556.

Callon, M. (1986). The sociology of an actor-network: The case of the electric vehicle. In M. Callon, J. Law, & A. Rip (Eds.), *Mapping the dynamics of science and technology* (pp. 19-34). Basingstoke: Macmillan.

Callon, M., & Latour, B. (1981). Unscrewing the Big Leviathan: How actors macro-structure reality and how sociologists help them do so. In K. Knorr-Cetina & A. Cicourel (Eds.), *Advances in social theory and methodology* (pp. 277-303). London: Routledge & Kegan Paul.

Couldry, N. (2000). *The place of media power: Pilgrims and witnesses of the media age.* London: Routledge.

Couldry, N. (2003a). *Media rituals: A critical approach.* London: Routledge.

Couldry, N. (2003b). Media meta-capital. Extending the range of Bourdieu's field theory. *Theory and Society, 32*(5-6), 653-677.

Couldry, N. (2005). Transvaluing media studies or, beyond the myth of the mediated centre. In J. Curran & D. Morley (Eds.), *Media and cultural theory* (pp. 177-194). London: Routledge.

Couldry, N., & McCarthy, A. (2004). Introduction: Orientations: Mapping mediaspace. In N. Couldry & A. McCarthy (Eds.), *Mediaspace: Place, scale and culture in a media age* (pp. 1-18). London: Routledge.

Foucault, M. (1980). *Power/knowledge.* Brighton: Harvester Wheatsheaf.

Gomert, E., & Hennion, A. (1999). A sociology of attachment: Music amateurs, drug users. In J. Law & J. Hassard (Eds.), *Actor network theory and after* (pp. 220-247). Oxford: Blackwell.

Hall, S. (1973). *The structured communication of events.* Stencilled occasional paper no. 5. Birmingham: Centre for Contemporary Cultural Studies.

Knorr-Cetina, K. (2001). Post-social relations: Theorizing sociality in a postsocial environment. In G. Ritzer & B. Smart (Eds.), *Handbook of social theory* (pp. 520-537). London: Sage.

Latour, B. (1991). Technology is society made durable. In J. Law (Ed.), *A sociology of monsters: Essays on power, technology and domination* (pp. 103-131). London: Routledge.

Latour, B. (1993). *We have never been modern.* London: Prentice Hall.

Latour, B., & Woolgar, S. (1979). *Laboratory life.* Princeton: Princeton University Press.

Law, J. (1994). *Organising modernity.* Oxford: Blackwell.

MacGregor Wise, J. (1997). *Exploring technology and social space.* Newbury Park, CA: Sage.

Mattelart, A. (1996). *The invention of communication.* Minneapolis: University of Minnesota Press.

Real, M. (1989). *Super media.* Newbury Park, CA: Sage.

Silverstone, R. (1994). *Television and everyday life.* London: Routledge.

Silverstone, R., & Hirsch, E. (Eds.). (1992). *Consuming technologies.* London: Routledge.

Tarde, G. (1969). *On communication and social influence.* Chicago: University of Chicago Press.

Taylor, C. (1986). Foucault on freedom and truth. In *Philosophical papers* (Vol. 2, pp. 152-184). Cambridge: Cambridge University Press.

Thompson, J. (1995). *The media and modernity.* Cambridge: Polity.

Woolgar, S. (1991). Configuring the user. In J. Law (Ed.), *A sociology of monsters: Essays on power, technology and domination.* London: Routledge.

NETWORK THEORY AND HUMAN ACTION

Theoretical Concepts and Empirical Applications

Thorsten Quandt

Network approaches are attracting a lot of attention these days and in particular from the general public. After September 11, 2001, the idea of networks has been widely discussed, primarily in reference to terrorist groups. Data mining algorithms based on networks algorithms have been applied in the search for Al-Qaeda members. Similar mathematical models are used to identify consumer behavior on the Internet or patterns in the DNA code. On a more general level, network metaphors have been used to characterize modern society as a whole, even in newspaper articles and on TV. Although many of these discussions are based on popular network ideas (and linked to similar phenomena such as the internet), some ideas actually stem from an academic debate that took place in recent years. There, one can identify several sources for such a discussion. The two major sources are: (a) mathematical concepts of networks derived from graph theory, and (b) sociological concepts based on the network metaphor.

In the second case, the central term *social connectivity* refers to a broad understanding of society being similar to a network, which arguably means a network of interlinked agents (i.e., individuals or groups). Especially in media and cultural studies, some researchers focus on the role of media in connecting such agents.

Although such an approach might be helpful in analyzing the relations between people and the media, it is not the only conceivable way to apply a network concept to human society. As an alternative way of employing network concepts, we want to present the idea of a network of action—a network that ultimately shapes the way we act, as well as the way we perceive and construct the world. We will argue that on the basis of our individual actions, structures are emerging that can most likely be described in terms of a network. This theoretical concept is supported by data from an observational study of online journalists. There, it became quite evident that human actions may be characterized by a network of action elements and also that suitable raw data taken during such observations can be analyzed by means of standard network analysis tools. In the last section, we will summarize the pros and cons of this new way of theoretical and empirical thinking suggested here.

NETWORK APPROACHES: SOME ROOTS

Network approaches are not as new as the current debate would lead us to believe. The concept of people forming a network is indeed an old one, and it was first introduced to sociology by researchers such as Georg Simmel (published in its entirety by Rammstedt, 1989 ff.) and Alfred R. Radcliffe Brown (e.g., Radcliffe-Brown, 1940) in the late 19th and first part of the 20th century. They used these ideas to describe social phenomena and structures, but mainly on a metaphorical level. Empirical work, such as the ethnographic studies of John A. Barnes on kinship and social structures pushed the sociological concept further ahead beyond its mere metaphorical meaning (cf. Barnes, 1954). Since then, the theoretical concept of networks in sociology and social sciences has been improved upon in many ways. In sociology as well as in economics, networks became a central concept for the description of structured phenomena: Williamson (1985) used this term to characterize a very efficient way of economic coordination; Perrow (1992) discussed the distribution of power and influence with the help of the network idea; Windeler (2001) applied the concept to organizations; and just lately Castells (2000) presented his vision of a network society, which has been discussed a lot since then, even outside the scientific community. These were just a few examples (cf. Scott, 2002, for a large overview of standard texts on networks).

On the other hand, there is another major field of network approaches that can be derived from the so-called "graph theory". The latter is the logical and mathematical basis for the formal description and analysis of networks and connections. A graph is a general type of structure, which can be represented by elements (nodes) and connections (links). The beginnings of graph theory date back to the late 18th century, starting with Leonhard Euler and his solution of the so-called Königsberg problem (Biggs, Lloyd, & Wilson, 1976). The mathematical graph theory was later refined in terms of a complex network theory, borrowing some ideas from chaos theory and the analysis of self-organizing systems (Barabási, 2002). With the increasing power of computer software, this kind of network analysis is becoming increasingly popular in many areas of research, ranging from the decoding of the human genome to the analysis of organizations or the uncovering of terrorist groups. The standard numerical tools include data-mining packages and the application of artificial intelligence–based analysis algorithms (cf. Klösgen & Zytkow, 2002). These tools open up huge possibilities for analyzing network structures in the social sciences as well. Due to the logical (and therefore empirically empty) quality of the underlying network concept, applications are truly universal.

However, this potential has not been fully explored by all disciplines. For example, sociological network thinking is usually restricted to a very specific approach. In most cases, the term "network" refers to society (or groups of people) forming a network of interlinked agents (which can be individuals or groups). So the *nodes* that appear in most sociological network theories are human beings, and the connections between these nodes are *relations* (with various definitions of what a relation might be).

We would like to argue that this approach is far too narrow and that network concepts can be applied to other social phenomena as well, especially to the basic category of human action. Actually, various companies on the Internet are already operating in the same direction. They try to model buying behavior using network algorithms: the nodes are the individual buying acts, which are connected to other buying acts, and in the end, there emerges a complex network of connected buying acts. This structure is what these companies are actually looking for in order to be able to predict consumer behavior. And there is already a general term for this kind of analysis: It is called *data mining* or *knowledge discovery* (cf. Klösgen & Zytkow, 2002).

In this chapter we will argue in the same direction: we will focus neither on a network of interlinked agents nor on individuals or groups, but rather on networks of actions. This does not mean that we want to leave out human beings or that we want to suggest that networks of individuals or groups would not be a helpful concept. But we believe that choosing them as network nodes might not be the only promising way of applying network theory to social or cultural phenomena. In the following section we would like to present some theory that will support our point of view.

THEORETICAL BACKGROUND: TOWARDS A NETWORK
APPROACH TO HUMAN ACTION

When describing human actions, it cannot be enough to just label the types of individual acts that are being performed by a certain person (asking "What is she or he doing?"). There are a number of factors that determine the way in which these acts are finally embedded into the flow of action. For example, there is the time and space framework ("where and when does she or he do this?"), contact persons or relations among subjects (". . . in contact with which person?"), the material resources (". . . with the help of what type of resource?") and the general sense making location of the act (". . . in which context?"). These elements may be looked upon as constitutional for human actions, and most of them have already been identified in the standard works on a sociological description of human action (cf. Schütz, 1981; Weber, 1972) and in more recent publications such as Giddens' structuration theory (Giddens, 1997). Although we can surely conceive of other elements as well, the elements described here may already be sufficient to characterize individual actions. Fig. 7.1, below illustrates these interconnected elements.

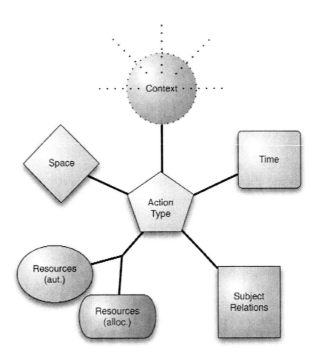

Figure 7.1. An Individual Act as a Star Network of Associated Elements

In this figure, we clearly observe a network structure: The constituent elements of each act are linked by the action itself, and therefore they constitute a small star network. Without its central node, the network would cease to exist, whereas some of its outer elements might eventually be missing under certain circumstances (which is true for relations among subjects and resources that are not essential for each and every individual human action). On the other hand, human actions do not exist as moments frozen in time. Instead, they are part of a constant flow in time, with one act followed by another. In our everyday life, we constantly do something, followed by another action and based on a certain history of acting. Such a history of action is only possible because we perceive actions as being related to each other, in particular when they take place in a temporal order.

An example: When we would like to call somebody, we know that we have to look up her or his number in the phone book (if we don't know the phone number), then we have to use the telephone, pick up the receiver, punch in the number, put the receiver near to our ears, we have to wait for the other person to answer the call, then we know that we have to say "hello" (and our name, if this person does not recognize us from our voice), and so on.

Another example from the everyday work in newsrooms (which relates directly to the empirical application later on): We may assume that the majority of journalists know which steps to follow when they have to write an article. They know their sources for research, they remember possible starting points from earlier work on similar topics, they know when they have to talk to somebody, and they know when they should stop researching and begin with writing things, and so on. They obviously remember single micro-steps as well as large coherent sequences.

In common language we call this *experience*. Sociologists and psychologists alike assume that humans remember actions through cognitive processes by means of what Schütz called a "stock of knowledge at hand" (Schütz, 2002, p. 153 ff.), which is a repertoire of basic rules at our disposal in order to develop strategies for our future actions. Such plans (or models) are based on the remembered relational and temporal structures of action elements. The plans do not have to be based on *conscious* reasoning: In most cases, we simply know what to do because we have developed rules for the respective actions (we know how to phone somebody, which resources we need to do so, where we can find these resources, in which context it is appropriate to phone somebody, in which temporal order we have to do things, etc.).

In the language of the network theory, these rules are operating as connection rules because they are able to describe the structures among various action elements such as resources, types of actions, personal contacts, contextual information, and the space and time framework itself. Therefore, this stock of knowledge is basically a huge network of relations that constitute human memory and that lay the foundations for further human actions, thereby creating the very identity of a person performing those acts (See Fig. 7.2).

Now what happens if several individuals, for example journalists in (different) newsrooms, have contact to similar subjects and similar resources, are working under certain material conditions, and are being confronted with similar actions? First of all, they will build up similar relations among certain action elements in their stock of knowledge. That does not necessarily mean that they are forming similar traces of memory in their brains. Actually, this is highly unlikely because the perceived actions usually relate to different elements in each individual stock of knowledge. But the important thing is that these subjects share the same relations. Let us take this chapter as a simple example: As a reader you will perceive our words in one way or another. And the way in which you relate the information contained in this chapter to your actual knowledge is a highly individual process, because we are all entering such a process with rather different memory structures. Nevertheless, you will share your relation to this chapter with any other reader, even if she or he is thousands of miles away and lives in a totally different environment.

So although the nature of links might vary, their relational qualities will basically be the same. They will also stay comparable if people share parts of their stocks of knowledge through communication or through co-orientation.[1] There may not be direct contacts between all the initial action elements, but at least there remain some links. For example if you (as a reader) would tell a friend what is explained in this chapter, say in a few days, this friend would most likely share a—somewhat weaker—tie to the present chapter (cf. Fig. 7.3).

So through their everyday practice, and through similar connections among actions, resources, contexts and so forth, people will build up comparable webs of sense-making relations (i.e., connections that allow for a complex behavior that creates options for subsequent human actions); therefore, the individuals are actually sharing some meaning (at least to a certain amount).

---

[1]The similarity between those relations can be explained through orientation towards similar phenomena and also through communication. However, similar structures are neither a necessary nor an exclusive effect of communication. The latter can be described as a special type of action that transfers parts of ego's memory structures into the stock of knowledge of the other.

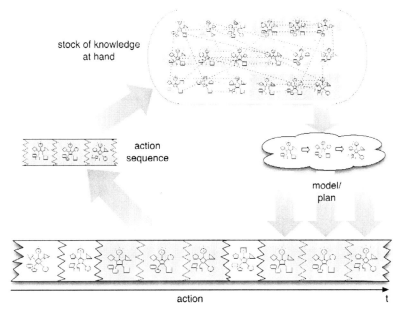

Figure 7.2. **Sequences of Actions are Being Transferred to the Stock of Knowledge**

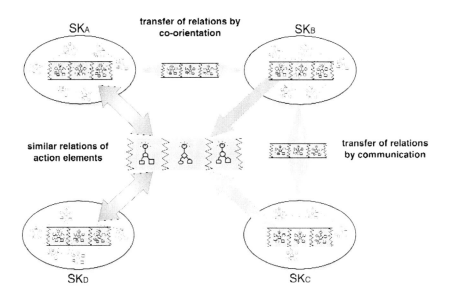

Figure 7.3. **Building Networks of Meaning Through Shared Relations**

EMPIRICAL APPLICATION: OBSERVATIONAL STUDY OF ONLINE JOURNALISTS

Design of the Study and Methodology

One of the advantages of network approaches is that they can easily be applied to empirical studies: After defining appropriate nodes and the relations among them, the structure of these networks may simply be described by graphs (which means that they form a logical structure that can be translated into a formal or mathematical language; cf. Scott, 2000; and Wasserman, Faust, & Iacobucci, 1994). The above-mentioned approach already provides us with the basic elements that may serve as categories for such empirical studies. The nodes of individual acts can be operationalized for direct use in (observational) studies. Surely, such an approach may also serve as the basis for surveys, but observations seem to be most natural way to analyze human action or behavior.

Based on the theoretical approaches mentioned above, a large observational study could actually be realized. During a 10-week study in the newsrooms of five German online newspapers, the actions of six online journalists have been observed.[2] The motivation for such a study was the idea that there might be some sort of professional rules evolving for this new area of journalism. At the time of the study, German researchers did do not know very much about real-life working conditions of online journalism (Neuberger, 2000, p. 37 f.). Therefore, a closer look at the everyday work of journalists and the underlying work rules and routines was certainly overdue. Following the abovementioned approach, such rules would be visible as recurring relations between observable action elements.

The operationalization of the individual action elements (types of actions, context, space, time, resources, subject relations) resulted in a codebook containing about 250 numerical and symbolic codes that had to be memorized by the observer. During our observations, the flow of action was broken down into individual acts[3] and the acts themselves into the constituent elements, which were itemized in the codebook.

---

[2]At the *Netzeitung* in Berlin, we observed two journalists due to some changes in the shift work during the observation.

[3]Acts were defined as being interconnected and coherent. Thus an act would end when at least one of its elements had changed. The question about the observed size of acts (the "granulation" of observation) is not answered by such a procedure, but this was not the central question when we were looking for patterns, because relationships will be visible even when the size of observed acts does vary. The relational structure will actually stay the same (cf. Quandt, 2004).

The graphics shown below should give us an impression of how this was done in principle (cf. Fig. 7.4): There, you can see a symbolic representation of the flow of action (lower part of the graphics). By using the observation codebook, it was split into individual actions (horizontal axis) and their constituent action elements (vertical axis). Different conditions or values of the individual elements are indicated by different shapes. The result of such a process is a matrix that can be analyzed for recurring patterns.

In addition to the observation codebook, several other empirical instruments were used. To provide a better understanding of the working environment, observational diaries were set up to write down open questions that could be answered during 11 interviews with the journalists and their editors in chief. In addition to that photographs of these workplaces were taken, and ground plans of the workplaces were drawn in order to get some impression of the working conditions of the journalists. But the core results were the coded observations. We obtained a data matrix with 11,671 acts (corresponding to 483 hours and 28 minutes of observation); each act consisted of about 50 variables that would describe its constituent elements in more detail.[4] Therefore the data basis for further analysis was quite large.

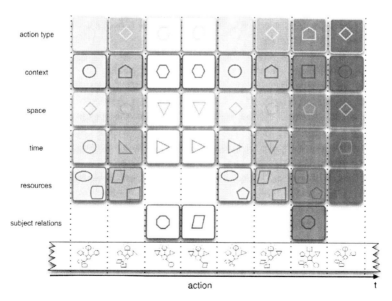

Figure 7.4.   **Breaking Down the Flow of Action into a Data Matrix**

---

[4]The high number of variables per case is partly due to individual coding for up to four resources, four (groups of) contact persons, and several context variables.

As mentioned above, the aim of the study was to identify patterns among the relational data contained in this matrix. Or to put it in other terms: We were looking for similarities and rules of action that might be typical for online journalists. Such patterns (work routines, rules of action) can evolve in different directions; first, there are frequent connections between different elements, which are called associations. Or one might find temporal patterns, which are called sequences.[5] The main question concerning the latter type of connection was the following: Are there certain actions that follow other actions on a regular basis?

RESULTS

Overall Distribution of Journalistic Action

The results of this study reveal some striking similarities in the observed actions of the different journalists, although there were no direct contacts between the observed individuals,[6] as they worked for different media organizations in different towns. Still, the schedule of their working days, as well as their general rules of action and their use of resources (including technological devices), followed comparable patterns. There appear to be invisible ties between the individuals and their actions, which is "net-work" in both senses of such an expression. This is quite astonishing, given the fact that online journalism is a relatively new field, with no original tradition of its own that would make it different from journalism as a whole. Even the literature on this subject has not identified special rules of online journalism (although there are many articles dealing with this subject). The abovementioned idea of human actions as being shaped through a network of relations seems to be useful in explaining this fact. It is assumed that the similarity of relations leads to the formation of comparable structure-building processes in the stock of knowledge, as well as among the observed actions. Some empirical data from our study will give us an impression of the abovementioned similarities. First of all, the overall distribution of types of actions was similar for almost all of the observed journalists (with the exception of one journalist who had a lot of technical tasks; this was actually due to the fact that he was the only online journalist in his media organization).

---

[5]Actually, a sequence is just a special type of association. However, because there is no term for nontemporal connections, we use the broader term "association" only for the nontemporal patterns.

[6]With the exception of the *Netzeitung* journalists; see also footnote 2.

The pie graph below (cf. Fig. 7 5) shows the overall distribution of time spent on different actions during a journalist's office hours. It is based on the data of an average journalist.[7] The biggest pieces are research, text production, interpersonal communication, the communication through media, and production jobs. That is roughly what one would expect from a journalist, although the high level of communication looks rather surprising (which mostly consists of co-ordination with colleagues, though; for example, through organizational talks). It is interesting to see how homogeneous the distributions of the individual journalists are. The following table (cf. Table 7.1) compares the amount of time spent on the individual actions for all of the observed journalists.

Action categories - % of observed time

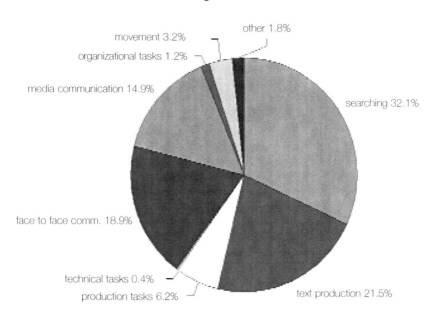

Figure 7.5. **Overall Distribution of Observed Actions Categories** (*Note*: Numbers for the smaller pieces of the pie have been omitted for the sake of clarity.)

---

[7]This average serves comparison purposes only. We calculated the mean of the distribution pies of the six observed journalists to have some reference line when comparing the journalists' values; therefore we did not have to compare each value of the individual journalist to the values of all the other journalists. We are certainly aware of the fact that the interpretation of this artificial person's data is problematic.

TABLE 7.1
Comparison of Distribution (Observed Action Categories, % of Overall Time)*

	NZ A	NZ B	FAZ	SVZ	TS	SPON	Ø-OJ.
searching	36.4	39.8	28.6	22.7	35.6	29.2	32.1
text production	28.5	26.7	30.5	6.9	17.9	18.5	21.5
production tasks	2.7	1.4	1.0	28.7	1.9	1,4	6.2
technical tasks	0.7	0.4	0.4	0.3	0.3	0.1	0.4
face to face comm.	12.6	13.7	18.0	19.3	29.5	20.2	18.9
media communication	14.5	12.2	17.9	14.8	5,1	24.7	14.9
organizational tasks	0.9	1.0	0.7	2.8	0.1	1.4	1.2
movement	1.9	3.1	1.4	1.6	1.7	0.9	1.8
other	1.8	1.7	1.3	3.0	8.0	3.5	3.2
Total	100	100	99.8	100.1	100.1	99.9	100.2

Basis: NZ A: 36:39:25 h; NZ B: 51:04:00 h; FAZ: 79:57:45 h; SVZ: 95:42:40 h; TS: 77:47:55 h; SPON: 64:44:05 h; Total: 405:55 h

*All numbers have been omitted for the sake of clarity.

There are obvious similarities, especially when looking at the central categories. The distribution values for the editors of the *Netzeitung* actually look as if they were from one and the same person. Both of them are doing almost the same things and spend approximately the same amount of time on similar actions, although they clearly are two different individuals.

Another example: The photographs below (cf. Fig. 7.6) depict the workplace of two online journalists. They look very similar: a lot of printouts and two flat screens. The journalists used the two screens for just the same reasons (content management system on one screen, agency news on the other). It is worth noting that in both cases, the flat screens were bought by the media companies because the journalists asked their management to do so. So that was not a structure that shaped the journalists' action in the first place, but they would ask for this setup due to their working necessities. This shows clearly that working rules and structures are reconstructed through the journalists' everyday action (and not only imposed by the management or tradition). The most surprising fact, however, is that the pictures were taken at two rather different media organizations; namely, the FAZ in Frankfurt and the *Tagesschau* in Hamburg. The main company of *Tagesschau* online is a public TV station like the BBC, and the main company of the FAZ is a conservative nationwide newspaper.

So we conclude that some individuals in the observed newsrooms have obviously developed comparable working patterns and that they are using comparable resources in similar working places. However,

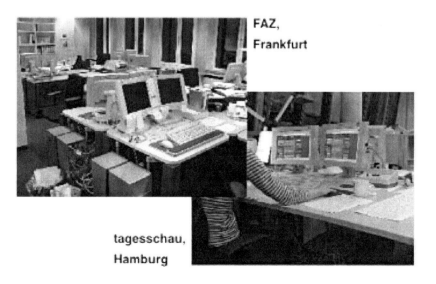

Figure 7.6.   **Workplaces of Online Journalists**

one could argue that this kind of research could be carried out without the background of a network approach, because we were using standard descriptive statistics for the above analysis. In the next section, we will show some analysis that is much more obviously related to the network approach.

Associations

According to the abovementioned theory, some actions refer to certain resources, resources to places or time frames, time frames to actions, and so on. The relations can be described by associations and sequences contained in the data matrix. With the help of the standard data-mining program Clementine, we carried out a network analysis of the associations. In principle, such an analysis counts the connections between the individual values of the coded variables and compares the actual number of observed connections between two values with the overall number of connections of the first value. Therefore it gives us an overall impression of the strongest connections (e.g., it will give you an impression about the strength of the ties between certain actions and resources). The network viewgraph shown below contains all the action types (on the left) and resources (on the right) that were observed during our study (cf. Fig. 7.7).[8]

Obviously, these connections are not evenly distributed. There are some strong ties and many weak ties, and quite a lot of nodes are not connected at all. A change of threshold within Clementine's network analysis algorithm will highlight the most frequent connections and delete all of the weaker ties (cf. Fig. 7.8).

As the number of connections shrink, one is finally left with just the strongest ties, which are of course very obvious links. For example, the communication acts are very strongly related to the resource *telephone*. That hardly comes as a surprise. Nevertheless, it is also a clear indication that the resources are closely defined and that they just serve one major purpose. Content management systems, on the other hand, are of a rather different nature. They are used as central nodes for many types of actions. This may indicate the importance of such tools for the production of news in online journalism. It is also obvious from the network diagram that most action types refer to a specific arrangement of resources (one action leads to one resource, which leads to another action, etc.). These relations create robust, meaningful patterns, because resources and actions are really "glued" together by such links.

---

[8]We are primarily interested in the shape and overall impression of the network graphs, as well as some extremely strong connections. Therefore an explanation of the individual values (and the German labels) is not necessary.

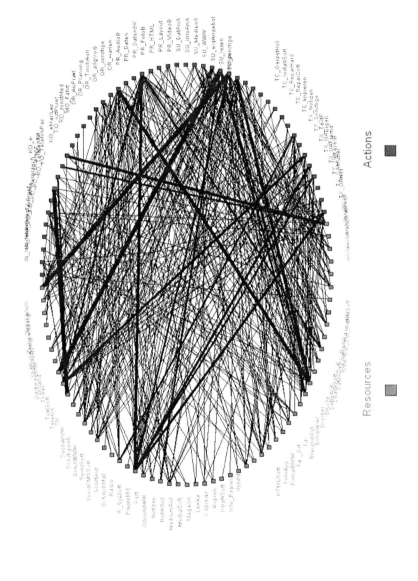

Resources

Actions

Figure 7.7. Association Analysis (Action Type x Resources)

125

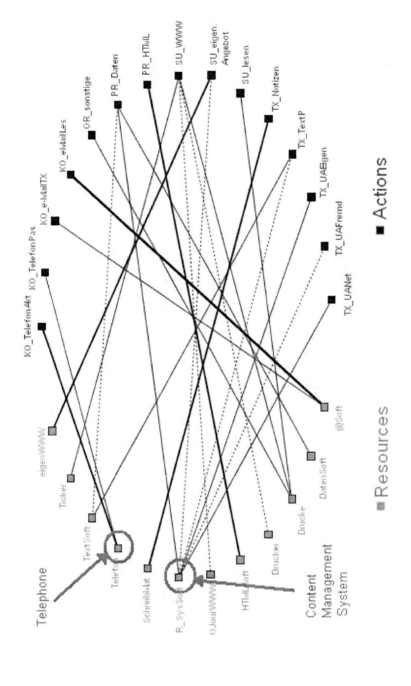

Figure 7.8. Association Analysis, Strongest Connections (Action Type x Resources)

126

Now if we take all the data from the observation and include all types of action elements as nodes, we should be able to identify the most important patterns and working rules of the journalists by analyzing the resulting data matrix. Empirically, this can be done with a more complex network graph. Here, the data-mining program locates the individual nodes according to the strength of relations to all the other nodes. In other words, the stronger the connections between the nodes, the closer they are to each other.[9] The output of such an analysis can be seen below (cf. Fig. 7.9a).

We can clearly identify several clusters in this network graph (cf. Fig. 7.9b). These clusters form the most coherent patterns observed in the study. The central core of the journalists' everyday work consists of traditional journalistic work patterns, based on researching, writing and editing news. Interestingly, technical tasks and their nodes aren't as central and the connections to the traditional work patterns are very weak. Scattered around the central core we can identify some more loosely connected mini clusters. The net structures observed here are woven by the everyday work of the journalists. We also believe that the journalists' are clearly aware of the work patterns and routines that form a coherent cluster. Although they might not be able to name them or consciously reflect on them, they know what to do in which contexts. Therefore, the clusters identified here also have some influence on the journalists' further action. One could say that the actions and the patterns in a cluster (or the working rules) are recursively connected to each other (for a similar concept, see Giddens, 1997). In other words, the clusters serve as orientation horizons for the journalists' further actions, and through these actions, the clusters themselves are reconstructed.

Another type of analysis focuses on the temporal sequences of individual acts over time. Although this can be carried out with the help of sequence analysis algorithms as well (like Clementine's CAPRI algorithm), we chose to carry out a graphical analysis first. As Keim (Keim, 2002; see also Klösgen & Zytkow, 2002, p. 226 ff.) notes, graphical analysis by a human being can be superior to computer algorithms, simply because humans easily detect certain patterns on the basis of their huge knowledge of similar observed phenomena. The granulation of the observation is a difficult problem for computer programs ("what is the size of the elements that should be observed, how long should the sequences be?" etc.). Similar problems appear when it comes to the

---

[9]This works more or less like gravity; each node is located according to the attraction force of the other nodes (with the attraction actually being the relational strength).

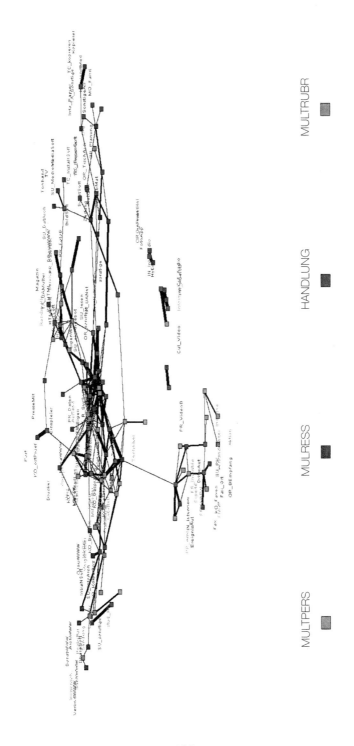

MULTPERS   MULRESS   HANDLUNG   MULTRUBR

Figure 7.9a.   Association Analysis, Strongest Connections (Action Type x Resources x Subjects x Topics)

128

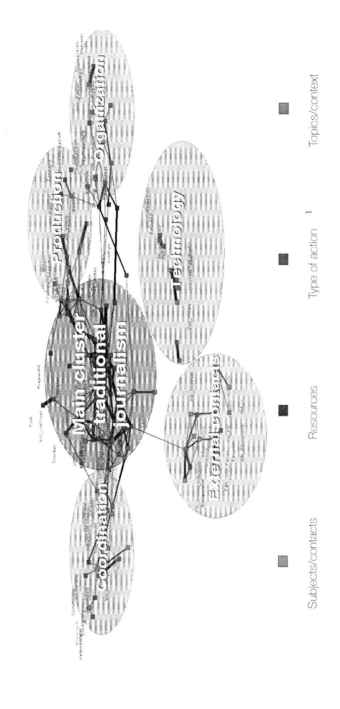

Subjects/contacts   Resources   Type of action   Topics/context

Figure 7.9b.

129

interpretation of raw data ("What kind of sequence is trivial, what kind of sequence is important?").

In order to analyze those sequences, we applied a "slicing" algorithm to the material, cutting the observed actions into 5-second pieces (the starting point and the end point of each action have been coded). The resulting data consisted of temporal cases, where each case represents an equal amount of time. Based on this transformed data set, it was possible to produce a graphic display of actions over time that may form the basis for further analysis (cf. Fig. 7.10 for an example).[10]

The picture below represents one selected working day. Each row shows one category of actions. The vertical lines depict the starting and end points of different phases of a working day. Early in the day (8.30 - 9.50), the online journalist is reading a lot of e-mails (media-based communication) and does not write very much, which is something like an orientation phase that marks the beginning of almost every working day. The following, bigger work phase shows quite a lot of research in the beginning (which also serves as a first orientation to collect interesting news), with more writing during the second half of this period. Then there is a break (13.30 - 14.30). After the break, there is a second working phase with almost no movement, but phone calls, e-mail exchanges, and long sequences of research. The last period of the day is characterized by writing and researching articles (those actions are usually bound to one news article/topic). There is almost no phoning or media-based communication going on (only a few contact persons were available after 16:00, although there was a big interview taking place afterwards, in this special case), and this period is dominated by long sequences of writing.

This is quite a common pattern for online journalism; we found similar sequences and phases in the data of most observation days. Obviously there is a constant stream of writing and research happening during the working day. There are no real production deadlines, but a constant need for researching and reworking news. Nevertheless, some of the communication processes seem to fade out by the end of a working day, which is dominated by writing. And despite the fact that there are no real production deadlines, we still observe orientation phases at the beginning of each working day and production peaks during the day. External contacts also seem to shape working patterns to a certain extent. Without going into the details, it may be noted that this finding is in clear contrast to various speculations that claim that online journalism may not be bound to the restriction of time.

---

[10]One of the biggest problems was the possibility of multiple actions taking place at the same point of time. But the "slicing" of the data would allow for the transformation of an action-based matrix (1 case = 1 action) into a time-based matrix (1 case = 1 time step, with new variables describing all the actions at this point of time).

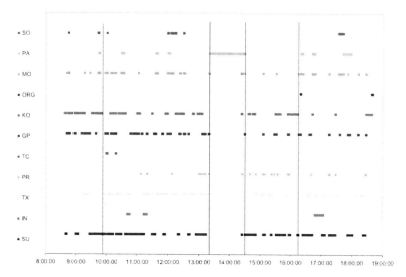

Figure 7.10. Time Based Graphical Analysis, "Piano Roll" Graph (for Action Types)

A detailed analysis of associations and sequences among our data (remember that we can go down to details of five seconds) also shows that there are interesting work patterns that seem to develop into rules of action. For example, writing and research routines seem to follow similar patterns in the vast majority of all cases, with a consistent use of content management systems and satellite or internet-based news agency information as basic working resources. This may illustrate some of the possibilities of the theoretical and empirical approach. We believe that it can be easily transferred to observation in other fields as well. Therefore, we don't want to go into the details of this very specific data set; the possible applications of the approach are much more universal, and the study presented in this chapter is just one example of its uses.

CONCLUSION: THEORETICAL AND EMPIRICAL POTENTIAL

The recent sociological discussion on network theory is somewhat conservative when it comes to the choice of network nodes: the term social network most commonly refers to the connection of individual actors. In this chapter, we argued that the network concept can be successfully applied to other network nodes, such as the basic elements of human action. Based on this premise, we developed a network approach to human action using concepts such as action elements, patterns, rules, and networks. Furthermore, we presented an observation study of online journalists' work routines that serves as an example of the empirical possibilities resulting from the theoretical approach. Using data mining software, we could identify recurring patterns in the action of the observed individuals. We could also show that these patterns form coherent clusters that might form orientation horizons for further action of the journalists.

However, as with every new approach, one has to ask: What might be the advantages and what might be the disadvantages of such an approach, compared to traditional ways of looking at society and action? In that sense, there are certainly some disadvantages to the network perspective: (a) The theoretical approach is only loosely tied to traditional perspectives on human action (this is especially true for the theoretical modeling of work in journalism); (b) It offers no simple, singular description of phenomena in the media; (c) It depicts complicated, fluctuating relations that may lead to ambiguities and sometimes even to contradictions.

Nevertheless, there are also advantages to such a procedure: (a) It takes into account the complexity of the social construction of reality; (b) As an analytical approach to the production of action networks and meaning in everyday action (similar relations of elements), it gives us more than just a handful of metaphors for describing social phenomena; (c) It is an inherently dynamic view, which is helpful if you want to look at changing aspects of social life; (d) The network-based observation of human action shows its potential when open for empirical research.

Empirically, it comes to a detailed description of working behavior. It can certainly be carried out, in addition to surveys, as a supplement and to correct certain aspects. One has to note, however, that observational studies cannot be carried out on a representative basis, because they are just too costly and would interfere with the editorial processes if carried out on a large scale. But they can be employed to create empirical conjectures, uncovering unknown relations with the help of data mining tools.

These tools have many applications beyond the few examples shown in this chapter. Algorithms based on (neural) networks (Klösgen & Zytkow, 2002) could lead to a deeper understanding of human behavior. We believe that for journalism research, this could open up a new way of theoretical thinking as well as new ways of empirical research and analysis.

REFERENCES

Barabási, A.-L. (2002). *Linked. The new science of networks.* Cambridge: Perseus.

Barnes, J. A. (1954). Class and committees in a Norwegian island parish. *Human Relations, 3,* 39-58.

Biggs, N. L., Lloyd, E. K., & Wilson, R. J. (1976). *Graph theory: 1736-1936.* Oxford: Clarendon Press.

Castells, M. (2000). *The rise of the network society.* Oxford: Blackwell.

Giddens, A. (1997). *Die Konstitution der Gesellschaft. Grundzüge einer Theorie der Strukturierung* [The constitution of society. Outline of the theory of structuration]. Frankfurt a. M., New York: Campus.

Keim, D. A. (2002). Data mining mit bloßem Auge [Data mining with the eyes only]. *Spektrum der Wissenschaft, 11,* 88-91.

Klösgen, W., & Zytkow, J. (Eds.). (2002). *Handbook of data mining and knowledge discovery.* Oxford: Oxford University Press.

Neuberger, C. (2000). Renaissance oder Niedergang des Journalismus? Ein Forschungsüberblick zum Online-Journalismus [Renaissance or decline of journalism? An overview of research on online journalism]. In K.-D. Altmeppen, H.-J. Bucher, & M. Löffelholz (Eds.), *Online-Journalismus. Perspectiven für Wissenschaft und Praxis* [Online journalism. Perspectives for science and practical applications] (pp. 15-48). Wiesbaden: Westdeutscher Verlag.

Perrow, C. (1992). Small-firm networks. In G. Eccles Robert & N. Nohria (Eds.), *Networks and organizations: Structure, form, and action* (pp. 445-470). Boston: Harvard Business School Press.

Quandt, T. (2004). *Journalisten im Netz. Über die Arbeit in Online-Redaktionen. Handeln-Strukturen-Netze* [Journalists in the net. Working in online newsrooms. Action-structures-networks]. Wiesbaden: Verlag für Sozialwissenschaften.

Radcliffe-Brown, A. R. (1940). On social structure. *Journal of the Royal Anthropological Institute of Great Britain and Ireland, 70,* 188-204.

Rammstedt, O. (Ed.). (1989 ff.). *Georg Simmel Gesamtausgabe* [Georg Simmel—Collected works]. Frankfurt a. M.: Suhrkamp.

Schütz, A. (1981). *Der sinnhafte Aufbau der sozialen Welt. Eine Einleitung in die verstehende Soziologie* [The phenomenology of the social world] (2nd ed.). Frankfurt a. M.: Suhrkamp. (Original work published 1932)

Schütz, A. (2002). *Theorie der Lebenswelt. Zur kommunikativen Ordnung der Lebenswelt* [The structures of the life-world, vol. 2] (rev. ed.). Konstanz: UVK.

Scott, J. (2000). *Social network analysis. A handbook* (2nd ed.). London: Sage.

Scott, J. (Ed.). (2002). *Social networks: Critical concepts in sociology.* London, New York: Routledge.

Wasserman, S., Faust, K., & Iacobucci, D. (1994). *Social network analysis: Methods and applications.* Cambridge: Cambridge University Press.

Weber, M. (1972). *Wirtschaft und Gesellschaft* [Economy and society] (5th ed.). Tübingen: Mohr. (Original work published 1921/2)

Williamson, O. E. (1985). *The economic institutions of capitalism: Firms, markets, relational contracting.* New York, London: Free Press/Collier Macmillan.

Windeler, A. (2001). *Unternehmungsnetzwerke. Konstitution und Strukturation.* [Organizational networks. Constitution and structuration]. Wiesbaden: Westdeutscher Verlag.

UNDERCURRENTS

Postcolonial Cyberfeminism, a Mailing List, and the Network Society

Maren Hartmann

... The power of flows takes precedence over the flows of power. ... . A network is a set of interconnected nodes. ... What a node is, concretely speaking, depends on the kind of concrete networks of which we speak. (Castells, 2000a, pp. 500-501)

The following pages are an exploration of the *power of flows* from the microperspective of a particular network. The purpose of this chapter is straightforward: it aims to extend and thereby problematize existing theorizations of the network society, especially in reference to Manuel Castells' concept (2000a, 2000b). It thereby hopes to draw out a specific point that has only been hinted at in Castells: that of the conflict between *the net* and *the self*. The chapter aims to do so through one specific case study. The case study concentrates on a postcolonial, cyberfeminist mailing list named Undercurrents. Certain exchanges from this list are analyzed in more detail within the chapter. The claims made are partly limited through the given example, but they nonetheless help to address this potentially problematic aspect of the network society concept. This problematic aspect is the nature and extent of conflicts in communicative exchanges that make up the networks.

To explore this point, underlying assumptions about new technologies as suggested in a concept such as the network society are here contrasted with the actual experience of the networked flow in a particular context. The tension between concept and experience is revealing. The particular case study, that is the Undercurrents mailing list, has been chosen for its focus on networking and its self-reflective nature. This network, as many others like it, is both technical and social.[1] It is one of many diverse elements that can be said to make up a possible network society. On first reading, Undercurrents appears to be a typical example for the assumed characteristics of such a society. As it turns out, this mailing list is typical not only concerning the possibilities that the new kinds of networks offer, but also in its warnings concerning network(ing) limitations.

The main claim made by the chapter is that the challenges encountered by a "lived" version of networks and connectivity could be an indication for the overall challenges that these theoretical notions will come across when applied more widely.[2] The chapter is explorative in nature and not based on completed research. The initial inspiration was provided by the claim of the book editors that the concepts of the network society and connectivity are crucial concepts for expanding current versions of communication theory. In basic agreement with this claim, the stress is here on potential limitations of these concepts. They are vital for their further development. A different inspiration for this chapter was a conference talk by Maria Fernandez, presented in December 2002. This talk told the (ongoing) story of the Undercurrents mailing list from the perspective of one of its moderators (Fernandez herself). The general theoretical context of the chapter can be found in postcolonial concepts, in cyberfeminist ideas and, obviously, in the network society concept. These notions can only briefly be introduced and explored but provide the underlying framework.

Method. For the purpose of this chapter, I studied some of the list's contents and interactions. The specific discussion threads from the mailing list that were chosen for closer analysis centre on the topic of *silencing.* Silencing is a process of social exclusion. In the Undercurrents context, it refers more specifically to the course of action in which some partici-

---

[1]The particular network under scrutiny has been made possible by technologies that emerged fully in the 1990s. In its simplest form, a mailing list is a computerized list of e-mail addresses to which information can be sent. This can have different forms: moderated or nonmoderated, open or closed, etc. The list presented here, as will be shown, is a closed, moderated mailing list with a publicly accessible archive.

[2]Castells himself "aims at communicating theory by analyzing practice" (Castells, 2002, p. 3). I am turning the process backwards, as it were, by questioning his theory through analyzing other practices.

pants in the mailing list were gradually excluded (or rather felt excluded) and thus stopped communicating with the rest of the group. Often they left the list. Silencing usually takes place with regard to certain topics, but is often also related to other, less easily traceable and more far-reaching issues. In the Undercurrents list, silencing supposedly took place as an act towards white women. Silencing was subsequently an important point of discussion, and it is this discussion that interests me. It became an important issue in this list despite very different initial aims. From day one of the list's existence, the active engagement with different forms of discrimination (especially racism, but also discrimination against women and the otherwise marginalized) had been defined as central: "We want to focus our attention on . . . why the colonialist symbols and stories that run rampant in computerized entertainment culture remain compelling in a supposedly post-colonial and post-racial world" (Undercurrents, 2002a). The extent to which their own practice would be influenced by similar mechanisms seems to have come as a surprise to many participants of the mailing list despite their heightened awareness concerning forms of discrimination. How silencing relates to the networked nature of communication in a network society remains to be seen.

Structure. The chapter begins with a brief introduction to the idea of the network society and gives a first hint at the idea of conflict within this concept. A very brief introduction to cyberfeminism and postcolonial theory provides the second step. This is followed by a description of the Undercurrents mailing list and a more detailed discussion of the list's conflict about silencing. This discussion finally leads to an examination of the relevance of this example for the conceptualization of a network society.

INTRODUCING THE NETWORK SOCIETY

As a historical trend, dominant functions and processes in the information age are increasingly organized around networks. Networks constitute the new social morphology of our societies, and the diffusion of networking logic substantially modifies the operations and outcomes in processes of production, experience of power and culture. (Castells, 2000a, p. 469)

Networks are increasingly becoming relevant as analytical categories in all areas of life (Rauner, 2004). The term "network society" (Castells, 2000a) describes a new form of social structure. This is based primarily on far-reaching changes in the economy and in technology, which subsequently lead to radical changes in media, culture, and social structures. The ways in which societies have been organized until now are questioned as part of this process. The economic principle is its informational emphasis, its global reach, and its networked nature. Most of these aspects are not new as such, but their current extent radically changes the consequences. Another important aspect of Castells' concept is the emphasis on alternative movements in society. These movements, ranging from feminism to alternative globalization movements, are important forces in the changes that Castells detects. They are in many ways contradictory forces to the economic structures that are emerging.

In Castells' network society concept, *the space of flows* plays a central role. It is summarized as "the technological and organizational possibility of organizing the simultaneity of social practices without geographical contiguity" (Castells, 2000b, p. 14). Underlying the space of flows is a network of communications. In the midst of the network communications hubs can be found. The different network strands cross each other in these hubs, and more and more the network replaces physical localities. Especially in cities and among certain social classes, the attachment is increasingly with the space of flows rather than with the localities. The diverse networks establish a new kind of global social order. This order is no longer tied to local, national or regional sociopolitical entities. Instead, this global social order can be envisioned as multilayered networks that are positioned on top of existing state borders. Thus these networks do not threaten the nation-state as such, but imply a reduction of its powers.

The new forms of social order are indifferent to established forms of identities, which used to consist of many local ties. This leads to a tension. The social identities, in their established as well as their reformed versions (the self)[3] and new global network society (the net) are anything but congruent (cf. Castells, 2002, pp. 1-2). Instead, the tension between the two characterizes the developments.

Castells stresses that in a network each node depends on the others and thus no hierarchy (in the well-known sense) is going to be established. He defines networks as neutral in terms of their values: "But once a network is programmed it applies its logic to all included actors without differentiation. Therefore, networks are value free: they can equally kill or kiss: nothing personal" (Castells, 2000b, p. 16; Landwehr, 2002, p. 5). This neutrality is questionable or at least problematic, especially seen in light of Castells' own problematization of identity in current times. Castells himself admits that some nodes can be at times more important than others. This is the case when they possess more information. This difference, however, he claims, is not based on any

---

[3]Changes to identity take place partly because of the increasing number and importance of the above mentioned alternative social movements.

intrinsic quality, but is simply a temporarily assigned role. The equality of network nodes is an important precondition for Castells' *power of flows*, that is, the change in power relationships based on the shift in information, communication and economic patterns.

The network society is defined as a structure of links, nodes and hubs. In a more concrete definition, networks are seen to organize community hypertextually (Bolter, 1997). Here, the structure of links consists of the discussion threads in a newsgroup. Together the threads make up the hypertext of the messages.[4] The basic structure of a network lies in its architecture of links and flows, its connectivity. Calling the whole concept a network society stresses that the network consists only partly of the basic technical infrastructure and that the exchange of ideas is much more crucial: this kind of connectivity represents dialogue. It relies on an exchange of communication and of ideas. Returning to Castells' power of flows, this exchange is thought to take place among "equals." The basic structures of networks suggest this and Castells does little to differentiate the concept.

Limitations of this idea become visible at the point where conflict emerges. Conflict is not necessarily a major aspect of the network society concept. Although clearly an important aspect of Castells' writing about the power of identity, dealings with different forms and consequences of conflicts are rarely explicitly dealt with. There is only a brief mention in a summary of Castells' ideas in which he states that social actors are "freely engaging in conflictive social practices" (Castells, 2000b, p. 5). This is not further explored nor is the agency of the individual actors in a structure such as the network addressed. Critics of the network society idea do not necessarily focus on this aspect either. Instead, Castells stresses—and in my view overstresses—the structural equality of networks. Equality is achieved by sharing the same aim, the same values. This can be seen in the following claim:

> Networks are open structures, able to expand without limits, integrating new nodes as long as they are able to communicate within the network, namely as long as they share the same communication codes (for example, values or performance goals). (Castells, 2000a, p. 501)[5]

---

[4]Jay Bolter (1997) goes as far as to claim that the individuals in question feel hypertextual in themselves: each is the sum of the links of all the communities they belong to at different times. In terms of most users' everyday experience of the medium, this is a far-fetched claim.

[5]Elsewhere he states: "New nodes can be included if they share the same communication codes, for example if they have the same goals. The goals of a network are defined by social actors who try to impose their own goals to the network" (Castells, 2000b, p. 16).

He thereby ignores intrinsic qualities of the nodes as such.[6] In my case study, the term network is researched via a very literal example of a network: a mailing list. The nodes within this network are the people who participate in online communication. Central hubs are the moderators. The case study suggests that shared values and goals were indeed the starting point of the participants in the mailing list that is being analyzed. In turn, however, the differences seemed to outweigh the commonalities by far. This again led to an extreme rupture in communication. For this reason, the primary engagement in this chapter is with these points of *rupture*, of *disturbance* within the particular network.

Rupture and disturbance are those points when or where the information and communication flow temporarily comes to a halt and then tends to erupt in an increased flow of communication. These points of conflict are crucial to an understanding of the dynamics of connectivity, of the interconnections between the participants. The extent of any potential disturbance of an interconnection or dialog is clearly not fixed, but it appears that too much conflict can hinder and threaten the exchange.[7] The claim is that the Undercurrents example questions the equality of the nodes and the openness of the network through its partial inability to accommodate the conflicts. The example underlines how differentiation and qualifications are necessary in any such analysis. However, while an inequality is reinforced in Undercurrents, it is also addressed and challenged. This is to a great extent due to the cyberfeminist, postcolonial nature of the network. The shared aims and values, then, do actually enable communication.

---

[6]Many early, mostly linear communication theories assumed equality between communication partners and simply assigned different roles for different actors in the communication process. Later theories tried to develop concepts of the power relationships among different actors, especially in relation to media communication processes. The network idea poses a new challenge. Due to its dynamic nature and the emphasis on the constant movement of and within communication, the network idea immediately challenges existing power structures. This challenge does not preclude inequalities, but it assumes at least the *potential* for equality among the network nodes. Thus Castells states, for example, that it "seems as though the symbolism of power embedded in face-to-face communication has not yet found its language in the new CMC" (Castells, 2000a, p. 390). But the question remains as to whether a new symbolism of power is emerging instead.

[7]The question that is not dealt with in this chapter is whether "too little" conflict hinders productive development. The constitutive nature of conflict for social relations is not seen to be questioned in the analysis presented here.

INTRODUCING CYBERFEMINISM

In its most general sense cyberfeminism simply puts an emphasis on the use of new technologies by women. Underlying cyberfeminism are the utopias of a nonhierarchical information use (the general utopia accompanying early new media use—cf. Hartmann, 2004) and the idea of a gender-neutral net existence (cf. Kuni, 1999, p. 467). Playfulness and creativity are widespread and important aspects. Instead of being alienated by new technologies, these technologies should be used as tools, used to be creative with, to work with, and to think with. Thus many cyberfeminists play an active role in the new media art scene.

The term "cyberfeminism" should, however, not create an illusion of unity. Cyberfeminism, like feminism, has many faces and many different approaches. For this reason, self-proclaimed cyberfeminists have either resisted or at least played with definitions of cyberfeminism. The German new media artist group Old Boys' Network and the participants of the Cyber-feminist International, for example, came up with a list of 100 antitheses to (or not to) describe cyberfeminism (OBN, 1997).[8] Interpreting this refusal to define or be defined, Faith Wilding, herself a self-proclaimed cyberfeminist (and a moderator of the Undercurrents list), detected "a profound ambivalence" in cyberfeminism (Wilding, 1998). This ambivalence refers not only to definitions, but also to the feminist inheritance and current technological developments. Instead, Wilding herself chose to begin by defining cyberfeminism negatively. Her summary of what she saw as common problems of diverse cyberfeminist approaches consisted of (a) a repudiation of "old style" (1970s) feminism, (b) cybergrrl-ism, (c) net utopianism, and (d) the fear of political engagement. Some of these points are (or were) only relevant in a specific historical context, but the struggle with the feminist inheritance remains an issue until today (cf. Fernandez, 2002).[9] Avoiding the problem, cyberfeminism mostly tried to avoid explicitly feminist aims or actions. Some cyberfeminists instead argued that a disolution of gender (and thereby of gender problems) was taking place online. Others concentrated on their artwork.

Overall, cyberfeminism mostly tried to differ from feminism not so much in terms of the overall aims as in the ways to achieve them. In a similar way (and on a more positive note), Wilding also claimed that:

---

[8]This does not prevent others (i.e., "non-cyberfeminists") labeling and categorizing cyberfeminism(s), for example, in terms of a distinction between radical and liberal cyberfeminism (Tsaliki, 2001, pp. 84-85).

[9]In terms of cybergrrl-ism, most cyberfeminist projects today would not choose to identify with it any more; however, it was strategically important in the mid-1990s to late-1990s. Similarly, net utopianism has by now moved to the core of cyberfeminist engagements as a point of attack rather than as a shared understanding.

> CyberfeminismS . . . can link the historical and philosophical prac-
> tices of feminism to contemporary feminist projects and networks
> both on and off the Net, and to the material lives and experiences of
> women in the New World Order, however differently they are mani-
> fested in different countries, among different classes and races.
> (Wilding, 1998)

On the more abstract level, cyberfeminism can be seen as a new form of
language and philosophy that questions ideas of subject, identity and
selfhood via technologies. The cyber prefix suggests control and therefore empowerment (cf. Fenton, 2001). Cyberfeminism tries to go beyond
the technologies (and art) by bringing the body and other social markers back into the equation. In that sense cyberfeminism deals with similar issues to other feminist projects in the past and present. The body
as a contested site is moved—once again—to the forefront, and other
social markers, such as class and race, also remain important issues.
Race and racism especially play a crucial role in Undercurrents. What
is new about all this is that it contradicts many of the dominant para-
digms about the nature of being online.

THE HISTORY OF CYBERFEMINISM

As hinted above, many cyberfeminists try to combine an artistic new
media output with (cyber)feminist ideas. This was initially started by
VNS Matrix, a group of four female Australian new media artists, in the
beginning of the 1990s (they lasted until 1997). VNS Matrix and the
British academic Sadie Plant (whose theories were important in early
cyberfeminism) are said to have coined the term "cyberfeminism" in
parallel (see Sollfrank, 2002). Plant claimed a particular—and privileged—relationship between women and computers (Plant, 1998). Her
description of this relationship was highly innovative, but also in the
end essentialist (therefore it was eventually dismissed by many cyberfeminists).

VNS Matrix, on the other hand, made their cyberfeminist efforts
well known through their Cyberfeminist Manifesto for the 21st
Century, which was first proclaimed in 1991 in Adelaide and Sydney. It
provocatively stated that VNS Matrix were "the virus of the new world
disorder, rupturing the symbolic from within, saboteurs of big daddy
mainframe, the clitoris is a direct line to the matrix [. . .]" (VNS Matrix,
1991). Installations, events, and public art works, produced with many
different media, were part of their range. Through these they set out
to challenge the notions of domination and control, which until then
had surrounded high-tech cultures. Much of cyberfeminism in the last

10 years has followed in the footsteps of VNS Matrix in terms of mixing new art forms with a playful, but nonetheless provocative version of feminism.[10]

From a practical perspective, cyberfeminism has resulted in several conferences, workshops, collaborations, publications, artwork, mailing lists, and so forth. Although it has in the meantime been dismissed for a lack of clear definitions and has also been used as "just another" label for feminist engagements with new technologies, cyberfeminism is still present today and has potentially reached a level of stability. Cyberfeminism (or cyberfeminisms) still consists of different approaches and diverse groups of women, some of which have turned to more political aims.

UNDERCURRENTS AS CYBERFEMINIST MAILING LIST

One cyberfeminist event not too long ago was the yearly conference Digitales in Brussels.[11] The conference took place in the beginning of December 2002 and consisted of lectures, workshops, tutorials, and other kinds of activities. As are many cyberfeminist gatherings, it was an action-oriented meeting mostly for women interested in new technologies.[12] At this conference, Maria Fernandez presented the talk that inspired this chapter. She is a Latina art historian based in the United States (at Cornell University), who is working around notions of postcolonial studies within the art history framework. Fernandez is also a self-proclaimed cyberfeminist. Her paper was entitled *Globalisation and Women's Networks*.[13]

---

[10]Other important groups in cyberfeminism were (and are), among others, the *Critical Art Ensemble* (of which Wilding is a part) and the organizers of the *Cyberfeminist International* (OBN is the driving force here). The latter is primarily based in Europe and grew especially in the late-1990s (after they partook in the Documenta 10), while the former has many U.S. based "members" and was most active in the mid-1990s.

[11]In terms of the naming of their event, the organizers add that they began with terms such as "network" or "bundle," because the conference concerns different organizations of women and feminists. Thus they themselves identify with a network idea.

[12]The invitation stated: "it is important for women to be able to use technology as a tool, it . . . can open a new space for thinking and creating" (Digitales, 2002).

[13]The author, Maria Fernandez, later let me know that no written paper was available. Her talk has, however, been made available as an audio file online by the conference organizers (Fernandez, 2003).

The focus of the talk was on the cyberfeminist mailing list Undercurrents, which has been active since February 2002. The list moderators' original intention was to get marginalized women to discuss among themselves. The list was meant to be a space for invited people to exchange their ideas (rather than an open list). However, due to a misunderstanding at the beginning, the list announcement was made known publicly on other mailing lists.[14] Subsequently many more people subscribed than originally anticipated. Today the Undercurrents list has a limited, but larger than planned number of subscribers. It is a closed list, but the list's archives are publicly accessible (see Undercurrents, 2002b).[15] The list was originally set up by Maria Fernandez, Coco Fusco, Faith Wilding and Irina Aristarkhova. The original announcement—spanning over nine pages—included a call to question libertarian characterizations of electronic culture and explored in detail how postcolonial ideas could be useful to execute this challenge. A main aim of Undercurrents is to address the racial politics of *net.culture*. In the original announcement, Undercurrents was described as "currents below the surface; hidden opinions or feelings often contrary to the ones publicly shown; electronic communication from other sites; heretofore unspoken questions about the racial politics of net.culture, new media and cyberfeminism" (Undercurrents, 2002a).

Undercurrents as a Postcolonial Mailing List

As the above quote already indicates, Undercurrents is not just a cyberfeminist, but also a postcolonial mailing list. In its broadest sense, postcolonial critique allows an investigation of power relationships in different contexts. It investigates the cultural, social, political, and economic practices that come up in reaction and resistance to colonialism (past and present). More concretely, many postcolonial theories study the relationships and interactions between the colonial nations and the societies they colonized. Major foci are those people (and their cultures) who have—in some way or other—been subjected to colonialism. Postcolonial theories also study racism in its current versions and many other related questions. The field of study began to emerge in the 1970s. At that point a lot of the work was still primarily concerned with literature. Today, the field encompasses many other cultural, social, and political aspects. The term "postcolonial" implies the question of whether former colonies (and their citizens) share not only certain experiences, but also qualities. Thus one of the questions postcolonialism

---

[14]The announcement was sent on to a public list by one of those initially invited.
[15]The mailing list's archives are publicly accessible at bbs.thing.net.

asks is what—despite the diverse nature of colonization—is potentially shared among those who were colonized.

Apart from literature as such, postcolonial theory has concentrated primarily on issues such as migration, identity, gender, and representation. The marginal plays a major role in postcolonial theory. It questions the nature of marginalization and traces the expressions of imperial domination. These expressions are located in several rather diverse fields, ranging from biology to art history. Different forms of resistance to these expressions are an important focus. In the postcolonial approach present in Undercurrents, the assumption is that media technologies represent possibilities of an extension or a new version of imperialist repression. The mailing list in the case study is dealing with one such extension of well-known differences.

THE UNDERCURRENTS CONFLICT

> I wish that others could have the courage to speak the way that all of you do in the list. Perhaps . . . [they] have understood that no matter how difficult the communication process is, the simple action of acknowledging each others words and position through their posting had marked the "difference" of Undercurrents. (Mem. 6, 15/06/02)

The positive note about Undercurrents quoted here only partly reflects the events and opinions that take place on the list. In her paper at the Digitales conference Fernandez explored some of the problems that the list has encountered since it was first set up. The problems she was referring to were mostly list-internal conflicts that had occurred in the summer of 2002. Similar conflicts have recurred regularly since then (and with even more force) (see Undercurrents, 2004). In the presentation, Fernandez asked herself what the nature of these conflicts was and whether they had been productive in the way they had occurred. The list had gone from discussion to anger on several occasions, and Fernandez took this to indicate the problematic nature of the conflicts. She herself appeared to be disappointed in both the high number and the nature of the conflicts encountered on the list. For her, these conflicts underlined that communication across cultural barriers remained problematic even when and where the technology in principle enabled easy engagement. For Fernandez it boiled down to a question of the extent of the antagonisms faced in such a discussion.

Fernandez had begun her argument with the premise that discussions with politically like-minded people can be important, but implicitly suggested that the women in the Undercurrents list were "not like-minded enough." She thus indirectly asked how a network in Castells' sense was possible among a group of diverse people. Through this question, the principal equality of the network nodes is examined. This is despite the fact that Fernandez' desired precondition for communication— that is, the like-mindedness of the participants—sounds very similar to Castells' earlier quoted claim that "new nodes can be included if they share the same communication codes, for example if they have the same goals" (Castells, 2000b, p. 16). In Undercurrents, this shared goal was assumed, but only partly achieved in the actual communication. The parallel idea of Castells and Fernandez—that is, that like-mindedness is a precondition for connectivity—is here questioned in terms of the nature and extent of the like-mindedness.

Silencing in Undercurrents

The focus of the analysis presented here concentrates on the same debate that Fernandez had referred to in her paper: the silencing of certain list members. This particular debate, which triggered widespread responses, emerged in August 2002. Its initial phase lasted only a few days. Similar topics had been debated before and have flared up again in different ways and with different labels several times since.[16] Although the debate had silencing as its core issue, it was later broadened to the question of the possible extent of conflicts within a mailing list.[17] Mixed in with the question of silencing are questions about the nature of online interactions and about the nature of private communications within such a semipublic space.

The silencing debate in August 2002 began with an initial exchange of posts between two women on the list, both of them moderators: Coco Fusco (a black artist and academic of Cuban heritage, but based in the United States) and Faith Wilding (a white artist and academic, originally from Paraguay, also based in the United States). The two have remained at the core of the conflict, but the repercussions have been felt beyond this personal engagement. As Fernandez puts it: "Several participants have been frustrated by misrepresentations and silences. I doubt that these can be explained by the presence or actions of a single

---

[16]See, for example, Coco Fusco's (Mod.1's) posting to the list on 03/04/2002 and the subsequent discussion and/or the discussion around the "Silencio Experience" in June 2002 (see Undercurrents, 2002b).

[17]Thus the conflict had the same topic as Fernandez' paper and this presented chapter. Despite these similarities, there are different frameworks of interpretation. Another major difference is that Fernandez was directly involved in the conflict she later reflected upon, whereas I am in the position of a distant observer.

person" (Mod.3, 15/06/02).[18] Nonetheless, even the initial posts in the thread were already personal and emotional.

The debate began to erupt when Coco Fusco added a comment to her posting about the detention of a (Mexican) journalist in Mexico. This comment said: "For all those on this list who have complained about feeling silenced, please read the following dose of realpolitik" (Mod.1, 18/08/2002). Fusco's reference was to earlier exchanges that had debated the issue of silencing. In fact, a few months earlier (April 2002), a debate had ensued around the notion of silencing in which Fusco and others had indicated that it might be appropriate that white list members should remain silent once in a while (this was based on the assumption that these people had voices elsewhere and that they could learn something from listening and from adopting the position of the subaltern for a brief period). In response to the above-quoted comment Faith Wilding stated in her post that the detention of the journalist should indeed be a reminder that one should be aware of any form of silencing,[19] but also that she was "disturbed and angry when (white) women get upset about being called on our racism on the list and then leave the list rather than stay and struggle" (Mod.2, 18/08/2002). The last comment was a direct response to Coco Fusco's recent posting, but also included a clear reference to the past debate on silencing. Although Wilding did not explicitly say so, she appears to accuse Fusco of having silenced others on the list, in a form of "inverted (or reverse) racism." This initial exchange between the two moderators triggered a number of further comments from other list members as well as from both these authors themselves (see Undercurrents, 2002b).

An important issue in the subsequent debate was the question of content and how personal content on such a mailing list should or could be. An often-repeated question was whether references to one's own feelings and circumstances did in the end deter from the real issues that needed to be discussed. This was argued primarily in terms of the need to provide this kind of localization and self-referentiality. In the fashion of existing traditions in feminism and postcolonialism, the personal was declared to be political and thus necessary. The danger of a related

---

[18]The abbreviations Mod.X and moderations thereof refer to the list moderators, and the abbreviations Mem.X, etc., refer to list participants without a moderating role. This step of increasing anonymity was introduced to acknowledge the ambivalent nature of private articulations made within a closed mailing list that are at the same time made public through the list archive. It was planned that the chapter be sent to one of the list's moderators, but there was no time in the process to include the potential reaction into the current version of the chapter itself. The position held by me, the author of this chapter, is that of a privileged voyeur in this context: a while female European, employed at a university and not a member of the mailing list that is being analyzed.

[19]This refers here to the broader definition of silencing.

increase in vulnerability or a change in the tone of discussion was not resolved, but simply stated as a problem.

The original discussion took yet a different turn when the list members began to look for reasons for both the eruptions (as also asked by Fernandez in her Digitales paper) and for the silence of others: "People only listen and don't speak for different reasons. It might be important to examine the circumstances of this as it operates on this list because I for one have little notion of who is actually on this list and why, why they stay and what they are thinking, what they are looking for?" (Mod.2, 19/08/2002). The search for the other members and their opinions was as much a recurring theme as the process of silencing, as another quote underlines: "I am deeply curious to know who all of you are, what you do" (Mem.4, 15/06/02). Thus, the topic of silencing went hand in hand with the topic of online silence (and related attempts to remove it). Eventually everyone was encouraged to break the silence.

Responses were manifold.[20] Some reasons given for the silence were relatively trivial, such as personal or other circumstances (too much work, for example). One woman reinforced the notion that not all silence was problematic. She stated that although she had been interested in the debate, she had not felt the need to articulate herself (up until the moment when she was explicitly encouraged to speak out). One other, crucial reason for the silence on this list was insecurity. The insecurity concerned either the tone of the debate or the academic expectations (different levels of knowledge) or other inequalities (such as different social and cultural circumstances). Thus one woman explained: "On this list, it seems that every word is analyzed to pieces! . . . individuals feel . . . that they must somehow defend their personal situation, position, standpoint" (Mem.1, 19/08/2002). With this statement the list member had—at least temporarily—broken her silence and uttered an alternative standpoint. She had also touched upon the core argument in this chapter: the position from which network participation (individual and otherwise) takes place is crucial to the make-up of the flows.

To briefly exemplify another aspect of the argument—that is, that it is the level of conflictual communication that threatens a network—here is another example from the list: a low point of the debate was reached a year after the above-quoted conflict. The same actors got involved in another personal attack on each other. A very similar debate erupted, with comparable arguments in tow. Here Fusco claimed that "Every time I have raised any critique of your colleagues' work . . . you have refused to address those criticisms, attacking me ad hominem or claiming that those criticisms are "not the point." Those are evasions . . ." (Mod.1, 14/08/2003). Later she added: "I've frankly been surprised by the extent to which all these women have felt personally emboldened to

---

[20]Through these responses the circle of silence was at least partly disrupted.

engage in nothing short of libelous attacks on my professional status and capacities offline" (Mod.1, 14/08/2003). This was a response to one of the most revealing moments in the debate, in which Wilding had accidentally sent a private mail to the list in which she called Fusco a "superbitch" (Mod.2, 11/08/2003). The point, however, is not these kind of accidents or extremes. More interesting is that the conflict moved from list-internal issues to the personal and that yet again several other list members had become involved in the debate and had started their assessment of the personal and conflictual nature of the exchanges. Life on the list continued, albeit not undisturbed.

DISCUSSION

Despite the list's aim to explicitly challenge diverse experiences of discrimination, prejudice seemed to be repeated on the list.[21] On a more positive note, some list members noted that diverse mechanisms of inequality (e.g., the ways in which "whiteness" can function) had been explicitly addressed on the list. Thus, a learning process had potentially been initiated (rather than presumed to have already taken place). Existing patterns of discrimination were actively challenged: inequalities were made explicit in the debate and some of the silences were at least temporarily broken. However, for many list members (and moderators), the result of the debates mentioned was a feeling that racist or other forms of discrimination were simply reinforced in this list and potentially made worse through the medium. They felt that the list could not provide what it was supposed to provide.

Fernandez describes the specificity of the communication through this kind of mailing list as more frustrating, but maybe less painful than other forms of personal communication (face-to-face, telephone, etc.). The frustration is partly based on the lack of body cues or similar markers. The lack of pain can be explained through the remaining distance in the communication. The displayed emotions are not channeled by existing offline communication conventions and thus manage to provoke quite thoroughly in the end. Similarly, silence online can be experienced as violence (as it cuts off any communication in this case). This is where the feeling of being silenced by someone has its origin. Added to this is, in this particular case, the topic of discussion and the self-reflexivity implied by the topic. They raise expectations that are not fulfilled.

In general, the mailing list provides a different communication sphere to other kinds of communication (see, e.g., Strate, 1996). At the

---

[21]This was experienced by both sides and cannot therefore simply be labeled as racism.

same time, this particular list does not operate on the same level of anonymity as others. Many list members were invited to participate because they were known to someone or through something. Some list moderators themselves (plus some of the list members) have actually met offline. On top of that, the chosen topic of this particular list enhances an emotional involvement. The conflicts encountered by the Undercurrents mailing list are therefore both exemplary and specific. The list's specificity can best be described through its cyberfeminist and postcolonial agenda; that is, the theoretical challenges it poses and encounters. Undercurrents' role as a feminist list, for example, explains to some extent the personal nature of some of the communication and the care that is taken to explain and explore one's positioning. It also explains the sensitivity towards the tone of the discussions. The list is struggling in real terms with the issues that it originally set out to discuss and thus poses a challenge to its participants.

Another characteristic of this network is the unusual *extent* of the list's conflicts and their personal nature. Emotions of this kind happen on several mailing lists, but the seemingly contradictory combination of caring and concurrent attacks is more extreme in Undercurrents. This is also the reason for Maria Fernandez' doubts about the appropriateness of the list's tone and consequently about its overall purpose (Fernandez, 2003). This doubt is shared by other list members, one of whom stated (in reference to the question of racism): "It was time for a new dialog then . . . it is now . . . the rhetoric is based on divisiveness and will do nothing but hamper any possibility of productive dialogs or consensus towards positive actions" (Mem.5, 15/06/02). Although the list started with the issue of discrimination and with a disillusion with the power of the net, many participants are not entirely sure about how to deal with the realities of a disillusion on their own list. A gap seems to exist between their original aim and its fulfillment. Reflexivity alone is not enough to close this gap.

Can the kind of emotional engagement presented here be clearly differentiated from other kinds of display of emotions online, such as flaming? Flaming has been described as uninhibited online communication due to anonymity, operationally defined as "name calling, swearing, insults, impolite statements, threats and put-downs, crude flirtations of a demeaning or sexually explicit nature, and attacks on groups or individuals" (Baym, 2003, p. 63; see also Strate, 1996). Flaming was for a long time predominantly discussed as part of the "cues-filtered-out-approach" in computer-mediated-communication—that is, the approach that defines online communication as context-free and therefore lacking certain well-known features of face-to-face communication. It is assumed that communication changes extensively due to the lack of these cues, of these features. Baym herself claims that flaming and similar forms of communication are context-dependent after all, because different norms develop in different online environments (Baym, 2003, p. 64). Baym does not deny the specificity of the cues-filtered-out communication environment, but simply stresses the importance of context.

In flaming, the medium's possibility for anonymity is used in order to attack someone: the medium "allows" the articulation of attacks through the combination of individual and mass communication; that is, through a form of personalized anonymity. It does not need much to hide. In the Undercurrents' list, however, the medium makes a difference in terms of the degree of engagement, but not in its nature.[22] Because the exchange is of a rather personalized nature, the conflict as such is not specific to the medium, but the extent and form of its articulation are. This confirms both Castells' and Fernandez' proclaimed precondition for communication: that of the importance of shared values. Hence, what this mailing list underlines is that each network node is a standpoint, an opinion. They are fluid and changeable, but also per se conflictual, as they work in contrast to other standpoints. They use antagonisms to create their own value. Within this, the *situatedness* of the nodes is important. And this is exactly the point where the particularity of this cyberfeminist, postcolonial mailing list returns: members are situated in everyday life positions that are signified through fights (be it against racism or other forms of discrimination), and thus an extreme sensitivity concerning attacks comes into play. The ensuing conflicts threaten but also further the network. The particular nature of this mailing list is crucial:

> List members keep getting upset about things getting personal, yet institutional racism operates on a personal level. . . . The issues that are dealt with here bring up all sorts of things that would get over-complexified and stagnant perhaps in the environment of a meeting space. (Mem.2, 19/08/2002)

OUTLOOK

A combination of topics emerges from the discussion above. To recapitulate: cyberfeminism, the framework for the emergence of the mailing list that has been analyzed, promoted networking through and with the new media, particularly (but not only) for women. In Undercurrents, cyberfeminism was brought together with another approach—postcolonial theory and practice. The primary emphasis is still on networking,

[22]Subsequently, this degree of engagement might, however, change the nature of the engagement.

but the overall approach is more explicitly political and less concerned with artistic and playful output. The postcolonial framework—although only marginally discussed here—can help to draw out some of the reasons that are part of emergence of the conflicts. One aspect is the difference between many white Western and many nonwhite, subaltern women in terms of their definitions of identity, embodiment, experience, and in terms of their everyday positioning.

The basic network idea describes networks as fluid, dynamic, and flexible. Most of all, they are said to restructure existing modes of interaction and communication. Power is reconstructed in new patterns, because networks are in principle made up of equal nodes. In Castells, the conflict is located between individual identities (the self) and global networks (the Net). This is one of the frameworks for the conflict displayed here. The conflict, however, begins earlier. Or, to use the words of another cyberfeminist: "Even if technically all people are related on the same level, there are always informational hierarchies which are installed through unofficial communication" (Sollfrank, 2002). And these hierarchies lead to conflict. Although necessary, these conflicts threaten the basic structures and forms of communication.

The newness in these kinds of networked communication does indeed lie in the erasure of context (as the cues-filtered-out approach suggests), but this context is only half or even less of what makes up a node. What is missing are not so much the clues as to whom one might be dealing with, but the context of situations, of people's everyday lives. The lack of context offers a chance to explore differences constructively (because the differences are there, but cannot easily be classified and thus pushed aside or cemented—their fluid nature is key), but it allows communication also to go into different extremes. These are not the extremes of anonymity, but the extremes of the personal situation.

The conflictual and situated nature of the nodes is a challenge for the further theorization of the network concept. It is also relevant for research that tries to use the concept to think through communication in relation to new technologies. Currently, analyses often stop too early. In order to properly understand the dynamics of such a network, a more diverse and multilayered approach is necessary. The concept must also clearly acknowledge potential points of conflict. In Castells' work, there is a harmonizing tendency that does not fully acknowledge the role of conflicts. When he calls a potentially conflictual interaction online "sincere" (Castells, 2000a, p. 389) and assumes that there is much support, but also many potential "casualties" in online communication, this description brushes aside what is taking place. In addition, Castells' proclamation that the flow of powers is replaced with the power of flows affords a differentiation. Instead of the removal of power structures, new power structures seem to emerge, which can only be understood with a multilayered approach (an important difference often exists between list members and moderators, for example). A thickening of the descriptive layers is essential.

The specificity of Undercurrents lies first of all in the self-reflective nature of cyberfeminism and postcolonial theory overall and of this list in particular. The list members set out to reflect on discrimination and then struggled to find it among their own.

> You . . . have posted a kind of disclaimer, you didn't mean to be so emotional. Perhaps if these "emotions" were kept in the public arena they could be channeled into constructive dialogues. (Mem.3, 17/08/2003)

Perhaps, indeed, more openness is the first step towards the constructive nature of communication that they all seem to aim for. And the willingness to deal with conflict is equally crucial:

> . . . it is a discursive list. . . . To try to unpick the institutional prejudices, biases that we carry around with us? . . . Which is . . . to say . . . that we *are* [italics added] prepared to examine, conflict, challenge ourselves and each other. And that sometimes it simply is going to be painful. (Mem.1, 19/08/2002)

The proclaimed need to begin with shared goals or other shared qualities needs to be at least partly rejected. Congruence of interests and opinion leads to a lack of challenge and thus of development and movement. The conflict is vital, but also potentially destructive for connectivity in a network society. What needs to be agreed upon is exactly the need for conflict (but also a level of restraint on the personal attack).

As the Undercurrents struggle shows, the focus on content such as postcolonialism increases the general awareness on the list concerning potential problems of discrimination, but the "location" from which the participants partake in this debate also comes back with more force than elsewhere. In a debate where the "standpoint" is a constant point of struggle, the networked nature of the communication does not make the nodes equal, even if it does challenge existing power relationships. Castells, it seems, would agree on the need for conflict, but does not see a way to combine embodied, situated, and thus specific identities with this conflict.

> . . . patterns of social communication become increasingly under stress. And when communications breaks down, when it does not exist any longer, even in the form of conflictual communication (as would be the case in social struggles or political opposition), social groups and individuals become alienated from each other, and see

the other as a stranger, eventually as a threat. In this process, social fragmentation spreads, as identities become more specific and increasingly difficult to share. (Castells, 2000a, p. 3)

To communicate despite the specificities is what Undercurrents attempts. The network conceptualization, as it has often been presented thus far, does not yet go far enough in terms of complexity. An initial hint for an extension has been given. It helps to further challenge illusions about net culture and a network society, and it also underlines their potential. It simply warns that too much noise can lead to quite a bit of silence.

REFERENCES

Baym, N. K. (2003). Interpersonal life online. In L. Lievrouw & S. Livingstone (Eds.), (2003), *Handbook of new media. Social shaping and consequences of ICTs*. London: Sage.

Bolter, J. D. (1997). Das Internet in der Geschichte der Technologien des Schreibens. In S. Münker & A. Roesler (Eds.), *Mythos internet* (pp. 37-55). Frankfurt a. M.: Suhrkamp.

Castells, M. (2000a). *The rise of the network society. The information age: Economy, society and culture* (Vol. I, 2nd ed.). Oxford: Blackwell.

Castells, M. (2000b, January-March). Materials for an exploratory theory of the network society. *British Journal of Sociology, 51(*1), 5-24.

Castells, M. (2002). *The power of identity. The information age: Economy, society and culture* (Vol. 2). Oxford: Blackwell. (Original work published 1997)

Digitales (2002). *Conference handbook.* Retrieved December 2, 2002, from http://www.digitales-online.org/

Fenton, J. (2001). *Contemporary surrealism, dérive and rêverie in the passages of Paris.* Retrieved October 2, 2001, from http://www.psychogeography.co.uk/contemporary_surrealism.htm

Fernandez, M. (2002, September). Undercurrents: A dialogue. In *eZine*, 16/September(09). Retrieved December 6, 2002, from http://www.msstate.ed/Fineart_Online/Backissues/Vol_16/faf_v16_n09/reviews/feature.html

Fernandez, M. (2003). *Digitales Presentation Audio File.* Retrieved March 8, 2004, from http://constant.all2all.org/%7Edigitales/sound.php

Hartmann, M. (2004). *Technologies and utopias. The cyberflâneur and the experience of being online.* München: Reinhard Fischer Verlag.

Kuni, V. (1999). Die Flaneurin im Datennetz. Wege und Fragen zum Cyberfeminismus. In S. Schade & G. C. Tholen (Eds.), *S Konfigurationen. Zwischen Kunst und Medien* (pp. 467-485). München: Wilhelm Fink.

Landwehr, I. (2002). *Netzwerke Küssen und Morden.* Retrieved February 16, 2004, from http://www.uni-weimar.de/medien/management/frames.html?url=/medien/management/sites/ss2002/netzwerke/netzwerke_scripts.htm&

OBN (1997): *100 Anti-theses.* Retrieved August 21, 2002, from http://www.obn.org/inhalt_index.html

Plant, S. (1998). *Zeros + ones. Digital women and the new technoculture.* London: Fourth Estate.

Rauner, M. (2004, February 26). Ziemlich verknotet. *Die Zeit, 10,* pp. 33-34.

Sollfrank, C. (2002). *Cyberfeminism: Revolution.* Retrieved June 16, 2004, from http://www.artwarez.org/aw/content/orange_revo.html

Strate, L. (Ed.). (1996). *Communication in cyberspace.* Cresskill: Hampton Press.

Tsaliki, L. (2001). Women and new technologies. In S. Gamble (Ed.), *The Routledge companion to feminism and cyberfeminism* (pp. 80-92). London, New York: Routledge.

Undercurrents (2002a). *Mailing list announcement.* Retrieved December 6, 2003, from http://lists.c3.hu/pipermail/artinfo/2002-February/000818.html

Undercurrents (2002b). *Mailing list archives.* Retrieved December 6, 2002, from http://bbs.thing.net/

Undercurrents (2004). *Mailing list archives.* Retrieved January 16, 2004, from http://bbs.thing.net/

VNS Matrix (1991). *Cyberfeminist manifesto for the 21st Century.* Retrieved November 29, 2002, from http://www.sterneck.net/cybertribe/vns-matrix/

Wilding, F. (1998). *Where is feminism in cyberfeminism?* Retrieved October 6, 1998, from http://www.obn.org/cfundef/faith_def.html

TOWARDS A
NETWORK SOCIALITY

Andreas Wittel

In this essay I want to introduce the phenomenon and concept of a net-work sociality.[1] The term "network sociality" can be understood in con-trast to community. Community entails stability, coherence, embedded-ness, and belonging. It involves strong and long-lasting ties, proximity, and a common history or narrative of the collective. Network sociality stands counterposed to *Gemeinschaft*. It does not represent belonging but integration and disintegration. It is a disembedded intersubjectivity that is somehow "lifted out" (Giddens, 1984). It is an immediate inter-subjectivity that is integral to what Rem Koolhaas calls the "generic city" (OMA, 1995). It is the social expression of a "liquid modernity" (Bauman, 2000). In network sociality social relations are not narrational but informational; they are not based on mutual experience or common history, but primarily on an exchange of data and on "catching up." Narratives are characterized by duration, whereas information is defined by ephemerality. Network sociality consists of fleeting and tran-sient, yet iterative social relations; of ephemeral but intense encounters.

---

[1]Many thanks to Scott Lash. The main arguments of this chapter emerged as a result of a dialog with him.

Narrative sociality often takes place in bureaucratic organizations. In network sociality the social bond at work is not bureaucratic but informational; it is created on a project-by-project basis, by the movement of ideas, the establishment of solely temporary standards and protocols, and the creation and protection of proprietary information. Network sociality is not characterized by a separation but by a combination of both work and play. It is constructed on the grounds of communication and transport technology. Network sociality, I suspect, is emerging alongside—and in some respects displacing—the community based sociality Richard Sennett (1998) talks about.[2]

As the title indicates, the theoretical precursor of this concept is Manuel Castells' (2000) notion of a network society. Castells' main concern is the outline of the global macrosociology of the information age. On the one hand, networks are comprised of subjects and technologies, and on the other the links between. They are open structures, able to expand almost without limits, and they are highly dynamic. As such, networks are "appropriate instruments for a capitalist economy based on innovation, globalization and decentralized concentration," and also for a "culture of endless deconstruction and reconstruction" (Castells, 1996, p. 470). I think it is worthwhile to translate this macrosociology of a network society into a microsociology of the information age—that is, not to focus on networks themselves, but on the making of networks. What kind of sociality is at stake in the information age?

My interest in the phenomenon of a network sociality shares certain objectives with mainstream social network analysis (Burt, 1980), yet differs widely from the latter in its approach. Firstly, standard network analysis features quantitative research, whereas my approach is based on an ethnographic perspective. Secondly, I am neither concerned with networks themselves and the mathematics of their formal properties, nor with the uncovering of models of social relations, but rather with the making of networks, with networking as a practice. How do people build, maintain, and alter these social ties? What means, tactics, and strategies do they employ? What kind of cultural capital do they need to increase their social capital? Bourdieu (1986), who originated the notion of *social capital,* has consistently analyzed the reproduction of more traditional social relations. How crucial is such social capital in the new informational fields that involve not the reproduction but the production of social relations (cf. Touraine, 1988).

I will argue with Rosi Braidotti (1994, p. 5) that "in-depth transformations of the system of economic production also alter traditional

---

[2]Sennett (1998) provides a strong ethnographic example for both kinds of sociality, separated by one generation only. Rico's social life has all the features of what can be understood as network sociality. His life is the life of a contemporary businessman being mostly on the move. His father's social life, however, is clearly based on community, on *Gemeinschaft.*

social structures." The rise of a network sociality is closely related to what has been called "late capitalism" (Jameson, 1991; Mandel, 1973), "new capitalism" (Sennett, 1998), or most recently "the new economy" (Castells, 2000; Dyson, 1998; Gilder, 2000; Kelly, 1999; Leadbeater, 1999) or the "weightless economy" (Giddens, 2001). It is connected to Foucault's concept of biopower and to what Michael Hardt and Antonio Negri (2000, p. xv) call "Empire," a form of sovereignty that "operates on all registers of the social order extending down to the depths of the social world." Furthermore, the rise of a network sociality is related to the development of information and communication technologies, to the processes of globalization and individualization, and to the fact that "modern society is society on the move" (Lash & Urry, 1994, p. 252).

I've suggested a rise of network sociality. Note the term "rise." Indicated here is a process, and this process has historical roots and it has limitations in terms of geography, class, and industrial sectors. Firstly, this process is not new; indeed, its historical roots are fairly old. Some features of network sociality have already been described in the first half of the last century by cultural theorists such as Georg Simmel and Walter Benjamin. However, as I will argue in the latter part of this essay, the rise of network sociality is not only a far broader and more visible phenomenon than it was a few generations ago, it is also new in terms of its formalization and institutionalization, and in terms of a somehow unashamed commodification of social relationships. Secondly the rise of a network sociality is especially visible in *urban (post)industrial spaces* and milieus. It is most visible among *the new middle class* of culturally educated and media- and computer-literate people.

One of the fields in which this network sociality is particularly visible is the cultural industry, especially the field of new media. The arguments presented here are informed by a two-year research project on the emergence of the new media industry in London.[3] Also, most of the examples used to illustrate these arguments are taken from this research. However, the networking practices described below are not merely a phenomenon of the new media field. They are paradigmatic more widely of the information society. This essay is meant to be read as an attempt to explore a cultural hypothesis. It is subdivided into three main parts. In the first part I want to introduce some examples that document the rise of a network sociality. The second part consists of a critique of some theoretical accounts on contemporary transformations of sociality. The third part is an attempt to outline the concept of network sociality.

---

[3]*Silicon Alleys: Networks of Virtual Objects*, the title of the research project (Scott Lash, Dede Boden, Celia Lury, Dan Shapiro, and Andreas Wittel), was part of the *ESRC Virtual Society?* program. It started in March 1998.

THE PHENOMENON

Example 1: New Media Industry as Social History. A few years ago, new media—the convergence of information and communication technology, old media, art, and design—started to emerge as a rapidly growing sector of the information society. New media, like all cultural industries, is predominantly an urban phenomenon (Indergaard; 2000; Pratt, 1998; Scott, 1997; Zukin, 1995). It started as an industrial sector, but soon was more. It became a business service for the whole industry. Probably all big players in every industrial sector now have a new media division, and the SMEs at least have a few employees with new media skills. The new media field leads and supports the economy in its preparation for the digital age. It is about to transform the economy into what recently has been called the "new economy" (Castells, 2000; Dyson, 1998; Gilder, 2000; Kelly, 1999; Leadbeater, 1999). This economic transformation includes a transformation of working practices. Or to sharpen this point; working practices become increasingly networking practices.

Whereas the structure of traditional industrial sectors is represented to a large extent by physicality and materiality (products, machinery, plants, transport and delivery systems), the structure of the net sector can best be understood by looking at work relations and the process of networking as social practice.[4] Indeed, the specificity of the net sector as industry is that it is mainly created on the grounds of social relations, as a bottom-up network. In the case of New York, Indergaard (2000) and Pratt (1998) both present a detailed analysis of the making of *Silicon Alley*. They persuasively show how Manhattan's new media industry is socially constructed on the grounds of networks and networking practices. The same is true for London's new media industry. "In the cyberspace economy, the commodification of goods and services becomes secondary to the commodification of human relationships" (Rifkin, 2000, p. 97). Indeed new media practitioners increasingly perceive working as networking and social relationships and networking as crucial tools and resources for a successful business. They talk about *relationship value*, claim the importance of *networking* and have reorganized their firms

---

[4]This is not to say that the new media industry is free from materiality. Many commentators (Latour, 1998; Löfgren, 2001) emphasize the materiality of the new media industry: computers, cables, modems, etc. The materiality of the new media industry is then used as an argument against claims of a "weightless" or "light economy." This argument is convincing to a certain extent. However it hides the fact that—compared with other industrial sectors—there is indeed a material lightness of the new media industry. For many new media firms in London and New York it was not unusual to move location several times between 1998 and 2000. Such frequency cannot be found in other industrial sectors. It can only be achieved because new media firms travel light; all they have to move are laptops and other computer-related equipment.

away from a focus on products towards a focus on clients, customers, and users. Pehong Chen, CEO of BroadVision, was asked by WIRED magazine (2000, p. 238) what e-tailers do wrong. His answer:

> It's smarter to try and get 30 percent of a person's lifetime value than 30 percent of today's market. Companies today deal with their customers on a troubleshooting basis, but at some point they're going to figure out that success is about building long-term relationships.

The *Silicon Alley Reporter*, one of the more influential magazines in the U.S. market on new media and the net economy rates once every year in a special issue the 100 most successful people of Manhattan's net sector. The ratings are based on five categories. One of them is called ability to network—another indication that networking is becoming a crucial skill in the competitive market of the new economy, that the economical success of a firm is deeply intertwined with the social skills of the people working for it. Scott Kurnit (1997), the CEO and founder of the Internet portal About.com, published an article in one of Silicon Alley's newsletters with the headline: "Creating Virtual Communities: It's the relationship that matters."[5] The CEO of NCCO—one of London's new media agencies—focuses on relationships and relationship technologies as a core business activity:

> We have our emphasis on people. So the type of consultancy that we offer is helping clients who want to understand what networking can do for their business and how they might use the network to rebuild their business. It will be about relationships in the future. The network prioritizes everything so adding value is going to be a function of differentiation in areas that are much less tangible. And the primary way of adding value is by building a relationship, which is delightful to engage in and sensitive to the consumer.

In June 2000 New York's Silicon Alley organized and performed a three-day think tank. The international managing director of BlueSky International is quoted in the following statement: "As the world becomes more global, personal relationships become more important"

---

[5]Scott Kurnit has a BA in Sociology and Communications and is, although he started much later, becoming a serious challenger for portals such as Yahoo and Excite. At the beginning of 2000, the traffic at About.com's website increased to 8.4 million unique visitors per month (*Silicon Alley Reporter,* Feb. 2000, Issue 30: 33). Today, About.com is one of the most popular destinations on the Net (http://ourstory.about.com/index.htm).

(*Silicon Alley Reporter*, June 2000).[6] The causality of this statement is hardly persuasive in terms of logic. But this is not the point. What is interesting here is the fact that personal relationships are perceived as becoming more important. That is to say, personal relationships are becoming more important in the economic field for the simple reason that more practitioners see them as a highly valuable business resource. This relevance of relationships seems to even diminish the importance of contracts with clients. One software developer explains:

> The contract kind of doesn't matter unless we were to completely screw it up or unless they were completely turning nasty as clients, and not paying us any money. If you've got a good client, then what you want is repeat business. In commercial terms, you either want repeat business or you want recommended business. And those are the two best kinds of business you can get because with the repeat business, you already know who you're dealing with and what the problems will be. As recommended business, the recommendation cuts both ways. If it's a client you like representing, normally they like you enough to tell you what your new clients are going to be like.

The shift from a focus on products towards a focus on users and clients is mirrored in the homepages of new media firms. In the period between 1995 and 1998 new media agencies highlighted on the homepages especially their products and services. Now most new media agencies highlight the list of clients they have. The products and services on Razorfish's website, for example, are nearly hidden. However this shift from products to clients is in no respect limited to the Internet industry. It is observable in many other industrial sectors as well. This shift may be described as the ultimate step towards flexible specialization.

The short history of business websites indicates this shift as well. A few years ago business websites had mainly the function of being an extended PR or marketing tool. Now they are interfaces as webs of connectivity. They connect the users with the firm behind the website. The short history of business websites indicates a shift from representation towards connectivity and interactivity (Wittel, Lury, & Lash, 2002). Now websites are a perfect example of what Karin Knorr-Cetina (2000) calls a "social object."

What is suggested is that this development of interfaces into connectivity networks is much more than an online phenomenon. It would seem to be more generally a characteristic of the new economy. At stake, however, is not merely a change of electronic communication. At stake is a change of face-to-face interaction. This transformation, iron-

---

[6]It would not be very difficult to list many more similar statements from high-ranking new media people.

ically, can be well studied in a field that is strongly associated with inter-face and with all forms of technologically mediated forms of communi-cation. This real side is the practice of networking.

As already said, networking has always been an important business practice. New, however, seems to be the broadness of the phenomenon. Until recently this practice has been associated with higher manage-ment. Now there seems to be a social trickling-down effect from the level of leadership and higher management to new media's "shop floor level." Networking now is as much performed on the ground of the cor-porate world as on the top. Also new seems to be the explicit acknowl-edgement of the importance of networking and the perception of social relations as social capital. Also new is the intensity of this practice. Finally, and as shown in the following example, the formalization and the institutionalization of this practice also seems to be new.

Example 2: Networking Events. In London we find a broad range of networking events in the new media field. Most of these events take place once a month. All of them were established between 1998 and 1999. Some of these networking events, such as *The Cultural Entrepreneurs' Club, Cybersalon* and *London Virtual Reality Group*, have a close affinity with the art world, but most of them are mainly placed as part and supplement of the industry. The best known is *First Tuesday*. It started in October 1998 in a pub in London. In June 2001 *First Tuesday* had more than 100,000 members worldwide. It branched out from London to other big cities in the United Kingdom and even spread to cities in Europe and the United States, operating in 100 cities across 46 countries. Other networking groups are *Digital People, Chemistry, New Media Knowledge, E-Futures, Surfs Up, The Ecademy, NetProZ* and *Boobnight* (Boob = bring our own beer). Additionally, women's networking groups such as *Hightech-Women, Webgrrls,* and *E-women* emerged with the aim to conquer the male-dominated world of e-business.

Some of these events are highly structured and organized. *First Tuesday*, for example, a network aiming to connect ideas and money, entrepreneurs and venture capital, found a particularly efficient way to enforce its networking practices. Internet entrepreneurs wear green badges, investors have red badges, and service providers get yellow ones. This way nobody loses time accidentally talking to the wrong per-son. Other networking groups (e.g., *Boobnight*) prefer a more playful approach and focus more on laid-back socializing than on a quick exchange of business cards. Some of the networks are open to everyone (*NetProZ*), others (*Chemistry*) are rather closed and work by invitation only. While some of them combine networking activities with presenta-tions or discussion groups (*The Ecademy, Digital People, E-Futures*), others focus purely on networking.

What unites all these networks is their inherent ambivalence: On the one hand they are instrumental and functional, on the other hand they're supposed to suggest the opposite. On the one hand the commodification of social relationships (doing a pitch, getting funds, finding work) is highly obvious, on the other hand it is important to hide this commodification by creating a frame (music, alcohol etc.) that makes people comfortable and suggests a somehow authentic interest in meeting people.

According to *First Tuesday* (www.firsttuesday.com), networks have the same function as a "medieval fair"; they are about exchange. This idea of commodification and exchange is also expressed on the website of the new media consultancy, Garol, a co-organizer of *NetProZ*. I quote from an article called *Get More Out of Networks* (www.garol.com/the-view):

> A network is based on a key principle—the exchange of currency. We're not talking about money . . . , we're talking about information. Networks thrive on a complex arrangement of exchange rates and credit facilities. To me a phone number might be nothing, but to you having it could change your life and put you in my debt. Effective networkers understand this. They play to it, offering a tidbit here and a bit of advice there, then calling in the slips when they need a favour. But they are not overt about it.

At the end of the article Garol comes up with seven "top tips for managing your network." One of them says: "Theft: Don't steal other people's contacts. If Joe tells you about Jack, ask him to introduce you. Don't just do it yourself." The expression "stealing contacts" is often heard and quite common in the new media field. The idea that contacts can be stolen is necessarily based on the premise that they are commodities.

Some of these networks establish informal rules on how to network. *First Tuesday* for example, recommends interaction with as many people as possible. It is seen as bad habit, one participant claims, to spend more than 5 or 10 minutes with the same person. Another regular guest describes the *First Tuesday* evenings as

> . . . promiscuous. It is naked in showing its promiscuity. Everybody's eyes are wandering all the time. Nobody wants to miss out. It is really important to check people out as quickly as possible. In a way it's like being in a gay bar without sex.

Why does networking become such a crucial practice for the net sector? What do these institutionalized networks do? Firstly, they circulate information and knowledge, secondly they circulate capital, thirdly they circulate labor, and fourthly they circulate clients and products. The net sector is highly flexible and highly open to change; thus, for the participants of this sector life and work is intrinsically insecure. Risk taking has become a necessity. Networks provide support. Thus networking reduces risk; it generates security. The bigger the networks are, the better for everyone who participates in them (Kelly, 1999).

So far, we do not have much ethnographical knowledge about the networking practices at these regular events. What are the main structural similarities and differences of these networking groups? How do the various groups articulate (make a pitch, get funds, find work) and hide (music, alcohol) a commodification of social relationships? How do they address the ambivalence between the more instrumental (functional, work related) and the more purpose free (playful, authentic) aspects of this form of socializing? Should these events best be analyzed as a form of social engineering? Do these gatherings have centers and peripheries? What concept of power underpins these events? How indeed do the participants network? How do they build, maintain, and alter social ties? What means, tactics, and strategies do they employ? There is a need for an ethnographic study of these events.

Example 3: E-mail Dinner Invitation. During my fieldwork in London's new media field I received by e-mail a dinner invitation. The text says:

> Please come to a dinner at my house to celebrate, well, everything. (and I have to add you are all doing interesting and interlinking consciousness industry shenanigans but you may discover that as we go along . . .)

The subject line of this e-mail has a somehow Marxist subtext: *consciousness and food.* It is not a habit of mine to bore readers with my private life. However, this invitation allows me to identify certain key characteristics inherent in network sociality. Particularly significant is the phrase in brackets.

Firstly, it suggests that the invitees of this dinner party don't know each other. The e-mail I received was sent to nine other people, and I didn't know any of the other invitees personally. Most of the names, however, seemed familiar to me. The host of this party mentioned these names on other occasions. During the dinner party itself I realized, indeed, that none of the invitees knew each other personally. The host works for an IT company in London, has an educational background in fine art, and is considerably involved in London's new media scene. It would have been easy for her to invite people who already knew each other. So we can assume that her decision to invite people who didn't was a very deliberate choice.

Secondly, the phrase in brackets informs each invitee about the work of the other participants. According to the message, we are "all doing interesting and interlinking consciousness industry shenanigans" and so, the message continues, we will "discover that as we go along." What is suggested here is that we will end up talking about our work rather than our private life. Furthermore, it is suggested that this practice of interlinking and exchange will be interesting and might even be useful for us, for our work and our careers. Indeed, at the dinner we did end up talking about our work. We had wonderful food, slowly but surely we got high and drunk, but we never stopped for a second talking about ongoing and future projects, events we participated in and ideas we had, about net.art, start-up companies, and interesting websites.

At stake here is a dinner party that is announced and presented as a networking event. This leads us to the third and most important reason why this e-mail is of significance. Of course parties and dinner parties always work and have always worked as networking venues—from the salon of the 19th century to contemporary business dinners on the level of higher management. Interesting in this case, however, is the fact that the function of the dinner party as networking event has been made explicit, that the connection between the private and the work-related aspects of the dinner party has already been addressed in the invitation. Here we again find explicitness in the acknowledgement of relationships as social capital. In fact this is the only information we get in the text of this e-mail (apart from the place and the date of the venue). Furthermore, the fact that the host of this dinner is part of the new middle classes is another interesting example of the above mentioned trickling down effect of reflexive networking practices from the elites (whether cultural or economic) to the new middle classes.

Example 4: Carole Stone. The last example is quite extreme and by no means representative of the social field I talk about. However, it might well be indicative in illustrating the historical transformations of sociality. It seems highly unlikely that a similar phenomenon could have been reported one or two generations ago. In April 2000, *The Guardian* (6 April 2000) featured as cover story in the supplement *G2* the networking practices of Carole Stone, who is according to the newspaper "London's networking queen" and "Britain's best connected woman." She holds monthly salons for 90 people. At least half of them are, according to *The Guardian,* regulars in the national press. The monthly event is "a party to which guests come alone, safe in the knowledge that however slight their connection to her, Stone will remember their names, occupations and who in the world they would most like to meet." Every Christmas, she gives a party to which she invites 1,000 guests. According to *The Guardian* she has 13,700 friends, all filed in a database. The database informs about their marital status, their CVs, and their history of attendance. In March 2001, *The Observer Magazine* (18 March 2001) featured her as well. However, at this stage she had 14,000 friends. This means that in less than a year she managed to make 300 new friends, which is roughly an average of one new friend every day.

For 10 years Carole Stone was the producer of BBC's radio program *Any Questions?* Now she runs a media consultancy business. Stone (2000) published a book called *Networking: The Art of Making Friends.* In the prologue she says: "Making friends is an art—an art that can be learned" (p. 5). But it is also an effort: "The effort I had to put in then is . . . fundamental to the art of making friends. Friends are made, they don't just happen. You have to work at it" (p. 7). She defines friends as "people you can help, and people who can help you—whether on a business or a personal level." Again we come across the theme of instrumentality and functionality of social relations, and the theme of art, skill, effort, and work in order to establish and maintain social relations.

Stone's book is a how-to-book. "How to go to parties with confidence and how to give them without worry, how to survive a snub and how to make successful small talk, how to network your friends and how to keep track of them all" (p. 9). The latter of course is particularly interesting: How to keep track of 14,000 friends? Stone writes:

> It's like everything else we rely on in life: don't skimp on the servicing. If you do, your friendship will break down, just as the central heating boiler does when the outlook's bleak and you really need some warmth badly. Friends have to be looked after and checked up on regularly to make sure they're in good working order. (p. 157)

For Stone a database must be a particularly helpful tool. In her book she doesn't mention the database and how she uses it. However, it is self-evident that the database—let's say compared to a collection of business cards—allows a far easier way to "nurture friends" (p. 160); that is, to contact them on a regular basis, to remember their birthdays, and to write them a thank you note (p. 161).

Lev Manovich (2001) calls databases the dominant symbolic form of the 21st century. In contrast to the image or the novel, to Manovich, databases do not have a narrative any more; no beginning, no end, no storyline, no hierarchy. They are a collection of individual items, each of them having the same significance and the same status. Databases grow; they are never complete. Mark Poster (1995) looks from a poststructuralist perspective at databases and explores how they reposition our identities. He analyzes databases as discourse (referring to Foucault's usage of discourse): they constitute subjectivity outside the immediacy of consciousness. In this respect there is a strong similarity with the panopticon. In contrast to the panopticon, however, databases can constitute subjectivity in absentia. Databases, so Poster continues, traverse and cancel the public and private distinction. Zygmunt Bauman (1998), taking up Poster's comparison between the database and the panopticon, points to another difference. Whereas the panopticon is above all an instrument of the state, the database is an instrument of the market. The main purpose of the panopticon is to instill discipline, to impose a uniform pattern of behavior, and to keep people in place. It is a weapon against difference. The database on the other hand, so Bauman says, is an instrument of separation, selection, and exclusion. All three perspectives on databases suggest structural similarities with many features of network sociality.

CONCEPTS OF THE TRANSFORMATION OF SOCIALITY

In the contemporary debate there are several attempts to capture the changes of sociality. I briefly want to introduce and comment on three of the more prominent concepts of current transformations of the social.

The Emergence of Virtual Communities

The growth of computer-mediated communication has produced a rapidly growing body of literature that seeks to explore the social implications of information and communication technologies (ICT). One of the core themes of this literature is the notion of *virtual community*. The term has been introduced by Howard Rheingold (1994) and has been quickly picked up by the media and social scientists (Jones, 1997; Stone, 1995; Turkle, 1995). Rheingold, like other virtual communitarians, is driven by a utopian aspiration. He starts as a critic of contemporary sociality and claims a decline of real community life. He talks about "the need for rebuilding community in the face of America's loss of a sense of a social commons" (p. 12). According to Rheingold, ICTs give us the chance to revitalize communities. What has been lost because of mobility and a growing relevance of consumption can now be reconstructed with a little help from a keyboard, a monitor, a processor, and a modem. In cyberspace, Rheingold and others believe, we will be able to revitalize the public sphere and construct new forms of community. Most of the literature on virtual communities has been based on similar utopian and techno-deterministic perspectives.

I do not consider the concept of virtual communities to be particularly helpful in understanding the contemporary transformations of social relations. It is misleading in three ways. Firstly, this techno-deterministic perspective does not interlink cultural and technological change. The assumption, that a cultural process—the disentanglement from communities—can be reversed with technological tools seems to be rather naïve. Or, as Kevin Robins (1995, p. 148) puts it: "For all its futuristic pretensions, Rheingold's imagination is fundamentally conservative and nostalgic."

Secondly, the usage of the term "community" in relation to electronic communication is at least problematic and confusing. Typically and in the tradition of Ferdinand Tönnies' view (1979), communities share a common geographic territory, a common history, a common value system, and they are rooted in a common religion. This definition of community is used by most commentators, including Rheingold (1994), who observe a decline of real community life. In this sense, the connection between community and the Internet is an oxymoron. However, in talking about online interaction, virtual communitarians refer to a quite different concept of community; to one that draws on the idea of the imaginary (Anderson, 1983) and that is based on Nancy's (1991) argument that communities are always constructed, never automatic, given, or natural.

Thirdly, the term "virtual" is misleading in that it suggests a doubling of reality. This demarcation line between a so-called virtual world and a real world has strongly shaped the debate on cyberspace and interactive media in the last few years. Virilio (1995), for example, suggests that we are facing a "fundamental loss of orientation. . . . A duplication of sensible reality, into reality and virtuality, is in the making." In contrast to this view I want to argue for a perspective that does not separate the virtual or online world from the real or offline world. In theoretical terms this emphasis on virtuality is problematic, because it suggests the existence of a "real" reality, a reality that is not mediated. And empirical research persuasively shows that e-mailing, online chatting, web surfing and other interactive practices are very real experiences for the people utilizing them (Miller & Slater, 2000). I do not intend to suggest that there are no fundamental differences between an online and a face-to-face sociality. To mention briefly the most important difference, any online communication lacks a common and mutual perception of the context. Online sociality cannot rely on exogenous (external) or contextual forms of structuration. Thus, any structuration of sociality has to be produced endogenously (internally) by the participants. However these differences do not justify a theoretical perspective that separates reality from virtual reality and thus constructs a doubling of the world.

The following two concepts are much more grounded and much more plausible than the social sci-fi construction of virtual communities.

The Erosion of Enduring Relationships

Richard Sennett (1998) is perhaps the most prominent commentator on the decline of long-term, sustained, and deep relationships. He focuses on the transformation of the organization of work, in particular on the human consequences of the new work regime. His inquiry: How can people generate meaning and identity under the condition of increased flexibility and risks? How can they maintain lasting and trustful relationships, and how are they to create a persistent narrative in a work environment that worships change and condemns routine? In general he argues that the replacement of linear time by serial time (e.g., short-term projects, short-term contracts) leads to a series of losses: a loss of trust among working colleagues; a loss of commitment towards the task in hand; and a loss of loyalty towards the organization. It is undoubtedly ironic that in an age characterized by teamwork and corporate culture we do not see an increase of social bonds between employees but rather a weakening of them. Informal trust, so Sennett notes, requires the duration of time.

Flexibility is another feature of the short-term economy. It produces a tolerance of fragmentation and generates a lack of attachment towards work and people. Networking seems to become more important than the ability to stick to a problem and solve it. This is as true for employees with a weak work identity as it is for highly motivated employees. The really successful employees seem to avoid the reckonings of the accountant's bottom line. "The trick is, let nothing stick to you" (Sennett, 1998, p. 79). Flexibility also affects loyalty to the company. If employees become unhappy, they are more likely to leave the organization rather than fight within it. And it affects skills and experience. Skills become portable and experience loses value. The ability to focus quickly on new tasks counts more than the accumulation of experience. Change becomes a value in itself and resistance towards change is taken as a sign of failure. In brief, short-term projects, short-term contracts, flexible tasks, and increasing fluctuation rates in organizations make it difficult for employees to develop a common narrative any more. Detachment is required, not involvement. A good team player should have the ability to stand back from established relationships. The result, to Sennett, is an erosion of deeper shared commitments, of loyalty, responsibility, and trust, of enduring and deep friendships.

In a way Sennett presents the counter story of the utopian statement of virtual communities. His observation of friendships becoming increasingly short-term and flexible is persuasive and based on empirical facts. However I hesitate to agree with the pessimistic undertone. His conclusion that this process jeopardizes the development of trust, commitment and loyalty seems to be debatable at least. Furthermore, Sennett implicitly suggests that these transformations are created by a small elite and they occur against the interests of the majority. Thus, he ignores the fact that the middle classes co-construct and actively participate within this process.

Postsocial Relationships

Postsocial theory analyzes the phenomenon of a disintegrating traditional social universe (Knorr-Cetina, 2000). Postsocial theory has one foot in individualization theory and another foot in actor-network theory and provides a framework for connecting both of them. Karin Knorr-Cetina assesses two "structural conditions of Western societies." The first condition is the current process of desocialization, the second is that of an enormous expansion of object worlds within the social world. It is important to note that postsocial theory does not claim a decline of the social. Instead it claims a shifting of social activities away from humans and towards objects. Here I will ignore the second condition—the expansion of objects—and merely focus on the assertion of a current process of desocialization.

The argument of a process of desocialization is placed in historical context that goes back to the beginnings of industrialization and modernity. Modernity is "associated with the collapse of community and the onset of individualization." While communities have been emptied of social meanings, larger scale organizations have attracted such meaning. Modernization is seen as an expansion of social structures. Knorr-Cetina claims the expansion of social structures is on hold in the contemporary climate; there is even a decline and retraction of social structures and a disintegration of community life in the private sphere. The conclusion being drawn is that social relations become flattened and thinned out.

The suggestion that there is a disintegration of a formerly strong link between communities and organizations and social life seems to be highly plausible. This is called desocialization. However, I hesitate to use this label. The historical and ongoing process of the disintegration of communities and organizations does not necessarily imply a retraction of social principles and structures. On the contrary: The example of Carole Stone seems to indicate an extension (or at least a quantification) of human interaction. Instead of perceiving this process as desocialization, I suggest a shift away from regimes of sociality in closed social systems and towards regimes of sociality in open social systems. Both communities and organizations are social systems with clear boundaries, with a highly defined inside and outside. Networks, however, are open social systems.

In the last part of this essay I attempt to outline a concept of "network sociality" by describing some of its main dimensions.

FEATURES OF A NETWORK SOCIALITY

Individualization

Individualization presumes a removal from historically prescribed social forms and commitments, a loss of traditional security with respect to rituals, guiding norms and practical knowledge (Beck, 1999). Instead, individuals must actively construct social bonds. They must make decisions and order preferences. The cultural sociologist Gerhard Schulze (1993) describes a change from *Beziehungsvorgabe* to *Beziehungswahl*, a change from pre-given relationships to choice. Pre-given relationships are not a product of personal decisions; they represent the sociality of communities. In contrast *Beziehungswahl* is defined by a higher degree of mobility, by translocal communications, by plenty, and by affluence of social contacts, and by a subjective management of the network. A few years earlier Touraine (1988) described this transformation in a very similar way. He talks about a shift from defensive identities towards offensive identities.

In the age of individualization identity depends increasingly on an awareness of the relations with others (Berking, 1996). Network sociality is not based on a shared history or a shared narrative. Instead it is defined by a multitude of experiences and biographies. The new media field contains subjects with a diversity of educational and geographical backgrounds. People are, so to speak, lifted out of their contexts and reinserted in largely disembedded social relations, which they must at the same time continually construct. In this respect their sociality is distanciated and immediate (Giddens, 1990).

Knowledge workers and people in the cultural industries are nomadic in their personal biography and in their nonlinear work biographies (Braidotti, 1994). They often move from one firm to another, from one occupation to another, "mixing and matching jobs as event organizers, web site designers, ad creatives, marketing advisers, conference runners, magazine publishers, sponsorship co-ordinators, club promoters, market researchers, PR officers and various kinds of consultancy" (Benson, 1999). To give a concrete example: In October 1998 the London-based new media firm Okupi had a staff of 10 employees. Eighteen months later the number of staff was 18 employees. However, only one of them had been part of the October 1998 team. Another indicator is the growing number of freelancers. More and more people work with and for firms, but not in firms any more. Possessed with an anticorporate ideology and a desire not to be committed to a single institution, the freelancers are paradigmatic for the work situation described by chronic network construction and maintenance. They are the most fully reliant on their own resources of social capital.

One aspect of individualization is the DIY-biography, the active construction of one's own life (Beck & Ziegler, 1997), in this respect the active construction and reconstruction of a social network. One constantly has to renew, refresh, and revalue the existing contacts. They are not taken for granted any more. That is one of the reasons why Carol Stone has to invite 90 people every month. It is the only way to keep up with 14,000 friends.

Ephemeral and Intense Relations

In the Internet industry as in most other industrial sectors business is increasingly organized in terms of short-term projects. As soon as a new project begins, talk (intrafirm talk as well as talk to the client) becomes intense, information moves to and fro rapidly at the same time that its wider circulation is tightly guarded (Boden, 1994; Sennett, 1998). For the duration of the project (usually between a couple of weeks and several months) new media people work long hours and give the project first priority. When the project ends, these collaborations are kept on a low flame and new projects, co-operations, and social ties are established or re-established.

The tendency towards ephemeral but intense, focused, fast, and overloaded social ties is also observable in nonwork situations. At parties, for example, the distinctive dimensions of network sociality are highly visible—the fleetingness of interactions, their intensity, and the fluctuation of social figurations. Parties are an occasion to talk to many people within only a few hours. One has to make decisions and selections about who to talk to and for how long. These decisions have to be made instantly. It would be useful sociological knowledge to find out how people make these decisions and on what grounds they select their conversation partners.

The development towards ephemeral but intense contacts is even visible in the realm of dating. For example, SpeedDating, founded in 1999 in Los Angeles and since then spread to a constantly growing number of countries, provides a service that allows participants to meet 10 people within 90 minutes. When the bell rings, eight minutes are reserved for each date, then the participating men and women have to rotate to another table and another person for the next date. After each date, participants fill in a yes or no answer on a rectangular card indicating whether they would like to see the person again. If a match is made, coordinators provide them with each other's phone number (*New York Times*, March 2000, p.35).[7]

The ephemerality of social contacts could be a consequence of affluence. It might be worth returning to the database of London's Networking Queen. It is not easy to manage 14,000 friends. The conclusion that Carol Stone can't afford to spend too much time with her friends on an individual base derives from simple mathematics. The more friends one has, the less time is available for every one of them. Here is an example from my own research. In February 2000, I attended a conference of new media practitioners in New York. Around 1,000 people participated in this three-day event. In the evening of the last day

---

[7]SpeedDating has in some countries reduced the eight min. interaction to a mere three min. interaction.

I asked one of the participants how many new contacts he had made during the day. He replied: "Not that many. I was a bad networker today. I got about 30 business cards." The quote is revealing, not only because of the number of contacts made in one day—according to my interlocutor a poor result. It is also indicative in another respect: He relates—or shall I say reduces—social contacts to the exchange of business cards. At the same conference another participant explained why he was willing to pay the conference fee:

> I mean the beautiful thing about New York is that a lot of people know each other, help each other, introduce each other, network ultimately. A lot of people forget you when they don't see you at these kinds of events. New York is small but at the same time it's very big as well. You live in the same area, you don't meet each other all the time, so you somehow lose contact. So these meetings and these conferences for me are about being seen and seeing other people again, saying hello, being sort of on the back of their mind and it's usually like a two-minute conversation like how are you doing, how is your business and that is all it needs.

Bauman (1996, p. 51) places these developments in a larger context: "Everything seems to conspire these days against . . . lifelong projects, lasting commitments, eternal alliances, immutable identities. One cannot build long-term hopes around one's job, profession, skills even; one can bet that, before long, the skills will cease to be in demand . . . one cannot build the future around partnership or the family either: in the age of confluent love, togetherness lasts no longer than the satisfaction of one of the partners, commitment is from the start until further notice, and today's intense attachment may only intensify tomorrow's frustrations."

From Narrative to Information

"Information," writes Lash (2001), "is compressed in time and space. It makes no claim to universality but is contained in the immediacy of the particular. Information shrinks or compresses metanarratives to a mere point, a signal, a mere event in time." Network sociality mirrors this distinction between the narrative and information on a micro-sociological level. Network sociality is not rooted in a common and shared history. As a consequence of this loss of a shared biography, subjects cannot rely on a common narrative, on shared experience. For this reason Sennett (1998) sees an erosion of enduring friendships, responsibility, and trust. However, this seems to be an open question. Certainly it should be worth looking at the possibility of a reconfigured trust being inscribed in informational social bonds, bonds based less in hierarchical relations and more in the complex, reciprocal intricacies of the transverse networks of information exchange. Trust here might be based less on continuous work relations of a long duration, and more on iterated work relations of a short duration, less on the knowledge of someone's character and more on the knowledge of someone's resources and his/her position in the social field. Trust here is constructed and produced as a social relation rather than already pre-given or reproduced. Giddens (in Beck, Giddens, & Lash, 1994, p. 186) calls this "active trust." It is a matter of mutual influence rather than mutual fatedness. Social relations of competition, too, are possibly becoming informational, based on the possession and strategic deployment of proprietary knowledge. Whereas ownership and use of some types of information are a legal matter (of contract, copyright, trademark, and patent), other kinds are less formally recognized, a matter of negotiation in the practice of networking (Lury, 1993).

To illustrate this shift from an experience-based sociality to an informational sociality, let me get back to SpeedDating. As mentioned, participants have only eight minutes to talk to each other before they decide whether they want to see the other person again. Within these eight minutes participants have to exchange information, not narratives. "What do you do for a living? Where are you from? What is the most exciting thing you've ever done? What do you do in your spare time?" These are the questions to be asked, according to the report in *The New York Times*. These questions are informational; the context resembles a job interview. It is an exchange of data rather than a romantic date.

Mobility and speed seem to be the primary reasons for this shift from a narrative or experienced-based to an informational sociality—mobility, because more and more people are on the move and thus somewhere else. In order to re-establish social contacts, catching up becomes an indispensable condition of social situations. Catching up is essentially informational. And the acceleration of speed in social encounters is additionally feeding the development towards an informational sociality. Narratives are time consuming; information is quick. A half-hour business meeting is a good example to illustrate this: Participants have to get to the point as fast as possible, they have to be focused, they exchange information not stories, discourses, and narratives.

The Assimilation of Play and Work

In network sociality professional ties become increasingly playful. Information exchange provides the infrastructure of the sector, and the ability to acknowledge the rules and conventions by which the creation, distribution, and protection of information occurs is crucial. Yet this does not preclude a playfulness; rather a playful attitude is frequently encouraged in the design and layout of work spaces (Goldwasser, 2000), which encourages the inhabitants to introduce the unexpected into their offices, and in the use of cafes and pubs for work meetings, where spontaneity and accidental encounters may spark new ideas or provide an occasion for the extension of networks. "Work has to be fun. Why bother to work so hard if it is not fun?" This is one of the most frequently heard statements of new media people. This playful attitude leads to an intensification of work. They listen to music while working, they do drugs while working, they spend a good deal of their work hours in pubs and cafes. And the purpose behind this integration of playfulness in work is to perform better.

Play is associated with creativity, experimentation, and innovation; it stands counterposed to bureaucracy and a Protestant work ethic. Some commentators use the term "playground" (Broeckmann, 1998; Schwarz, 2000) to describe the activities in the field of cultural industries and digital media. Although play is intentional it involves the elaboration of nonpurposive rationality (Gadamer, 1990). This is an activity that, although still rule-bound, is not subordinated to any pre-given aims or constrained by the developmental constraints of narrative. As such, it provides the basis of new symbolic resources in the workplace.

The assimilation of work and play corresponds with the blurring of boundaries between work and private life, between colleagues and friends,[8] and between colleagues and clients. From my fieldwork in London's new media industry it became clear that many firms established very close relationships with their clients. Both sides have to embark in a real collaboration. In these interactions, the boundaries between producer and client are fading. Sometimes the clients have been so deeply involved in the production process that they become part of the production team.

But the assimilation of work and play works in both directions. Not only is play invading work, we also experience the invasion of work into the realm of play. Parties, dinner parties, Carole Stone's monthly salon, SpeedDating—all this is strongly related to work. Networking events such as *First Tuesday*, *NetProZ*, and *Chemistry* can be seen as a perfect symbiosis of work and play, of instrumentality and nonpurposive rationality. Parties, for example, work particularly well in combining both dimensions. This might be one of the reasons for the popularity of parties in the cultural industries and in the new media field. Many new media companies, for example, Pseudo and Razorfish—have become well known for their parties. The *Industry Standard,* a San Francisco–based new economy magazine, is "famous for its Friday night parties" (*The Guardian*, 9 January 2001, p. 3). Furthermore, most of the new media conferences start and finish with a party. However, all these par-

---

[8]*It Really Pays to Treat Staff as if They Are Your Friends* is the headline of an article in *The Times* (27 July, 2000).

ties are not just pure fun. Indeed, they are hard work, as David Brooks (2000, pp. 200-202) humorously describes:

> Bobos (Bourgeois Bohemians—A.W.) have taken the ultimate symbol of Dionysian release, the party, and merged it with work. . . . Now parties tend to be work parties; a glass or two of white wine, a little networking with editors and agents, and then it's home to the kids. . . . More Bobos pass out business cards at parties than pass out under the table.

Technology

Network sociality is a technological sociality insofar as it is deeply embedded in communication technology, transport technology, and technologies to manage relationships. It is a sociality that is based on the use of cars, trains, buses, and the underground, of airplanes, taxis, and hotels,[9] and it is based on phones, faxes, answering machines, voicemail, videoconferencing, mobiles, email, chat rooms, discussion forums, mailing lists, and web sites. Transportation and communication technologies provide the infrastructure for people and societies on the move.

A community-oriented sociality does not rely as much on transport and communication technology. Network sociality is delocalized, it is a sociality on the move, a sociality over distance, a sociality based on *technogene Nähe*, on technogenic closeness (Beck, 2000). In this essay I have mainly focused on face-to-face sociality, however it is impossible to separate face-to-face interactions from interactions over distance. In urban spaces the idea of an uninterrupted face-to-face sociality disentangled from technological devices is becoming the exception. More and more we are experiencing an integration of long-distance communica-

----

[9]*The Observer* (4 July 1999, p. 7) recently warned that in terms of air traffic in the London area "we will shortly be descending into chaos." According to *The Observer*, Heathrow's two runways now handle an average of 85 aircraft every hour. Some 45 arrive and leave from Gatwick, 35 pass through Stansted, Luton handles 20, London City 20, and Northolt in west London 12. "All this adds up to 220 planes an hour, hitting runways once every 16 seconds." According to *The Observer*, the air traffic in the London area will double in the next 20 years. If we assume an average passenger rate per plane of 200 (a rather low estimate), then there are currently more than one million passengers entering or leaving London every day. This is due to a massive rise of the tourism industry (Urry, 1990), but maybe even more to the rise of business mobility. Pico Iyer (2000) recently published an ethnographic report about the effects of an increasing need for mobility. It is an exploration of life on the run and a world full of hotels, airports, and shopping malls.

tion in our realms of face-to-face interaction. Just consider the implications of the advance of mobile phones in the last decade. It is hard to imagine a dinner of let's say four businessmen without a mobile phone ringing. The ringing phone disrupts the previous social figuration, and a new figuration has to be constructed. This new figuration, however, is transformational. It has to be renegotiated as soon as the conversation on the mobile phone is finished.

The third form of technology necessary for the development of a network sociality is the technologies to manage social relationships; that is, business cards, databases in e-mail applications, and databases in mobile phones. Until recently, business cards were the most popular mode to archive and order information about friends, colleagues, and acquaintances. However the weaknesses of business cards as technology to manage social relationships became increasingly apparent. Firstly and in stark contrast to databases, they only allow for one system of order and categorization (e.g., alphabetically, temporally, according to profession). Secondly, business cards might be a helpful instrument to manage social relationships, but they don't guarantee that the owner of a business card collection will be able to relate all cards to persons or encounters. The size of the collection is particularly significant: the bigger the collection of cards, the more likely that the owner has to apply additional techniques to master the collection. Most of my interviewees have developed specific strategies to relate business cards to faces. One interviewee told me he writes on every new business card the date and the place of the encounter. Another person writes on the back of business cards one or two key words of the conversation she had. However, all the people I talked to had something in common. They admitted that they have business cards they can't identify any more. It will be interesting to observe if the rise of the database will reduce the attractiveness of business cards.

CONCLUSION

I argue for the acknowledgement of an emerging model of sociality. The concept of network sociality is, however, fairly incomplete. So far networking as social practice is considerably under-researched, it lacks solid empirical data, and it especially needs ethnographic exploration. One of the areas under scrutiny would be the *private-public dichotomy*. How private and how public are these social bonds? Is it indeed feasible to conceptualize the private-public relation as dichotomy or could network sociality best be understood as a hybrid, as an amalgam of private and public aspects?

Another area that deserves empirical attention is the relation between different *forms of capital* (economic, social, cultural, and symbolic). Bourdieu (1986) emphasizes the convertibility of these different forms of capital. How is, for example, social capital transformed, transferred, translated, and exchanged into economic capital? How is the antagonism between functionality and morality renegotiated in network sociality? Finally, a third area worth closer inspection is the *microdynamics* of network relations. Aspects such as trust, loyalty, hierarchy, power, and conflict need to be addressed and investigated in the context of networking. One strategy to improve an understanding of these aspects might consist in an attempt to re-examine sociological and anthropological studies of groups and to relate these findings to networking practices.

To conclude: My hypothesis is that network sociality will become the paradigmatic social form of late capitalism and the new cultural economy. After describing the phenomenon of the rise of networking as social practice and critically introducing three of the currently prominent theories of transformations of sociality, I have outlined my concept of a network sociality: it is a sociality based on individualization and deeply embedded in technology; it is informational, ephemeral but intense, and it is characterized by an assimilation of work and play. Furthermore I suggest that certain features of the practice of networking might be "new": its widespread practice in urban postindustrial spaces; its framing and institutionalization in the form of new media networking events, parties, conferences, art openings, mailing lists, and digital discussion forums; its increasing commodification and the increasing perception of social relationships as social capital; and finally, a process from having relationships towards doing relationships and towards relationship management. Network sociality is about social bonds that are continuously produced, reproduced, and—as Bauman (2000, p. 163) points out—"consumed."

In social science the assertion of novelty is always a tricky enterprise. Objections against such a perspective can easily be raised. Of course, all social changes contain elements of continuity. This cultural hypothesis of the rise of network sociality, however, has been developed in the spirit of the following remark by Castells (2000, Vol. 3, p. 356): "After all, if nothing is new under the sun, why bother to try to investigate, think, write, and read about it?"

REFERENCES

Anderson, B. (1983). *Imagined community: Reflections on the origin and spread of nationalism.* New York: Verso.
Bauman, Z. (1996). Morality in the age of contingency. In P. Heelas, S. Lash, & P. Morris (Eds.), *Detraditionalization: Critical reflections on authority and identity.* Oxford: Blackwell.

Bauman, Z. (1998). *Globalization: The human consequences.* Cambridge: Polity.

Bauman, Z. (2000). *Liquid modernity.* Cambridge: Polity.

Beck, S. (Ed.). (2000). *Technogene Nähe.* Berlin: Akademie Verlag.

Beck, U. (1999). *Individualization.* London: Sage.

Beck, U., Giddens, A., & Lash, S. (1994). *Reflexive modernisation: Politics, tradition and aesthetics in the modern social order.* Cambridge: Polity.

Beck, U., & Erdmann-Ziegler, U. (1997). *Eigenes Leben. Ausflüge in die unbekannte Gesellschaft, in der wir leben.* München: Beck.

Benson, R. (1999, February 2). Flexecutives. *The Guardian.*

Berking, H. (1996). Solidarity individualism: The moral impact of cultural modernisation in late modernity. In S. Lash, B. Szerszynski, & B. Wynne (Eds.), *Risk, environment and modernity.* London: Sage.

Boden, D. (1994). *The business of talk: Organizations in action.* Cambridge: Polity.

Bourdieu, P. (1986). The forms of capital. In J.G. Richardson (Ed.), *Handbook of theory and research for the sociology of education.* New York: Greenwood.

Braidotti, R. (1994). *Nomadic subjects: Embodiment and sexual difference in contemporary feminist theory.* New York: Columbia University Press.

Broeckmann, A. (1998). Towards a European media culture—which culture, which media, which Europe? Retrieved January 12, 1998, from http://www.v2.nl/~andreas/texts/1998/europeanmedia-en.html

Brooks, D. (2000). *Bobos in paradise. The new upper class and how they got there.* New York: Simon & Schuster.

Burt, R. (1980). Models of network structure. *Annual Review of Sociology, 6,* 79-141.

Castells, M. (2000). *The information age: Economy, society and culture* (2nd ed. Vols. 1, 2, & 3). Malden, MA: Blackwell.

Dyson, E. (1998). *Release 2.1: A design for living in the digital age.* New York: Broadway Books.

Gadamer, H.-G. (1990). *Wahrheit und Methode.* Tübingen: Mohr.

Giddens, A. (1984). *The constitution of society.* Cambridge: Polity.

Giddens, A. (1990). *The consequences of modernity.* Cambridge: Polity.

Giddens, A. (2001). Anthony Giddens and Will Hutton in conversation. In W. Hutton & A. Giddens (Eds.), *On the edge: Living with global capitalism.* London: Vintage.

Gilder, G. (2000). *Telecosm: How infinite bandwidth will revolutionize our world.* New York: Free Press.

Goldwasser, A. (2000). Building Dilbert's dream house. *The New York Times Magazine,* pp. 68-71.

Hardt, M., & Negri, A. (2000). *Empire.* Cambridge, MA: Harvard University Press.

Indergaard, M. (2000, August). *The bullriders of Silicon Alley: New York places its bets.* Paper presented at the annual meeting of the American Sociological Association.

Iyer, P. (2000). *The global soul. Jet lag, shopping malls, and the search for home.* New York: Knopf.

Jameson, F. (1991). *Postmodernism, or, the cultural logic of late capitalism.* London: Verso.

Jones, S. (Ed.). (1997). *Virtual culture. Identity and communication in cybersociety.* London: Sage.

Kelly, K. (1999). *New rules for the new economy: Ten ways the network economy is changing everything.* New York: Viking.

Knorr-Cetina, K. (2000). Postsocial theory. In G. Ritzer & B. Smart (Eds.), *Handbook of social theory.* London: Sage.

Kurnit, S. (1997). Creating virtual communities: It's the relationship that matters. Retrieved August 8, 1997, from @*NY.*

Lash, S. (2001). *Critique of information.* London: Sage.

Lash, S., & Urry, J. (1994). *Economies of signs and space.* London: Sage.

Latour, B. (1998, April). *Thought experiments in social science: From the social contract to virtual society.* 1st Virtual Society? Annual public lecture, Brunel University.

Leadbeater, C. (1999). *Living on thin air. The new economy.* London: Penguin.

Löfgren, O. (2001). *European ethnology and life in the experience economy.* Opening lecture at the 7th SIEF-Conference, Budapest.

Lury, C. (1993). *Cultural rights.* London: Routledge.

Mandel, E. (1973). *Der Spatkapitalismus.* Frankfurt a. M.: Suhrkamp.

Manovich, L. (2001). *The language of new media.* Cambridge, MA: MIT Press.

Miller, D., & Slater, D. (2000). *The internet.* Oxford: Berg.

Nancy, J.-L. (1991). *The inoperative community.* Minneapolis: University of Minnesota Press.

OMA, Koolhaas, R., & Mau, B. (1995). *S, M, L, XL.* Rotterdam: 010 Publishers.

Poster, M. (1995). *The second media age.* Cambridge: Polity.

Pratt, A. (1998). *Making digital spaces: A constructivist critique of the network society.* Unpublished paper.

Rheingold, H. (1994). *The virtual community: Finding connection in a computerised world.* London: Secker and Warburg.

Rifkin, J. (2000). *The age of access.* London: Penguin.

Robins, K. (1995). Cyberspace and the world we live in. In M. Featherstone & R. Burrows (Eds.), *Cyberspace, cyberbodies, cyberpunk.* London: Sage.

Schulze, G. (1993). *Die Erlebnisgesellschaft:Kultursoziologie der Gegenwart.* Frankfurt: Campus.

Schwarz, M. (2000). *Digital media in the technological culture—Perspectives for arts and cultural policy.* Advice commissioned by the State Secretary for Education, Culture and Science of The Netherlands.

Scott, A. (1997). The cultural economy of cities. *International Journal of Urban and Regional Research, 21*(2), 323-340.

Sennett, R. (1998). *The corrosion of character. The personal consequences of work in the new capitalism.* New York, London: W.W. Norton.

Stone, A. (1995). *The war of desire and technology at the close of the mechanical age.* Cambridge, MA: MIT Press.

Stone, C. (2000). *Networking: The art of making friends.* London: Vermilion.

Tönnies, F. (1979). *Gemeinschaft und Gesellschaft. Grundbegriffe der reinen Soziologie* (8th ed.). Darmstadt: Wissenschaftliche Buchgemeinschaft.

Touraine, A. (1988). *Return of the actor. Social theory in postindustrial society.* Minneapolis: University of Minnesota Press.

Turkle, S. (1995). *Life on the screen: Identity in the age of the internet.* New York: Simon & Schuster.

Urry, J. (1990). *The tourist gaze: Leisure and travel in contemporary societies.* London: Sage.

Virilio, P. (1995). *Speed and information. Cyberspace alarm. CTHEORY.* Retrieved January 12, 1998, from http://www.ctheory.com/a30-cyberspace_alarm.html
WIRED 8.06 (2000, June). Interview with Pehong Chen, p. 238.
Wittel, A., Lury, C., & Lash, S. (2002). Real and virtual connectivity: New media in London. In S. Woolgar (Ed.), *Virtual society? Get real!* Oxford: Oxford University Press.
Zukin, S. (1995). *The cultures of cities.* Oxford: Blackwell.

CONCEPTUALIZING PLACE
IN A WORLD OF FLOWS

Shaun Moores

In the context of arguments about "the rise of the network society" (Castells, 1996) and the need for a 21st-century "sociology of fluids" (Urry, 2000), I want to focus in this chapter on the character and significance of places, and on the relations between places in contemporary social life.[1] How are we to conceptualize place, then, in a world of flows, including those information flows that are facilitated by modern media of communication? What role do the media play, alongside other institutions and technologies, in transforming experiences of locality and in creating new sorts of social situations for interaction? Attempting to answer these questions will involve us in a critical discussion of ideas put forward by various social and communication theorists. To begin

---

[1]Much of the material in this chapter has been discussed with staff and students in the Department of Sociology and Communications at University of Rome *La Sapienza*, during my stay there as Visiting Professor of Communications in Spring 2003. Subsequently, the material was presented on a visit to the Department of Communication Science and Performing Arts at University of Milan *Cattolica* in Autumn 2003. An earlier version appeared as an electronic working paper entitled *Media, Flows and Places* (Media@lse, London School of Economics and Political Science, 2003).

with, it is appropriate to consider certain aspects of work done by Manuel Castells and John Urry (the two theorists cited in the opening sentence of my chapter), because each of them raises important issues to do with media, flows, and places in their accounts of global social change. I will then be looking back at work done by Doreen Massey (see especially Massey, 1995), Joshua Meyrowitz (1985, 1994), and Paddy Scannell (1996), who have reflected, respectively, on place as permeable, marginalized, or pluralized.

SPACE OF FLOWS AND SPACE OF PLACES

There is much to say about Castells' wide-ranging account of what he names the network society (Castells, 1996),[2] but for the specific purposes of this chapter my main interest is in his social theory of space, and particularly in the distinction that he draws between the *space of flows* and the *space of places*. I should state at the outset that, although Castells' work seems to me to be helpful in making sense of current social transformations, his conceptualization of space has its problems. As I will try to show, those problems have to do with an apparent contradiction in the way in which place is understood.

Space is defined by Castells (1996, p. 411), in general terms, as "the material support of time-sharing social practices," although he is keen to stress that time-sharing practices today do not necessarily rely on the physical contiguity of participants in social interaction. Indeed, in his view, "it is fundamental that we separate the basic concept of material support of simultaneous practices from the notion of contiguity" (Castells, 1996, p. 411; and see Thompson, 1995, p. 32, on the "altered experience of simultaneity" or "sense of now" in modern life). This is because there is a new spatial form (Castells calls it the space of flows) that is characteristic of the network society,[3] which facilitates relationships across physical distances in simultaneous time. Castells (1996, p. 412) tells us that "our society is constructed around flows: flows of capital, flows of information . . . flows of organizational interaction, flows of images, sounds, and symbols." In turn, these flows are made possible by the social development of technologies such as microelectronics, telecommunications, and broadcasting systems.

---

[2]For a general discussion of the concept of *network* as "a set of interconnected nodes" and for some concrete examples of networks, including "the global network of the new media," see Castells (1996, pp. 470-471).

[3]It is worth remembering that there are those who would have their doubts about the newness of the developments identified by Castells, contending that the principle of networking has a long history (Mattelart, 2000; see especially Standage, 1998).

It is at the point where Castells advances his ideas on the space of flows that he first deals with the fate of place in the network society. Here it is proposed that whereas the "structural logic" of the space of flows might be *placeless*, in fact "places do not disappear," rather they "become absorbed in the network," in which "no place exists by itself" since its position and meaning are "defined by flows" (Castells, 1996, pp. 412-413). In my view, this conception of places in relation to flows, as well as to other places, is generally a productive one. As will become clear later in the chapter, it is potentially compatible with Urry's perspective on places as *multiplex* and with Massey's discussion of the *openness* of places. However, when Castells moves on to present a more detailed analysis of the space of places, offering a specific example to illustrate his case, I believe there are certain difficulties that arise as a result of him seeing the space of flows as constructed in opposition to the space of places (so that these two forms of space may eventually constitute *parallel universes* [Castells, 1996, p. 428]).

Having initially understood place in relational terms, Castells (1996, p. 423) proceeds to assert that: "A place is a locale whose form, function and meaning are self-contained within the boundaries of physical contiguity." What puzzles me about this assertion, given the way in which he previously spoke of places as being defined by flows, is the notion that a place can be self-contained. His claim becomes even more puzzling when he refers to the example chosen to illustrate his discussion of the space of places, the district of Paris known as Belleville. He explains that his knowledge of this place originated when he arrived in France as a political exile in the early 1960s and was "given shelter" there by a Spanish immigrant worker who introduced him to the "tradition" of the neighborhood. Years later, in the 1990s, he observes how "new immigrants (Asians, Yugoslavs) have joined a long-established stream of Tunisian Jews, Maghrebian Muslims, and Southern Europeans, themselves the successors of the intra-urban exiles pushed into Belleville in the nineteenth century" (Castells, 1996, p. 423). In addition, the district has been "hit by several waves of urban renewal," because in recent years "middle-class households, generally young, have joined the neighborhood because of its urban vitality" (Castells, 1996, p. 424).

Judging by Castells' account, Belleville is surely far from being self-contained. I have no difficulty at all in seeing that this district of Paris is a physical location with its own distinctive character, but every one of the factors mentioned in the description, including the circumstances of his own arrival there many years ago, involves a connection with somewhere else and with forces from beyond the locale. Indeed, we could say that the place's distinctive character has been molded precisely out of these links that stretch across the city and out across various parts of the globe. As he recognizes: "Cultures and histories, in a truly plural urbanity, interact in the space, giving meaning to it" (Castells, 1996, p. 424). Curiously, despite writing about a *stream* of people moving into

Belleville, this does not register with Castells as a kind of *flow* (it would count for Urry, though, whose broader definition of a flow will be discussed shortly).

Castells appears to choose Belleville as an example of the space of places because, according to the interpretation he makes of this place, it is "socially interactive and spatially rich" (Castells, 1996, p. 425). Of course, his value judgment presupposes the existence of other places that must be considered less well off in physical and symbolic terms. Drawing on the writing of Allan Jacobs (1993), Castells (1996, p. 425) points to "the difference in urban quality between Barcelona and Irvine (the epitome of suburban Southern California)," arguing that although Irvine is indeed a place, it is a spatially impoverished one in which "experience shrinks inward toward the home, as flows take over increasing shares of time and space." No doubt lay individuals (not just academic authors such as Jacobs and Castells) make value judgments about places too, some of them presumably preferring a quiet suburban life to the urban vitality of a Belleville or a city such as Barcelona, but in my view there are further problems that arise as a consequence of this type of place discrimination in Castells' work. There is evidently an assumption here that staying home to watch television, say, is necessarily a worse or less valid cultural experience than going out and encountering people in the street, that physical copresence in public contexts is somehow better or more authentic than media use in private, domestic settings. In addition, there is no mention of the fact that, even for most residents of urban places such as Belleville and Barcelona, experience of the social world will still be constituted, at least in part, by technologically mediated flows of images, sounds, and symbols.

To sum up this section of the chapter, then, I am suggesting that Castells is quite right to begin by identifying the relation between flows and places as central to any social theory of space in the network society, but quite wrong to think of the space of flows and the space of places as diametrically opposed forms with completely separate logics.[4] As he

---

[4]Castells' thinking here is based, to some extent, on a distinction between places that serve as nodes in networks associated with dominant functions in contemporary society (such as "stock exchange markets, and their ancillary advanced services centers, in the network of global financial flows" [Castells, 1996, p. 470]) and the sorts of place inhabited by subordinate social groups, which, he concludes, are "increasingly segregated and disconnected from each other" (Castells, 1996, p. 476). Although I can see the value of his distinction as part of an attempt to deal with dimensions of power and inequality in social change (see also my commentary on Massey), it makes little sense to me to conceive of the multiple space of places as more disconnected than hitherto. Having said that, there are certain places, particularly in rural regions of the so-called developing world, which are relatively excluded from contact with what Castells terms the space of flows. This point has been well made by geographers interested in the non-uniform or uneven process of "time-space convergence" (Janelle, 1991; Leyshon, 1995).

goes on to acknowledge in his subsequent reflections on space, "the geography of the new history will not be made, after all, of the separation between places and flows, but out of the interface between places and flows" (Castells, 2000, p. 27), and as the detailed portrait he paints of Belleville seems to indicate, a place can be thought of as a distinctive location, the significance of which is actively produced at the site of multiple and complex connections with a wider world beyond that place.

SOCIAL AS MOBILITY AND PLACES AS MULTIPLEX

Pursuing a line of argument that overlaps in some respects with Castells' commentary on the rise of the network society, Urry (2000) sets out a bold manifesto for sociology in the 21st century, the main emphasis of which would be on the study of various transnational (and translocal) flows or *global fluids*, "upon heterogeneous, uneven and unpredictable mobilities" (Urry, 2000, p. 38).[5] One way in which his work differs from Castells', though, is that this proposed emphasis on *the social as mobility* leads him to question the central concept of his own academic discipline to date, interrogating the whole idea of the "social as society" (Urry, 2000, p. 2), including, presumably, even the idea of a *network society*. For Urry (2000, pp. 5-6), the concept of society in sociological discourse is too closely tied up with "notions of nation-state, citizenship and national society" to be usefully deployed in the analysis of flows that now criss-cross the "porous borders" of nations. Instead, he advocates "sociology beyond societies." Whether or not we agree with him on this matter of terminology (quite frankly, I find myself wondering why he rules out any possibility of rearticulating the sign of society to suit contemporary circumstances), his general call for social theory to focus in future on various sorts of mobility does merit serious consideration here.

To the kinds of flow listed by Castells, Urry adds others. He talks, for instance, about flows of waste products that bring with them new risks, the mobilities of objects such as consumer goods and, crucially, flows consisting of people on the move (not just "the social actors who operate the networks," in their "global corridors of social segregation" [Castells, 2000, p. 20], but the movements of many ordinary individuals too). In his discussion of modern forms of *corporeal travel*, he observes that: "The scale of such travelling is awesome. There are over 600 million international passenger arrivals each year. . . . International travel now accounts for over one-twelfth of world trade" (Urry, 2000, p. 50).

---

[5]An earlier version of this thesis on the need to understand fluidity or mobility as increasingly constitutive of modern life is to be found in Scott Lash and John Urry (1994).

These figures are indeed awesome, although we need to remember that, for the vast majority of people making journeys abroad, there will be a return home, where day-to-day life will continue to be lived in and around their local places of work and residence. For this reason, John Tomlinson (1999) is correct to criticize Urry for an overly bold assertion, made in a book co-authored with Lash (see Lash & Urry, 1994, p. 253), "that the paradigmatic modern experience is that of rapid mobility [understood as physical movement] across often long distances." Instead, Tomlinson (1999, p. 9) proposes "that the paradigmatic experience of global modernity for most people . . . is that of staying in one place," where they experience what global modernity "brings to them" (and see Giddens, 1990, p. 19, on place as "increasingly phantasmagoric"). This case is also put by David Morley (2000, p. 14), who, having quoted statistics indicating that over half the adults in Britain still live within five miles of their place of birth, states that it is "in the transformation of localities, rather than in the increase of physical mobility (significant though that may be for some groups), that the process of globalization perhaps has its most important expression."

The arguments made by Tomlinson and Morley point us usefully, in my view, away from any "generalized nomadology" (Morley, 2000, p. 13) and towards a consideration of how places are changing today as part of those broader transformations that are often referred to as *globalization*. However, I think Urry's account of the social as mobility can be defended in two main ways. Firstly, his later book does not seek to privilege the experience of corporeal travel over that of other fluids or mobilities, rather it situates physical mobility in relation to, for example, forms of *imaginative* and *virtual* travel. Secondly, far from ignoring place, he offers an enabling conceptualization of places as multiplex. Let me try to explain these aspects of his work in turn.

By imaginative and virtual travel, Urry means the instantaneous mobilities that are facilitated by broadcasting and computer-mediated communication, which media users can experience "without physically moving" (Urry, 2000, p. 70). Providing specific examples of instantaneous mobilities made possible by television, he writes: "We imaginatively travel and are at Princess Diana's funeral, in war-torn Bosnia, seeing the world record being broken, with Mandela being released from jail and so on" (Urry, 2000, pp. 67-68). His employment of travel as a metaphor for the experience of watching television (he goes on to speak of private consumers being "thrown into the public world" by radio and television) suggests that viewers can feel transported elsewhere by the medium, not just on big occasions like the ones in his list of examples but in their routine viewing practices too (see Larsen, 1999, for empirical evidence that some viewers do feel this sense of transportation). On the other hand, Urry (2000, p. 69) also employs language that is closer to Tomlinson's, talking about how distant events, personalities and happenings are constantly brought into the living room by television, helping to transform everyday life. Either way, whether it is better thought of as the viewer "going places" or as the medium "bringing it all back home" (Moores, 2000), Urry is raising important issues to do with broadcasting's role in connecting the local and the global.

When he discusses instances of virtual travel via the computer screen, Urry's most interesting observation is that although the Internet is evidently used to create and sustain relationships across physical distances (providing participants with a virtual copresence), members of *virtual communities* may occasionally feel the need to meet up physically.[6] The reason I am particularly interested in this observation is that it indicates the potential links between corporeal and noncorporeal travel, the fact that physical and other mobilities can sometimes be closely connected. Perhaps the best examples of such links are provided by contemporary *diasporic* cultures (see also Morley, 2000). Referring to James Clifford (1997, p. 247), Urry (2000, p. 155) points to how dispersed peoples, who have made their homes away from "homelands," live in a cultural context of to-and-fro cross-border connections made possible by modern technologies of transportation and communication (and see Appadurai, 1996, on relations between global *ethnoscapes* and *mediascapes*).

Despite his strong emphasis on global fluids, Urry does not neglect the issue of the transformation of localities raised by Tomlinson and Morley. Indeed, we might say that he sees flows and places as parts of the same issue, contending that local places "can be loosely understood . . . as multiplex, as a set of spaces where ranges of relational networks and flows coalesce, interconnect and fragment" (Urry, 2000, p. 140). A place, for Urry (2000, p. 140), is a "particular nexus" between "propinquity characterized by . . . co-present interaction" and "fast flowing webs and networks." It is at this nexus that the meanings of place are constructed and these meanings will be multiple. Taking the example of a city such as Edinburgh, then, Karen Qureshi (2003) names one of its multiplex spaces "Pakistani Edinburgh." Her ethnography, which focuses on the reflexive negotiation of identities among young people who were born and brought up in Scotland, but whose parents migrated there from the Punjab, makes it clear that Pakistani Edinburgh is not a self-contained unit. It is characterized by specific kinds of physical contiguity or propinquity, and yet it has highly permeable boundaries, being formed through physical, imaginative, and virtual travellings in and out of it, while overlapping with what Qureshi terms mainstream Edinburgh.

---

[6]This point is developed further in Urry (2002). For a recent ethnographic study of an Internet forum in which some of the participants interact face-to-face as well as online, see Lori Kendall (2002).

THE OPENNESS OF PLACES

When he outlines his understanding of places as multiplex, Urry acknowledges a debt to the work of Massey, a geographer who has written extensively on place (see Massey, 1993, 1994, 1995), partly as a consequence of her engagement with debates in that discipline about the value and purpose of locality studies. She confirms that places should be thought of as "not so much bounded areas," but rather as open and porous, "constructed through the specificity of their interaction with other places" and having multiple significances, "since the various social groups in a place will be differently located" (that is, differently located "in terms of the spatial reorganization of social relations") (Massey, 1994, p. 121). In her view, each place has its own *uniqueness*. However, this special quality is not simply the outcome of "some long internalized history" (Massey, 1993, p. 66). What defines the uniqueness of any place has to do with the particular "mix of links and interconnections" to a beyond, "the global as part of what constitutes the local, the outside as part of the inside" (Massey, 1994, p. 5).[7]

Massey's concern, therefore, is with what she calls "the openness of places" (Massey, 1995, p. 59) in global times, although she is careful to qualify her remarks about the *permeability of localities* in the contemporary period. To begin with, this openness is "not a new phenomenon, just as globalization itself is not" (Massey, 1995, p. 61). Like Stuart Hall (1991, p. 20), Massey asks us to guard against "historical amnesia" when it comes to thinking about the globalizing process, pointing to the case of a port city such as Liverpool, which has formed its own distinctive character out of links with other places through trade and migration over the past three centuries. What is new about globalization in its current phase, she suggests, is that "the speed of it all—and its intensity—have increased dramatically in recent years" (Massey, 1995, p. 46). A further qualification is related to her more general argument about "the power-geometry of it all" (Massey, 1993, p. 61), by which she means the inequalities associated with global (and local) social change. Experiences of locality and interconnectedness are highly uneven, even among people who are living in the same place. This leads her to see place and its multiple meanings as a matter of political, as well as geographical and cultural, importance.

Having briefly set out Massey's theoretical and political position on place, I now want to spend some time looking at empirical evidence that

---

[7]Implicit here is a rejection of the idea that globalization necessarily leads to greater cultural homogeneity, and a proposal that the heterogeneity of places may actually be intensified by the globalizing process. A complementary perspective on the ways in which transnational connections give rise to distinctive cultural mixes or confluences in local settings is offered by Ulf Hannerz (1996).

she provides, which arises out of research into specific localities. This research was designed to map the spatial locations and connections, which Massey (1995, pp. 54-55) refers to as "activity spaces," of members of different social groups inhabiting a number of small country villages in Cambridgeshire. As we will see, the reach of these groups' activities varies enormously.

At one extreme, then, there are "high-tech scientists, mainly men, whose work is based in Cambridge, though they often have computers with modem links at home as well," who are "in constant contact with, and physically travelling between, colleagues and customers all around the world" (Massey, 1995, p. 59). The activity spaces that they move in, both physically and virtually, are thoroughly multinational. "At the other extreme," Massey (1995, p. 59) reports, "are people who have never been to London and only rarely have made it as far as Cambridge . . . in order to go to the shops or maybe to the hospital." Members of this group are known as the locals, and most of them work on farms or in village shops and services. Other people in these villages work more or less locally, but are employed as cleaners or caterers by multinational firms for which "this is just one group of workers among many scattered over the globe" (Massey, 1995, p. 60). Finally, there are women who are the partners of the "high-tech men," several of whom are "occupied in a daily round of nurseries and child-minders, often being the heart and soul of local meetings and charities" (Massey, 1995, p. 60). They tend to drive into Cambridge to do their shopping, maintain contacts with extended family outside the local area and like to go on holiday somewhere exotic.

Clearly, Massey's account of the different social groups shows how place is far more permeable for some (in this case, the middle-class incomers and out-goers) than it is for others. In addition, within that middle-class group, there are gender differences in the shaping of activity spaces. Still, even the more "rooted," less *routed* (Clifford, 1997) working-class people here are increasingly "touched by wider events." Farm workers, for example, are subject to agricultural policy decisions made in London or Brussels, and the cleaners and caterers who work for multinational firms in the area might well feel the force of global economics if those companies were to cut back on jobs.

NO SENSE OF PLACE?

In what remains of this chapter, my focus shifts more fully onto the role of media (or, to be precise, *patterns of information flow*) in the constitution of what Meyrowitz (1985, p. 6) productively terms "the situational geography of social life." It should be evident, given the ground covered so far, that I am not advocating a media-centered approach to the study of global social change. My preference is for that change to be "understood as a multifaceted . . . differentiated social phenomenon" (Held et al., 1999, p. 27). However, media use does play an important part in what Massey calls the "spatial reorganization of social relations," and I would argue that Meyrowitz's theory of *situations as information-systems* (Meyrowitz, 1985, pp. 35-38; Meyrowitz, 1994, p. 59) goes some way towards enabling us to appreciate this particular aspect of contemporary spatial (and temporal) transformations. As with my earlier reading of Castells' work on flows and places, though, I will be appropriating Meyrowitz's ideas critically and selectively, taking serious issue with his assertion that in today's electronic society, people increasingly have *no sense of place.*

Making a seemingly improbable link between Erving Goffman's sociology, which is mainly concerned with situations of face-to-face interaction in which "individuals are physically in one another's response presence" (Goffman, 1983, p. 2), and Marshall McLuhan's version of medium theory, which relates developments in media technology to time-space transformations (see especially McLuhan, 1964), Meyrowitz (1985, p. 7) argues that electronic media are altering our *situational geography* by undermining "the traditional relationship between physical setting and social situation." He is interested, broadly speaking, in how information flows serve to create and define situations. This concern by no means invalidates the work done by Goffman on copresent encounters in physical settings, but it does extend the study of situations to include a range of interactions and "quasi-interactions" (Thompson, 1995, pp. 84-85) in and with "media settings."

The best way of illustrating Meyrowitz's theory of situations as information-systems, which might appear from my commentary to be highly abstract, is by referring to a concrete instance of communication discussed in his book on electronic media. He takes the example of two friends who are speaking to one another on the telephone, noting that the situation they are "in" is only marginally related to their respective physical locations, before adding that "the telephone tends to bring two people closer . . . in some respects, than they are to other people in their physical environments" (to the extent that those in the same room sometimes respond jealously by asking: "Who is it?," "What's she saying?," "What's so funny?") (Meyrowitz, 1985, p. 117). In his example, the telephone is a medium that helps its users to "override" their physical separation and engage in an instantaneous mediated encounter in which there is a sort of closeness at a distance. It has been suggested, in fact, that the telephone has the capacity to be an especially intimate means of communication, given that the voice of the person on the other end of the line is electronically proximate, "next to the ear" (Gumpert, 1990, p. 148; see also Hutchby, 2001, p. 31, on how intimacy at a distance "is afforded by the telephone"). Although this is undoubtedly the case, a caller's immediate physical context is still significant in the shaping of any telephone conversation.[8] What the two friends in Meyrowitz's example say, then, is likely to depend in part on whether, and if so by whom, the talk is being overheard. For that reason, I think telephone use, and electronic media use more generally, is best seen as a pluralizing setting as opposed to removing somebody from one situation, which becomes marginal, and putting them in another. We will be returning to this point in the following section of the chapter.

Like Massey, Meyrowitz recognizes the permeability of localities, emphasizing the role of electronically mediated information flows in weakening the power of physical boundaries to segregate different spheres of social life: "Electronic messages seep through walls and leap across great distances" (Meyrowitz, 1985, p. 117). He writes, for instance, about the changing character and significance of the domestic sphere: "The walls of the family home . . . no longer wholly isolate the home from the outside. . . . Children may still be sheltered at home, but television now takes them across the globe before parents give them permission to cross the street" (Meyrowitz, 1994, p. 67) (this is strikingly similar to Urry's observations on the instantaneous mobilities of imaginative travel). Meyrowitz (1985, pp. 117-118) even goes so far as to suggest that the "meaning of a prison . . . has been changed as a result of electronic media of communication," because "those prisoners with access to electronic media are no longer completely segregated from society." In his terms, physical incarceration no longer necessarily implies informational isolation.

Let me come now to what I believe to be the main problem with Meyrowitz's thesis on media and social change, namely the way in which he conceptualizes place. The use of the word "place" in the title of his book, he explains, is intended as part of a "serious pun" in which it is supposed to signify "both social position and physical location" (Meyrowitz, 1985, p. 308). Running those two meanings together, his key argument is that social roles and hierarchies, through which people have traditionally come to "know their place," are transformed as electronic communication transcends the limits of physical settings. He offers us a dramatic (though problematic) example of this process at work, stating that: "A telephone or computer in a ghetto tenement or in a suburban teenager's bedroom is potentially as effective as a telephone or computer in a corporate suite" (Meyrowitz, 1985, pp. 169-170). His statement is rightly questioned by Andrew Leyshon (1995, p. 33), who asks if the technology is really as effective in the way that Meyrowitz

---

[8]For instance, if the telephone users are supervised workers in a call center, they are required to make a certain number of calls per hour, often operating with a script or prompt sheet (Cameron, 2000).

suggests, for although "the inner-city resident, the suburban teenager and the corporate executive may all be able to telephone a bank . . . they would not all necessarily enjoy the privilege of being granted an audience with the bank manager." Meyrowitz's perspective on the transformation of place as social position is, therefore, rather too optimistic about the prospects for challenging established social hierarchies.

My difficulty with Meyrowitz's ideas, however, has more to do with his proposal that the relevance of place (understood as geographical location) is being increasingly marginalized in contemporary social life. We live a relatively placeless existence today, he contends, and so it is necessary to move "beyond place" when theorizing communication and culture.[9] Although I would agree, of course, that many physical places have a greater degree of openness or permeability than they had in the past, and although I have also made a case here for considering the flows that connect places, this should not lead us to assume that people are experiencing a loss of the sense of place. On the contrary, my position is that, through practices of electronic media use, place is instantaneously *pluralized* (and see Moores, 2004).

THE DOUBLING OF PLACE

I am borrowing (and extending) the idea of the "doubling of place" from the work of Scannell (1996), a theorist and historian of broadcasting, who believes one of the remarkable yet now largely taken-for-granted consequences of radio or television use is that it serves to "double reality" (Scannell, 1996, pp. 172-173). He develops this line of thought in his analysis of public events and of the changing experiences of "being-in-public" in modern life: "Public events now occur, simultaneously, in two different places: the place of the event itself and that in which it is watched and heard. Broadcasting mediates between these two sites" (Scannell, 1996, p. 76). In proposing *a phenomenological approach* to the study of radio and television (see also Scannell, 1995) that is concerned with the "ways of being in the world" that have been created for viewers and listeners, Scannell (1996, p. 91) goes on to argue that for the audience members in their multiple, dispersed local settings, there are transformed "possibilities of being: of being in two places at once." Of course, it is only ever possible for any individual to be in one place at a time physically, but broadcasting nevertheless permits a live witnessing of remote happenings that can bring these happenings experi-

---

[9]To be fair to him, he does concede, ultimately, that modern life is not completely placeless, acknowledging the fact that "regardless of media access, living in a ghetto, a prison cell, and a middle class suburb are certainly not equivalent social experiences" (Meyrowitz, 1985, p. 312).

entially close or "within range," thereby removing the "farness" (see Heidegger, 1962, p. 140, on the "conquest of remoteness" and the "de-severance of the world" and Scannell, 1996, p. 91).

My feeling is that Scannell's conception of the *doubling of place* and the reflections he offers on the altered possibilities of being for media users, although they appear in a book devoted to the study of broadcasting, might also be applied more generally in the analysis of those electronic media such as the Internet and telephone, which share with radio and television a capacity for the virtually instantaneous transmission of information across sometimes vast distances. Broadcasting, as Scannell has shown in his historical investigations (see especially Scannell & Cardiff, 1991), has its own distinctive communicative features, which mark it out in various ways from computer-mediated or telephone communication. However, I want to contend that radio and television can be considered alongside the Internet and telephone precisely because of the common potential that all these media have for helping to construct experiences of simultaneity and liveness in what have been called "non-localized" (Thompson, 1995, p. 246) (I prefer *translocalized*) spaces and encounters.[10]

In order to try to illustrate my argument about extending the application of Scannell's writing on the doubling of place, I will discuss a couple of examples of electronic media use, each of which is drawn from recently published research. The first is taken from Kendall's ethnography of an Internet forum or "multi-user domain" (Kendall, 2002) and is a personal reflection by the author on her day-to-day practices of computer use. "Online interactions can at times become intensely engrossing," Kendall (2002, p. 7) comments, but if "the text appearing on my screen slows to a crawl or the conversation ceases to interest me, I may cast about for something else offline to engage me." That "something else" may involve picking up the day's mail, flipping through a magazine, leaving the computer to get food, or talking "to someone in the physical room in which I'm sitting" (Kendall, 2002, p. 7).[11]

Kendall's account is clearly about a pluralizing of place (and of social relationships). Indeed, she notes that "although the mud [the multi-user domain] provides for me a feeling of being in a place, that place in some sense overlays the physical place in which my body resides" (Kendall, 2002, pp. 7-8). While "hanging out" with others in

[10]Film and print media could be seen to facilitate a doubling of place for their users, too, although these media do not have the potential for instantaneous communication across large distances and therefore do not afford the same senses of simultaneity and liveness that are available from radio, television, the Internet, and the telephone.
[11]Interestingly, Kendall's description could easily be an account of routine, distracted television viewing in the home, if we were to substitute the references to computer use with ones to glancing at a television screen.

a virtual place,[12] then, her corporeal presence is in a physical setting. This is a simple yet crucial point that needs to be recognized when studying global Internet cultures, because as Daniel Miller and Don Slater (2000, pp. 4-7) assert, much of the early academic literature in this area has tended to focus on the constitution of "spaces or places apart from the rest of social life" rather than treating the Internet "as continuous with . . . other social spaces" and "as part of everyday life" (see also Wellman & Haythornthwaite, 2002). As in the analysis of television cultures, our attention must be given both to the "presencing" (Scannell, 1996, p. 92) of places on the screen and to those places in which the screen is viewed and interacted with, including a modern public context such as the Internet café (see McCarthy, 2001, on television viewing in various locales 'outside the home' and Wakeford, 1999).

The second example of electronic media use to be discussed here comes from the work of a conversation analyst, Emanuel Schegloff (2002). He relates a story, told to him by an old friend, which is set on a train carriage travelling through New York. At the center of this narrative is a "young woman . . . talking on the cell phone, apparently to her boyfriend, with whom she is in something of a crisis" (Schegloff, 2002, p. 285). Other people in the carriage, we are told, busy themselves "doing not overhearing this conversation": Except for one passenger. And when the protagonist of this tale has her eyes intersect this fellow-passenger's gaze, she calls out in outraged protest, "Do you mind?! This is a private conversation!" (Schegloff, 2002, p. 286).

A further echo of Scannell's writing on the doubling of place is to be found in Schegloff's own commentary on that story of mobile phone use (Americans tend to refer to it as a cell phone). The young woman in the tale is, in his words, "in two places at the same time—and the railroad car is only one of them" (Schegloff, 2002, p. 286). "The other place that she is is on the telephone," Schegloff (2002, pp. 286-287) adds, stating that "there are two theres there." We are not accustomed to thinking of speaking on the telephone as an instance of what philosopher Edward Casey (1993, p. xv) calls "being-in-place," and yet the participants in this telephone conversation (at least one of whom is physically "moving-between-places" [Casey, 1993, p. 280]) share an occasion of "talk-in-interaction," in which there is a simulated copresence rather like that created by synchronous Internet chat.

---

[12]It is worth noting that a virtual place is often known as a *room*. This word, traditionally employed to describe a local physical setting, is being used there in an effort to contextualize social relations between participants who are physically separated (to simulate what John Thompson [1995, p. 32] calls "the spatial condition of common locality").

Although Schegloff does not say so explicitly, the story is, in my view, one in which there are plural and competing information flows, and therefore plural and competing *definitions of the situation*. The protagonist whose body resides in the physical place of the railroad car is, she protests, having a private conversation (see also Sussex Technology Group, 2001, on mobile phones as technologies for private talk in the company of strangers). This claim is something of a surprise, given that her voice is loud enough to be clearly audible to other people in the same carriage. She appears not to care about being overheard. Nevertheless, Schegloff (2002, p. 286) still identifies certain features of the talk that could support her indignant expression: "this young woman is talking to her boyfriend, about intimate matters, in the usual conversational manner—except for the argumentative mode, and this also, perhaps especially, makes it a private conversation." Indeed, almost all of the fellow passengers collaborate to support this woman's interpretation. They cannot help overhear the argument (one side of it, that is) but pretend not to hear, looking down at their reading materials or else out of the carriage windows, avoiding eye contact with the mobile phone user so as not to intrude openly on intimate matters. There is a single passenger, though, who refuses to accept the performed pretense, perhaps as a result of being irritated by the intrusion of private talk into a public setting. What I am suggesting is that at the precise moment when eye contact with the protagonist is made, the two "theres" there end up colliding.

CONCLUSION

Readers of this chapter will no doubt notice that it has a narrative of a sort, consisting of a series of related sections on the work of relevant social and communication theorists. That narrative implies a conclusion, which I am now ready to state explicitly. In marked contrast to the view that contemporary social life is increasingly placeless (a view expressed in Meyrowitz's analysis of the impact of electronic media), my preference is to see place as constituted at the interface with flows (Castells), as multiplex (Urry) and open (Massey), and as doubled (Scannell), virtually instantaneously, in the process of using radio, television, the Internet, and the telephone. Of course, in recounting this narrative, I realize that there is a certain amount of slippage in my use of the term "place." At different stages of the chapter, then, the emphasis shifts between the material and the symbolic, or the experiential, dimensions of place, and between place as physical setting and as virtual or simulated location. If we are adequately to conceptualize place in a world of flows, though, it is necessary for us to recognize and synthesize these multiple aspects, engaging in a cross-disciplinary dialogue of the kind that can only be suggested here.

REFERENCES

Appadurai, A. (1996). *Modernity at large: Cultural dimensions of globalization.* Minneapolis: University of Minnesota Press.

Cameron, D. (2000). *Good to talk? Living and working in a communication culture.* London: Sage.

Casey, E. (1993). *Getting back into place: Toward a renewed understanding of the place-world.* Bloomington: Indiana University Press.

Castells, M. (1996). *The information age: Economy, society and culture. Volume 1: The rise of the network society.* Oxford: Blackwell.

Castells, M. (2000). Grassrooting the space of flows. In J. Wheeler et al. (Eds.), *Cities in the telecommunications age: The fracturing of geographies* (pp. 18-27). New York: Routledge.

Clifford, J. (1997). *Routes: Travel and translation in the late twentieth century.* Cambridge, MA: Harvard University Press.

Giddens, A. (1990). *The consequences of modernity.* Cambridge: Polity.

Goffman, E. (1983). The interaction order. *American Sociological Review, 48*(1), 1-17.

Gumpert, G. (1990). Remote sex in the information age. In G. Gumpert & S. Fish (Eds.), *Talking to strangers: Mediated therapeutic communication* (pp. 143-153). Norwood, NJ: Ablex.

Hall, S. (1991). The local and the global: Globalization and ethnicity. In A. King (Ed.), *Culture, globalization and the world-system: Contemporary conditions for the representation of identity* (pp. 19-39). Basingstoke: Macmillan.

Hannerz, U. (1996). *Transnational connections: Culture, people, places.* London: Routledge.

Heidegger, M. (1962). *Being and time.* Oxford: Blackwell.

Held, D. et al. (1999). *Global transformations: Politics, economics and culture.* Cambridge: Polity.

Hutchby, I. (2001). *Conversation and technology: From the telephone to the internet.* Cambridge: Polity.

Jacobs, A. (1993). *Great streets.* Cambridge, MA: MIT.

Janelle, D. (1991). Global interdependence and its consequences. In S. Brunn & T. Leinbach (Eds.), *Collapsing space and time: Geographic aspects of communication and information* (pp. 49-81). London: Harper Collins.

Kendall, L. (2002). *Hanging out in the virtual pub: Masculinities and relationships online.* Berkeley, Los Angeles: University of California Press.

Larsen, P. (1999). Imaginary spaces: Television, technology and everyday consciousness. In J. Gripsrud (Ed.), *Television and common knowledge* (pp. 108-121). London: Routledge.

Lash, S., & Urry, J. (1994). *Economies of signs and space.* London: Sage.

Leyshon, A. (1995). Annihilating space? The speed-up of communications. In J. Allen & C. Hamnett (Eds.), *A shrinking world? Global unevenness and inequality* (pp. 11-46). Oxford: Oxford University Press, Open University.

Massey, D. (1993). Power-geometry and a progressive sense of place. In J. Bird et al. (Eds.), *Mapping the futures: Local cultures, global change* (pp. 59-69). London: Routledge.

Massey, D. (1994). *Space, place and gender.* Cambridge: Polity.

Massey, D. (1995). The conceptualization of place. In D. Massey & P. Jess (Eds.), *A place in the world? Places, cultures and globalization* (pp. 45-77). Oxford: Oxford University Press, Open University.

Mattelart, A. (2000). *Networking the world, 1794-2000.* Minneapolis: University of Minnesota Press.

McCarthy, A. (2001). *Ambient television: Visual culture and public space.* Durham, NC: Duke University Press.

McLuhan, M. (1964). *Understanding media: The extensions of man.* London: Routledge and Kegan Paul.

Meyrowitz, J. (1985). *No sense of place: The impact of electronic media on social behavior.* New York: Oxford University Press.

Meyrowitz, J. (1994). Medium theory. In D. Crowley & D. Mitchell (Eds.), *Communication theory today* (pp. 50-77). Cambridge: Polity.

Miller, D., & Slater, D. (2000). *The internet: An ethnographic approach.* Oxford: Berg.

Moores, S. (2000). *Media and everyday life in modern society.* Edinburgh: Edinburgh University Press.

Moores, S. (2004). The doubling of place: Electronic media, time-space arrangements and social relationships. In N. Couldry & A. McCarthy (Eds.), *MediaSpace: Place, scale and culture in a media age* (pp. 21-36). London: Routledge.

Morley, D. (2000). *Home territories: Media, mobility and identity.* London: Routledge.

Qureshi, K. (2003). *Performing selves and belongings: The reflexive negotiation of identities among Edinburgh Pakistanis.* Ph.D. dissertation, Faculty of Social Sciences, Open University.

Scannell, P. (1995). For a phenomenology of radio and television. *Journal of Communication, 45*(3), 4-19.

Scannell, P. (1996). *Radio, television and modern life: A phenomenological approach.* Oxford: Blackwell.

Scannell, P., & Cardiff, D. (1991). *A social history of British broadcasting. Volume 1. 1922-1939: Serving the nation.* Oxford: Blackwell.

Schegloff, E. (2002). Beginnings in the telephone. In J. Katz & M. Aakhus (Eds.), *Perpetual contact: Mobile communication, private talk, public performance* (pp. 284-300). Cambridge: Cambridge University Press.

Standage, T. (1998). *The Victorian internet: The remarkable story of the telegraph and the nineteenth century's online pioneers.* London: Weidenfeld and Nicolson.

Sussex Technology Group (2001). In the company of strangers: Mobile phones and the conception of space. In S. Munt (Ed.), *Technospaces: Inside the new media* (pp. 205-223). London: Continuum.

Thompson, J. (1995). *The media and modernity: A social theory of the media.* Cambridge: Polity.

Tomlinson, J. (1999). *Globalization and culture.* Cambridge: Polity.

Urry, J. (2000). *Sociology beyond societies: Mobilities for the twenty-first century.* London: Routledge.

Urry, J. (2002). Mobility and proximity. *Sociology, 36*(2), 255-274.

Wakeford, N. (1999). Gender and the landscapes of computing in an internet café. In M. Crang et al. (Eds.), *Virtual geographies: Bodies, space and relations* (pp. 178-201). London: Routledge.

Wellman, B., & Haythornthwaite, C. (Eds.). (2002). *The internet in everyday life*. Malden, MA: Blackwell.

ABOUT THE AUTHORS

Nick Couldry is Professor of Media and Communications at Goldsmiths College, University of London (UK). He is the author or editor of six books and more than forty articles and book chapters, including *Media Rituals: A Critical Approach* (Routledge, 2003), *The Place of Media Power: Pilgrims and Witnesses of the Media Age* (Routledge, 2000) and *Inside Culture* (Sage, 2000); his latest book *Listening Beyond the Echoes: Media, Ethics and Agency in an Uncertain World* was published by Paradigm Press (2006). His main research interests are media power, social theory, media anthropology, and the methodology of cultural studies.

Maren Hartmann is Assistant Professor of Communication Sociology at Berlin University of the Arts (Germany). Before her return to Germany, she worked at the Universities of Sussex, Westminster, and Brighton in the United Kingdom and the Free University of Brussels in Belgium, both in research and teaching positions. She is the author of *Technologies and Utopias: The Cyberflaneur and the Experience of "Being Online"* (Reinhard Fischer, 2004) and co-editor of *Domestication of Media and Technology* (Open University Press, 2006). Her publications also include a range of articles and book chapters. Her main research interests are cyberculture, media in everyday life, and media ethnography.

Andreas Hepp is Professor of Communications and Head of the Institute for Media, Communication and Information (IMKI) at the Faculty of Cultural Studies, University of Bremen (Germany). He is the author of *Fernsehaneignung und Alltagsgespräche: Fernsehnutzung in Perspektive der Cultural Studies* (Everyday Talk and the Appropriation of TV: Television in a Cultural Studies Perspective, Westdeutscher Verlag, 1997), *Cultural Studies und Medienanalyse* (Cultural Studies and Media

Analysis, Westdeutscher Verlag, 1999, second edition Verlag für Sozialwissenschaften, 2004), and *Netzwerke der Medien: Medienkulturen und Globalisierung* (Networks of the Media: Media Cultures and Globalization, Verlag für Sozialwissenschaften, 2004). His publications have also included numerous journal articles, book chapters and co-edited books. His main interests are in media, communication and cultural theory, media sociology, inter- and transcultural communication, cultural studies, media change, methods of qualitative media research, and audience studies.

Friedrich Krotz is Professor of Communication Research at the University of Erfurt (Germany). He worked for more than a decade as a Researcher and Scientific Head of Department at the Hans Bredow Institute for Media Research, as a Lecturer at the University of Zuerich (Switzerland), and Professor at the Universities of Jena, Potsdam and Muenster (all Germany). To his recent publications belong books on the mediatization of communicative action and on theory generating methodologies such as grounded theory and ethnography. He is also co-editor and author of books on methodology, on the concept of mediatization, and on globalization topics. In addition to other memberships, he is (co-)Head of the "Psychology and Public Opinion" Section of the International Association for Media and Communication Research (IAMCR). Currently, the main areas of his research are digital and interactive media, the social and cultural change induced by media development, intercultural communication, and methodology.

Shaun Moores is Professor of Media and Communications at the University of Sunderland (UK). He was formerly Associate Professor of Media and Communications at the University of Melbourne (Australia), and Visiting Professor of Communications at University of Rome La Sapienza (Italy). He is the author of *Interpreting Audiences: The Ethnography of Media Consumption* (Sage, 1993), *Satellite Television and Everyday Life: Articulating Technology* (John Libbey Media, 1996), *Media and Everyday Life in Modern Society* (Edinburgh University Press, 2000) and *Media/Theory: Thinking About Media and Communications* (Routledge, 2005). His publications have also included numerous journal articles and book chapters, as well as a book in Italian translation entitled *Il Consumo dei Media: Un Approccio Etnografico* (Il Mulino, 1998). His main interests are in qualitative empirical research on media uses in daily living, and in linking the analysis of media and communications with key themes in contemporary social theory.

Thorsten Quandt is Assistant Professor of Journalism at Berlin Free University (Germany). He is author of *Journalisten im Netz* (Journalists in the Net, Verlag für Sozialwissenschaften, 2005) and co-editor of *Die* *neue Kommunikationswissenschaft* (The New Communication Studies, together with Martin Löffelholz, Westdeutscher Verlag, 2003). He has also published numerous journal articles and book chapters. His current research topics include journalism, online communication, and media innovations, and he is interested in advances in both media theory and empirical research alike.

John Tomlinson is Professor and Head of Research in Communications, Media and Cultural Studies and Director of ICAN, Nottingham Trent University (UK). His books include *Cultural Imperialism* (Pinter, 1991) and *Globalization and Culture* (Polity Press, 1999) both of which have been extensively translated (8 languages). He has published on issues of globalization, cosmopolitanism, modernity, and media and culture across a range of disciplines from sociology, communications and cultural studies to geography, urban studies and development studies, and has lectured extensively in Europe, Latin America, Asia and North America. His latest book is *The Culture of Speed* (Sage, 2007).

Carsten Winter is Professor of Media and Music Management at Hanover University of Music and Drama (Germany). His co-edited books include *Kulturwandel und Globalisierung* (Cultural Change and Globalization, Nomos, 2000), *Grundlagen des Medienmanagements* (Foundations of Media Management, second edition, Fink, 2002), *Medienentwicklung und gesellschaftlicher Wandel* (Media Development and Social Change, Westdeutscher Verlag, 2003) and *Globalisierung der Medienkommunikation* (Globalization of Media Communication, Verlag für Sozialwissenschaften, 2005). His publications have also included numerous journal articles and book chapters. His main interests are in media and communication management, convergence, media history, and media development.

Andreas Wittel is Senior Lecturer in Social Theory at the School of Arts, Communication, and Culture, Nottingham Trent University (UK). He was formerly research associate at the Centre for Cultural Studies, Goldsmiths College (UK), and at the Institut fuer Arbeitswissenschaft, Ruhr-Universitaet Bochum (Germany). He is the author of *Belegschaftkultur im Schatten der Firmenideologie: Eine ethnographische Fallstudie* (Employee Culture in the Shadow of Corporate Ideology: An Ethnographic Case Study, Sigma, 1997) and co-editor of *Arbeitskulturen im Umbruch: Zur Ethnographie von Arbeit und Organisation* (Work Cultures: Ethnographic Research on Work and Organisations, Waxmann, 2000). His main research interests focus broadly on contemporary sociocultural change and on the intersection of culture and economy. In particular, he is interested in digital media, work, social relationships, and ethnographic research.

INDEX

A

actant 8, 21*f*, 96, 100-104, 138*f*
actor network theory (ANT) 8, 93-109
action 8, 21*f*, 24, 84, 94, 96, 100-104,
    111-132, 191
agent 96, 101*f*, 111
Americanization 35
appropriation 51-54
articulation 46, 78
audience 99, 104ff 194*f*

B

belonging 47, 83*f*, 152
biography 172

C

capitalism 3*f*, 27*f*, 158*f*
centrism 33, 48
change 15, 20-25, 43, 45*f*, 68, 70, 73*f*,
    78-81, 137*f*, 168-170, 192
civil society 29, 86*f*, 89*f*
civilization 16
code 37-39, 139, 146
commercialization 25-28
communication theory 136
community 15*f*, 46*f*, 157*f*, 168*f*, 171,
    177*f*
complexity 14*f*, 21, 24, 40*f*, 70-72, 75,
    78*f*
compression 2*f*
computer 7*f*, 64, 69, 71, 142, 195
conflict 9, 35, 135, 139*f*, 145, 148-154
connectedness 2, 37, 78, 83-87, 105

connectivity 2, 6*f*, 13-29, 33-58, 71-73,
    76-79, 111, 162
container-thinking 36, 46
control 27, 61, 79, 142
convergence 7, 59, 69-92, 160
cosmopolitism 67*f*
critical theory 27
cultural industry 27, 159*f*, 176
cultural studies 33*f*, 41*f*, 78
culture 6*f*, 18-21, 33-58, 76*f*, 103, 144
cyberfeminism 135-156
cyberpunk 73
cyberspace 64, 72, 168*f*
cyborg 64

D

database 166-168, 178
deconstruction 34, 95, 102, 159
deterritorialization 5, 36, 43-54, 60
diaspora 5, 43*f*, 51, 53, 189
diffusion 19, 46
digital divide 51*f*
digital media 24*f*, 28
digitalization 73
discrimination 137, 149, 153
disembedding 4, 157
distance 2*f*, 62*f*, 66*f*, 177*f*, 189, 192*f*,
    195
doubling 10, 77, 169, 194-197

E

elite 29, 166, 170
enlightenment 19, 79, 81

ethnography 52*f,* 112, 165, 189, 195
everyday life 18, 23-26, 40, 43*f,* 53,
    60, 62-65, 104*f,* 115, 151*f,* 188*f*
experience 3, 60, 70, 75, 83, 99, 104,
    106, 115, 136, 169*f,* 174*f,* 186, 188,
    194*f*
e-mail 60, 130, 165*f,* 169

F

face-to-face 24*f,* 27, 162*f,* 169, 177*f,*
    192
family 15, 89, 193
feminism 135-156
figuration 16, 178
film 5, 42, 195
flaming 150*f*
flexibility 170
flow 4*f,* 17, 39-42, 82*f,* 138*f,* 183-187
fluid 4*f,* 39*f,* 70-72, 187
fragility 63, 94
fragmentation 80, 106
Frankfurt School 60
freedom 75, 84*f,* 88*f*
functionalism 16, 40, 95, 96, 99

G

Gemeinschaft 86, 157
geography 43, 61, 187, 190, 191*f*
global city 38
global culture 35, 41
global village 21, 35
globalization 2-4, 13-15, 19*f,* 21*f,* 26,
    34-37, 41, 43, 60, 70, 158*f,* 188,
    190
graph theory 112*f*
group 38, 106, 163, 165, 191

H

hegemony 6, 14, 28
homogenization 21, 35, 190
human action 24, 99, 112, 113, 114*f,*
    120, 131*f*

I

idealism 95, 97
identity 26, 28, 45*f,* 47, 53, 138, 139,
    152, 153*f,* 167, 172, 189
ideology 77, 88
imagined community 46*f,* 169
imperialism 6, 50
individualization 19, 20-22, 26, 171,
    176*f*

inequality 3, 48-54, 75, 149
information 4, 26, 38*f,* 71*f,* 78, 105*f,*
    138*f,* 152, 157*f,* 174*f,* 191-193
infrastructure 51-53, 73*f,* 107, 177*f*
innovation 19
institution 16, 22*f,* 27, 77, 90, 98*f,* 104,
    159
integration 22*f,* 36*f,* 94, 157, 170*f,*
    177*f*
interaction 17*f,* 52, 85, 152, 162*f,* 171,
    173, 177*f,* 184, 192
interactivity 24, 162, 169
Internet 4, 42-45, 52, 65, 71-74, 105*f,*
    169, 189, 195*f*

J

journalism 8, 118-133

K

knowledge 95, 101, 104, 113, 115-
    117, 172, 175

L

landscape 41, 51
laptop 64, 69*f,* 72*f,* 80, 90
lifestyle 22, 59, 62
lifeworld 16-18, 23, 25*f,* 28
liquid modernity 39, 61*f,* 157
liveness 105*f,* 195
locality 2, 7, 45*f,* 52, 148, 190*f*
location 7, 62, 82*f,* 153, 187, 190, 192*f*
logic 4, 26, 35, 70, 72, 138

M

mailing list 9, 135-137, 140, 143-155
market 21-23, 27, 59, 74, 161
marketing 59*f,* 162
McDonaldization 14, 35
media and communication studies 95*f,*
    98
media culture 7, 34, 42-47, 50, 53*f,* 73,
    90, 138
media environment 17, 25
media theory 33*f,* 78, 94-96, 99*f,* 106*f*
mediality 69, 71, 73, 76-79
mediation 64, 76, 98, 103
mediatization 20*f,* 23-29
medium theory 23, 78, 191-194
migration 5, 44*f,* 190
miniaturization 62, 64, 71
mobile phone 7, 59*f,* 64, 66, 106, 178,
    196*f*

mobility 5, 43*f*, 61*f*, 71*f*, 75, 172, 175, 187-189
modernity 36, 61, 161-163, 97*f*, 171, 188
multiplicity 187-189

N

narration 61, 157*f*, 170, 172, 174-177
nation-state 5, 17, 36, 138, 187
nature 43, 61, 93, 95
network sociality 9, 157-159, 165*f*, 171-179
network society 3*f*, 13-21, 135-140, 158, 183-187
networking 66, 72, 136, 151, 158-168, 176-179
new economy 159-162
new media industry 159*f*, 176
news 39, 104*f*, 130*f*
newsroom 115*f*, 118, 123
node 3*f*, 15, 37-39, 48-50, 113, 127, 138-140, 152
nomadology 188

O

object 93, 95*f*, 102-104, 171
openness 39, 139*f*, 171, 190*f*
organization 4, 15, 38, 48-50, 158, 169-171

P

paradox 39, 50, 104
phenomenology 194*f*
place 2*f*, 9*f*, 60-63, 179-197
placeless 185
play 158, 175-177
post-colonialism 135, 143-145, 151-153
postsocial theory 170*f*
poststructuralism 34
power 3, 38-41, 61, 71*f*, 81*f*, 96-104, 140, 152, 190
preacher 7, 42, 74, 80-82
proximity 2, 35, 64
public sphere 17, 82, 168

R

racial politics 137, 144
racism 137, 140, 147, 149-151
radio 7, 46, 73, 75, 194*f*
railway 61

rationality 76*f*, 176
relationship 2, 60, 63, 76, 85, 96, 142, 160-162, 169-172, 178*f*
religion 7, 76-84, 169
representation 43*f*, 50*f*, 162
risk 165
ritual 76*f*, 79, 87, 90, 96*f*
rupture 9, 140

S

scape 35, 40*f*, 83, 189
self 16*f*, 36, 135, 138
self-organization 40, 113
sexuality 53
shrinking 2
silencing 136*f*, 146-148
situatedness 9, 151
situation 26, 191-193, 197
social capital 158, 163, 179
social institution 15, 23, 77
social life 13-24, 28, 96, 193*f*, 196*f*
social movements 38, 47
social order 93, 98, 107, 138
social sciences 8, 36, 94, 112, 179
social theory 3, 6, 9, 71, 100, 186*f*
sociality 9, 157-159, 166, 168*f*, 171*f*, 175, 177-179
society 15-17, 18-23, 26-29, 36, 76, 88, 95, 97*f*, 111*f*, 138, 187
sociology 15, 18, 34, 36, 41*f*, 76*f*, 93-95, 103*f*, 112*f*, 187
software 62, 113, 132
solidarity 69*f*, 77, 80, 87, 89*f*
space 2*f*, 40*f*, 61*f*, 71*f*, 100, 106, 138, 184-187, 191
spatiality 2, 41, 100, 186, 191*f*
speed 44, 84, 175
stability 19, 39, 43, 93
standardization 35
structuration theory 114
struggle 17, 141, 153
subject 102, 116, 158, 172, 174
switch 36-38
system 17, 39, 76, 94, 171, 192

T

technology 3*f*, 52, 59-68, 69*f*, 73-75, 93-98, 105, 107, 141-143, 158, 160, 168, 177-179
television 7, 27, 44, 46*f*, 50-53, 75, 78, 82-84, 94, 104-106, 188*f*, 194-196

temporality 19, 100*f,* 115
terminal 60-63
territoriality 36, 47-54, 61
text 102, 105
theorizing 33*f,* 36-38, 41*f,* 46, 53*f,* 135
thickening 41*f,* 46-48, 50*f*
tradition 15, 22, 170*f*
transculturality 51-54
translocality 5, 7, 44-54, 74, 195
transnationalism 5, 36, 51, 74, 187
traveling 5, 38, 42*f,* 61*f,* 71*f,* 187-189

U

ubiquity 62*f*
universality 33*f,* 41*f,* 81*f*

V

value 22, 59, 61*f,* 84, 104, 121, 138-140, 160*f,* 186
virtual community 168-170, 189
volatility 44

W

whiteness 147, 149

Printed in the United States
205176BV00001B/196-219/P

9 781572 738577